TH

NEW GROWTH

JASMINE NICHOLE COBB

VISUAL ARTS OF AFRICA
AND ITS DIASPORAS
A series edited by Kellie Jones
and Steven Nelson

DUKE UNIVERSITY PRESS
Durham and London 2023

Printed in the United States of America on acid-free paper ∞
Production editor: Lisa Lawley
Designed by Courtney Leigh Richardson
Typeset in Portrait, Gill Sans, and Trade Gothic
by Copperline Book Services

Library of Congress Cataloging-in-Publication Data
Names: Cobb, Jasmine Nichole, author.
Title: New growth : the art and texture of black hair /
Jasmine Nichole Cobb.
Other titles: Visual arts of Africa and its diasporas.
Description: Durham : Duke University Press, 2023. | Series:
The visual arts of Africa and its diasporas. | Includes
bibliographical references and index.
Identifiers: LCCN 2022020085 (print)
LCCN 2022020086 (ebook)
ISBN 9781478016434 (hardcover)
ISBN 9781478019077 (paperback)
ISBN 9781478023708 (ebook)
Subjects: LCSH: Hairdressing of Black people—Social aspects. |
Hairdressing of African Americans—Social aspects. | Hairdressing
of Black people—History. | Hairdressing of African Americans—History. |
Black people—Race identity. | African Americans—Race identity. | BISAC:
SOCIAL SCIENCE / Ethnic Studies / American / African American &
Black Studies | HISTORY / Social History
Classification: LCC GT2290.C633 2023 (print) | LCC GT2290 (ebook) |
DDC 391.5089/96—dc23/eng/20220701
LC record available at https://lccn.loc.gov/2022020085
LC ebook record available at https://lccn.loc.gov/2022020086

Cover art: Lorna Simpson, *Jet Double Sit-in*, 2012. Collage
and ink on paper. Unframed: 11³⁄₁₆ × 8¹¹⁄₁₆ in. (22.1 × 28.4 cm).
Framed: 12 × 9½ × 1½ in. (30.5 × 24.1 × 3.8 cm). © Lorna Simpson.
Courtesy of the artist and Hauser & Wirth.

FOR ALI AND ASA

INTRODUCTION

1

2

3

4

CONCLUSION

CONTENTS

FIGURES

PLATES ●●●

Writing this book has been a journey filled with numerous personal and professional transformations. I could not have completed this work without the generosity of friends and acquaintances who were willing to share hair stories with me. People have been forthcoming with private, anecdotal, and transformative experiences around the wearing or styling of Afro-textured hair; strangers opened their businesses to me for taking pictures and asking questions—from a Dominican salon in the Netherlands to cosmetic stores in Barbados. Early funding from the American Academy of University Women was pivotal, helping to signal the value of this work while also providing me with space to explore diverse topics, at Taliah Waajid's World Natural Hair, Health & Beauty Show in Atlanta, Georgia; the archives at the Schomburg Center for Research in Black Culture of the New York Public Library; and at the Studio Museum in Harlem.

Friends and colleagues helped me reimagine Black coiffure. Keyana Pompey, Lynette Lee, and Precious Daniels still share their growth journeys with me and I am thankful. Also, Robin Stevens, Tshepo Masango Chéry, GerShun Avilez, Khadijah White, and Aymar Christian shared products and personal experiences; Shawnika Hull accompanied me to hair salons and beauty supply stores throughout Philadelphia. John L. Jackson Jr., Robin Means Coleman, Maghan Keita, and Deborah Thomas, along with E. Patrick Johnson, D. Soyini Madison, Jacqueline Stewart, Joshua Chambers-Letson, Jasmine Johnson, and Miriam Petty, urged me to push forward in my intellectual curiosity about Black hair. Joycelyn K. Moody has been a guide and a mentor. Ellen Scott has consistently lent her wisdom, kindness, and cheer since graduate school. Likewise, C. Riley Snorton has remained a constant friend and inspiration, hearing these concepts in their crudest forms and encouraging me the entire way.

Colleagues working on visual culture have magnified my thinking on this subject. Huey Copeland has been unendingly generous, and his insights transformed my approach to the representation of Black hair. He, along with Krista Thompson, Deborah Willis, Kellie Jones, Steven Nelson, and especially Richard Powell, guided me toward diverse forms of illustration and inspired me to take chances. Some of this experimentation took place at the From Slavery to Freedom Lab at Duke's John Hope Franklin Humanities Institute, which I have codirected with Powell and Lamonte Aidoo, who has been a charitable collaborator. Our work together added much excitement to my life at Duke. Our lab is just one of many forms of institutional support that I have received from Valerie Ashby, Sally Kornbluth, Kevin Moore, and Ranjana Khanna. My departmental colleagues have also enlarged my thinking and teaching about blackness, the diaspora, and art history. Mark Anthony Neal has been a tireless advocate. Tsitsi Jaji, Joseph Winters, Anne-Maria Makhulu, Charlie Piot, Sam Fury Childs Daly, Wahneema Lubiano, Michaeline Crichlow, Tommy DeFrantz, Kerry Haynie, Lee Baker, Thavolia Glymph, Charmaine Royal, Karin Shapiro, Stephen Smith, Karen Jean Hunt, John Gartrell, and Heather Martin as well as Kenya Harris, Stacy Nicole Robinson, Tyra Dixon, and Wilhelmina Green have been a caring intellectual community. Likewise, Beverly McIver, Victoria Szabo, Mark Olson, Gennifer Weisenfeld, Kristine Stiles, Esther Gabara, Thomas Rankin, William Seaman, Neil McWilliam, Paul Jaskot, Sheila Dillon, Stanley Abe, and Trevor Schoonmaker have also been cheerful colleagues. At Duke University Press, my editor, Ken Wissoker, and Joshua Gutterman Tranen have been gentle guides and engaged readers from our first conversation about this project.

Much of the heavy lifting required to bring a book to fruition could not have been done without the generous support of graduate-student colleagues. Emily Mohr, Brandee Newkirk, Jessica Orzulak, and Fati Abubakar helped me complete this work; Serda Yalkin, Jacqueline Allain, Ayanna Legros, and Ashleigh Smith have been wonderful interlocutors. LaCharles Ward, Cecilio Cooper, Shoniqua Roach, Rhaisa Williams, and Jared Richardson have helped to keep questions about Black freedom at the forefront of my work.

As for the practical matter of writing, I could not have completed this book at this moment in my life without the support of writing groups. Before the pandemic, I found the most unlikely community in Duke's Faculty Write program, a group in which participants had no overlapping intellectual interests and came from different places in life. Yet, despite those differences, I found in this group a support that helped me keep at it. A special thank you to Jennifer Ahern-Dodson and Charlotte Sussman for fostering these spaces. Through the pandemic, however, I found a crew and a reinvigorated friendship with Kathryn Sophia Belle. Also from different phases and places in life, *our group* has deepened my commitment to my work and helped me embrace the fullness of life that happens around it. Together, we wept about the murder of George Floyd while urging one another toward deeper self-love and self-care. For you all I am eternally grateful.

Family still cheers for me through life's changes, expanding and growing in ways I could not have imagined. On this particular journey toward completion, reclaiming time with my brother, Brandon Cobb, has bought so much joy to my life. I am thankful for his love, his enthusiasm, and his faith. I look forward to more time and more family. My sister, Danielle Walters, and my mother, Caryl Harris, as well as Monique Walker-Bryant, Jean Webster, Marilyn Johnson, Dana Abernethy, and Fay McCready, still teach me so much.

Finally, I have been blessed with a new squad since writing my last monograph. My partner, Kenyon, remains with me through more transitions than I can count and is still the first and last person with whom I share my ideas. Loie is still here, too. In the process of writing this book, however, Ali and Asa joined our lives. Some days I did not know how this work would get done, but I leaned into them and found the crux of concerns laid out in this book—liberation, amplified by tender and kind forms of contact in the everyday of Black life. You all love me and inspire me, always. Thank you.

NEW GROWTH

INTRODUCTION

A tentative freedom is tangled in Afro-textured hair. Post-black artist Rashid Johnson suggests as much in his *Self-Portrait with My Hair Parted like Frederick Douglass* (plate 1), in which the artist, dressed in a black suit, a white collared shirt, and a striped necktie, sits at a left-facing angle with his dreadlocks parted on the right side.[1] Like other images in his *New Negro Escapist Social and Athletic Club* series, Johnson's portrait is citational, referencing the fugitive–free abolitionist with words and image. The pronounced side-parted hair of Douglass's 1847 daguerreotype, taken by photographer Samuel Miller (figure I.1), is the inspiration for Johnson's illustration. In this reference, it is not simply the legacy of photographic practice that connects these two images, but also the hair: Douglass's crown of thick and textured coils and Johnson's once-fringe dreadlock style, now presented as thin, organized cords and paired with formal attire. Douglass's hair suggests care—implies that it was touched, perhaps by his hand or another's, and parted in a deliberate manner to create a style. This clue about

I.I
Samuel J. Miller,
Frederick Douglass,
1847–52. Photographic
plate, 5½ × 4⅛ in.
(14 × 10.6 cm). Courtesy
of the Art Institute of
Chicago.

self-fashioning distinguishes Douglass's photograph from many midcentury
images of unfree people. For instance, Joseph T. Zealy's photographs of Renty,
Alfred, Delia, Drana, Fassena, Jack, and Jem, commissioned by Louis Aggasiz,
show them "stripped" of clothing, and not simply naked, deprived of a chance at
self-presentation.[2] Relatedly, when Dolly ran away from South Carolina planter
Louis Manigault, he fashioned a runaway notice by cutting her image from a
family portrait that shows Dolly dressed in work attire and her hair covered
with a scarf.[3] Dolly's off-center pose, seated as she is in a wooden chair, is reminiscent of other "family" photographs of the period, wherein white children appear alongside the unfree Black women charged with their care, such as in this
photograph of Lucy Cottrell (figure I.2).[4] These images portray limits on the
Black subject's autonomy, indicated in strictures of undress, personal grooming,
and posture. Conversely, Douglass's solitary portrait, formal attire, and impressive mass of parted textured hair mark his image with a personal touch so that
self-styling distinguishes the abolitionist from other Black images of the period.

1.2

Lucy, Holding Charlotte,
ca. 1845. Kentucky
Gateway Museum
Center, Maysville, KY.

Despite the distinctions of Douglass's hair and attire, these features, like the photograph itself, do not clearly indicate the activist as a free man. Shawn Michelle Smith describes Miller's portrait of Douglass as "perplexing, as it represents a legal freedom defined both against and according to the terms of the institution from which he escaped."[5] This illustration of a nominally free Douglass shows him as "liberated" at the hands of white abolitionists who purchased the activist so that he could continue his work on the abolitionist circuit without capture. The freedom and aesthetic choices often read into Douglass's portrait imply autonomy, but in actuality it is the various signals of touch and feeling associated with the textured surface that is his hair that help stake such claims. Douglass's part marks care and separates the fugitive not just from other nineteenth-century photographs of unfree Black people but also from later portraits of Douglass in which his hair appears longer and the part is absent. Accordingly, it is through the photographic medium and through his hair that Johnson's image speaks to a concept of freedom. Choosing to have his hair "parted like Frederick Douglass," Johnson's coiffure appears tamed. His locs are not separated like those of fellow artist Jean-Michel Basquiat, for example, whose polaroid portrait by Andy Warhol shows his hair, shirt collar, and tie organized in a less orderly fashion (plate 2). In directing our attention to the part, hair becomes central to the "aesthetic means" by which Johnson speaks to the past and to the present, to "the promised freedoms" and to the "productive constraints" that concern many post-black artists.[6] Johnson's hair signals a kind of liberation in the current moment but carries within it histories of repression and efforts to revise dictates on feeling and touch that have rendered dreadlocks unacceptable. Johnson's citation, then, presents hair and touch in two frames: radical in the context of Douglass's photograph and staid in the context of the artist's own twenty-first-century image. The result is an impermanent freedom, conveyed through hair as visual material to be read as anticapitalist, diasporic, and commodified.

New Growth: The Art and Texture of Black Hair explores issues of touch, texture, and feeling as they relate to the idea and the image of "natural hair." Throughout the book, I refer to "natural hair" and "Black hair" interchangeably to describe textured hair among people of African descent—the opposite of coifs presented in straight strands and loose curls and attributed to people not identified as "Black." Afro coiffure, or the character of hair associated with people of African descent, in the absence of chemical and mechanical straighteners includes a variety of curls, coils, and kinks, even on a single individual; various within itself, this human surface is best thought of as densely textured. Within this focus, I propose a haptic exploration of Afro coiffure, with the visual representation of textured hair providing a vehicle for reorganizing the sensual experience of blackness. Not just photography but also Black hair's textural distinction, such as is emphasized in the images of Douglass and Johnson, points to both the image surface and the human surface as central for rethinking engagements with a palpable Black raciality. Here, I explore how hair has been a site for the sedimentation of slavery's inscription of "black" as a feeling in multiple registers and worthy of particular kinds of touch or physical engagement. Alongside this reading of hair as a representation, I also ask, How do images bring viewers closer to a sensuous engagement with blackness? Likewise, How do images foster distance?

In this focus on Afro-textured hair, specifically, my aim is to avoid some of the dichotomous thinking that has ruled everyday conversations about blackness. This includes popular culture debates about "good" and "bad" hair texture and theories of self-hate as a consciousness underpinning the choice to straighten textured hair. In electing to focus on hair read as "natural," or "Black," I mean to ignore the choice to straighten hair as I try to better understand the significations ascribed to the textured surface. This is not to say that commentary on the *quality* of Black hair textures or the appreciation of coiffure in the *absence* of chemical straightening products is irrelevant to the study, since wearers of textured hair are still subject to aesthetic and moral judgments about style in popular parlance. However, in my focus on natural hair explicitly, I mean to examine mythologies about blackness as a surface realized in the dual sensation of seeing and feeling. Along these lines, I am interested in the ways that image-cultures have helped to shore up or negate those mythologies without regard to a set of alternative options such as heat-straightened hair, for example.

Central to this book is the question of liberation. Over and again, in different time periods and geographic locales, Black coiffure is part of a conversation on the aesthetics of liberation. Frequently, hairstyles such as the Afro, dreadlocks, or simply "the natural" have been typified as "Black" for the way in which these styles embrace unique hair textures common among people of African descent. Black hair's characteristic coils and matting capability have been used to code wearers of textured hair as "pro-Black," suggesting a larger investment in "Black" aesthetics. Art historian Kobena Mercer's canonic essay "Black Hair/Style Politics" details Afros and dreadlocks in particular as "specifically diasporean" aesthetic practices that do not naturally occur but that are carefully crafted and may employ artifice as a way to enhance the "natural."[7] Similarly, art historian Judith Wilson extends this argument to explore the pairing of aesthetic and moral judgment of Black hair in various artistic projects, including film, photography, and installation works by creatives of African descent. *New Growth* is a project in Black visual culture that speaks to these concerns but that also draws upon "art, popular media, exhibitions, public and domestic environments, new media, politics, and commerce," as photography historian Deborah Willis describes, to limn a better understanding of hair within and through Black visual culture.[8]

Here, I read textured hair for "meaning-making" about the Black body. Black aesthetics are central to "creating and maintaining black life-worlds" and are indicative of Black humanity, as these notions are "symbiotic."[9] Thus, a diverse array of images about Black hair are central to the cultural production of Black hair. Afro-textured hair corresponds to Black aesthetics engaged with the hand and with the eyes; it has often figured in recalcitrance from racial capitalism, whether among fugitives from slavery in the nineteenth century or among Black professionals in the twenty-first century. Along these lines, slavery matters; the Middle Passage and chattel slavery are significant not merely for excavating the possibility of a Black aesthetics under duress but for marking a significant point in time from which to explore the means by which racial capitalism's characteristic violence and accumulation helped shape conceptions of blackness.[10] Jennifer Morgan explains that physiognomy had no relevance before New World conquest; the "cultural deficiency" ascribed to the hair, skin, and facial features of African-descended women would be actively created.[11] Along these lines, hair has been a reccurring topic for Black cultural producers, coupled with issues of coloniality and bondage, as a means by which to reject theories of inferiority and create alternate systems of value for Black aesthetics on the terrain of the human surface.

The Struggle with Black Hair

In the context of slavery, concomitant with the life of Frederick Douglass, Afro-textured hair served as a marker of status—Black or not, free or not—while its proper management in the twenty-first century, neatly parted such as in Johnson's self-portrait, determines social acceptance. Black hair was socially significant in the nineteenth century not only to people like Douglass, who wanted to illustrate personal upkeep, but also to white legislators, enslavers, and would-be scientists looking for other forms of corporeal evidence of racial variety. Even white abolitionists made meaning about hair and the presumption of blackness in the discussion of race mixture. In each instance, Black hair appears imbricated in a much longer arc of racial capitalism that extends back to slavery, even as Black coiffure was not a known, salable commodity. Thus, the ways of doing Black hair and its corollary significations have made and remade textured hair into a symbol and site of Black freedom in visual representation.

The economic stability attributed to the labor of Black hair is among the earliest illustrations of Black liberation associated with coiffure. Capitalist appeals to entrepreneurship and consumerism have been highlighted as key among Black hair's liberatory potential. Some of this signaling results from notable labor opportunities associated with Black hair care, where African Americans have found occasions for financial stability through barbering, for example.[12] No figure signifies the complicated freedom achieved through hair and accumulation like Madam C. J. Walker—businessperson, entrepreneur, and first woman millionaire born in the United States. Walker is often accused of suppressing textured hair with the hot comb (which she did not invent), but her birth in 1867 also renders Walker as symbol of the transition from enslavement to freedom, informing views of Walker as moving from the destitution of (post) slavery to redemption found in the lucrative embrace of white beauty norms. Noliwe Rooks locates Walker among a number of Black women, situated between complex values of beauty and enterprise, who connected "dark skin and slavery."[13] Rooks speculates that visual exemplars for beautiful hair would have been derived from styling habits of white women enslavers, thus framing "the merchandising of hair-care products" for African Americans in print culture up into the early twentieth century.[14] But Walker is among a long line of Black women entrepreneurs; historian Tiffany Gill argues that a number of Black women obtained financial freedom and participated in political activity through work in hair care, where "lines between producers and consumers" were blurred by a diverse cadre of people who expanded the definition of "entrepreneur" with forays into hair care as well as product manufacturing. The financial freedom attributed to Walker and others has helped to make the business of Black hair a pathway toward stability and autonomy.[15]

But more than financial freedom, violence is the chief imprint on textured hair's imbrication in struggles for Black liberation. The spectacular prevalence of natural hair in 1960s Black politics, worn by youth organizers resistant to integration who demanded a synergy between activism and personal style, has endured in pictures that connect natural hair to a radical Black consciousness. Among them, even those activists with straightened hair and formal attire faced attack. In preparation for harassment, activists of the Student Nonviolent Coordinating Committee (SNCC) practiced having their hair pulled (figure I.3). Eventually, and for practical reasons, many of these same women let go of straightened styles after having food thrown at them during lunch counter sit-ins in the South. According to historian Tanisha Ford, women of SNCC rejected the aesthetics of the "respectable body" and "bourgeois beautification," since by 1963 the brutality faced by activists spurred the adoption of unprocessed hairstyles and denim as the preferred radical aesthetic. Thus, the "SNCC women served as early models" for Black radical women of the 1970s.[16] While personal style shaped the political significance of textured hair, these instances also reveal violence as a central story as whites perpetrated aggression against those wearing both straightened and natural hair.

Illustrations of Black protest in the mid-twentieth century also locate textured hair in the midst of state violence, making this period iconic for its representation of Black hair. But activist and scholar Angela Davis argues that the historic photos of the 1960s and 1970s served as sources of terror in their moment of circulation—when images of Davis with her Afro spurred persecution of other Black women wearing this hairstyle at the height of its popularity—before entering an "economy of journalistic images" that has since fueled the commodification of '60s style and radical aesthetics.[17] The embrace of the natural emerged in a politically fraught context captured in civil rights photog-

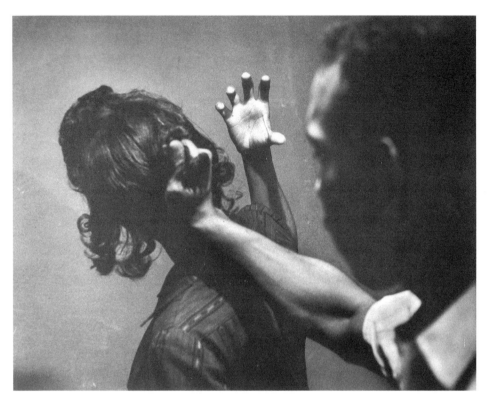

1.3

James Karales, *Passive Resistance Training, Student Nonviolent Coordinating Committee*, 1960. © Estate of James Karales. Reproduced by permission of the Howard Greenberg Gallery, New York.

raphy, and it went on to appear in both political and popular representations, whether in Black Power propaganda or in the consumer market for Soul Music, food, and fashion.

Finally, the imbrication of Black hair in a critical cultural consciousness also helped it to signify freedom. Black hair as explored in the visual works of Black creatives reflects various social values. For example, purveyors of a "New Black Aesthetic" produced images that lampooned "the black nationalist movement" or an "official, positivist black party line," often turning to hair as a way to give mass audiences a peek inside Black culture.[18] Most notably, director Spike Lee's film *School Daze* (1988), about life on the campus of a fictional historically Black university, Mission College, took up the mantle of a blackness as divided between those who are socially conscious and those who are not and recognized in part by the appearance of dark skin and textured hair or light skin with straightened hair. The film's iconic "Good or Bad Hair" show tune pits its representative women against one another to reveal the emotional, social, and psychological significance of hair and aesthetic judgment. George C. Wolfe's *Colored Museum* skit "The Hairpiece" is similar, centering on a dispute between two wigs with differently textured hair about who has more fun. In these works, Black hair is framed not just as a sign of liberation but as a material in need of liberation—to be freed from self-hate among people of African descent. Hair becomes a vehicle through which individuals might reconcile the psychic ramifications of imperialism, colonialism, and chattel slavery. Learning to accept and appreciate features characterized as inherently Black, such as textured hair, became central to a visual culture interested in denouncing white supremacy. Historically rooted in images of Black businesspersons, combined with illustrations of textured hair on the heads of Black activists, the visual narrative of textured hair as an embrace of blackness is solidified and expanded upon by contemporary cultural productions.

Blackness and Texture

Textured hair, and not just images of textured hair, functions as a visual material for reimagining sentiment and sensuousness in the cultural aftermath of slavery. To think of Black hair as visual material culture is to think through the ways in which its look and feel are mutually significant, and in this way, its style and care operate as "culture made material."[19] Dictates on how to comb or how to view the simple stuff of Black hair textures—the curls, kinks, and coils—help to mark it as racially distinct, while at the same time igniting particular acts of ritual and communal practice around its grooming that further grant it a distinct materiality. This visual materiality is commonly conveyed through dichotomous discursive formations—such as good or bad hair, straight or natural hair—and is buttressed by both practices (ways of touching) and opportunities (hiring) attributed to each designation. Such qualitative distinctions about texture fit among a larger constellation of beauty as dichotomous and tether together skin colors and hair textures into disparate polarities, as if these couplings represent singular phenotypes.[20] At the same time, acts of ritual, creativity, and productivity involved in the working of textured hair into unique styles render it a Black diasporic visual material, linking up people of African descent across time and space through practices of invention and craft.[21] Hair textures and common modes of handling textured hair help tether together dispersed peoples of African descent and approaches to care and styling that represent a way of "practicing" diaspora.[22] Thus, as Afro-diasporic visual material, hair shows up on people and in illustrations, warranting a closer examination of how its significations traffic in legacies of power and cross-cultural contact. While hair texture has a communicative value—read as a racial signifier of genetic makeup when a tight curl is present or absent—it is presuppositions about the feel and character of a coiffure that shape the perception of racial identity. Judgments about upward mobility, sensibility, and raciality attributed to Black hair are based on the look, the feel, and the *look of the feel* of Black hair altogether. It is this dual significance of the visual and the material that undergirds David Hammons's installations made of discarded hair clippings and in which Afro-textured hair represents the Black body in the abstract, with a unique materiality that lends itself to building *Hair Pyramids* made from clippings or a *Nap Tapestry* from woven dreadlocks (figure I.4). While these works draw upon the visual capacity to feel hair texture, Hammons also acknowledges Black coiffure as a container for sentiment, describing hair as a "filter" and a "potent" material that retains spirit, making it difficult for him to acquire clippings of Black hair and compelling him to move on to other artistic materials out of self-protection.[23] Thus, as aesthetic material, Black hair represents both exterior and internal conceptions of feeling, complicating the sale of works from human hair and demanding caution from the artist handing material.

Marked by both textural and etheric qualities, Black hair conjures multiple registers of feeling or appeals to the haptic. First, Black hair functions as absorbent, bearing what Stefano Harney and Fred Moten theorize as "hapticality" or "the interiority of sentiment." Constituted in the ship's hold through the Middle Passage, they describe this "feeling of the shipped," hapticality, as the set of feelings produced in the multiple displacements of diaspora; hapticality yields "the capacity to feel through others, for others to feel through you, for you to feel them feeling you." This feeling, they argue, "is unmediated, immediately social," the result of "skin, against epidermalisation, senses touching."[24] These multiple vectors of feeling are produced under strained conditions and then birth other possibilities for feeling, such as through music and visual arts. Born under duress, hapticality becomes representational and presents the means by which the shipped remain legible to each other, culled together as a diasporic people through multiple sensualities rendered on multiple surfaces. The "haptic as an explicitly minoritarian aesthetic," according to Rizvana Bradley, or as "a specific set of material negotiations between bodies, spaces and objects," it is a chance to think about interpersonal and imagistic interactions, to consider "non-normative sensuality" on a variety of surfaces.[25] Thus, I take up hair as a human surface for thinking through alternate sensuous encounters with Black

1.4

David Hammons, *Nap Tapestry*, 1978. Photograph by Dawoud Bey.

I.5

Colin Quashie, *SlaveShip Brand Sardines*, 2012. Sardine can, 3 × 4½ × ⅞ in.
(7.6 × 11.4 × 2.2 cm). Collection of the Nasher Museum of Art at Duke University,
Durham, NC. Gift of Mark Sloan and Michelle Van Parys in honor of Trevor Schoonmaker, 2016.13.2. © Colin Quashie. Image courtesy of the Nasher Museum of Art.

raciality, and in its hapticality I find a continual reckoning with the legacies of
the hold and the cultural consequences of transport.

The visual legacy of slavery often directs scholarly attention toward the
flesh. Artists remark on this emblematic inheritance from the torment captured
in Joseph Turner's *Slave Ship* to Colin Quashie's *SlaveShip Brand Sardines*, signifying on the antislavery image of bodies crammed in a cargo hold (figure I.5).
These illustrations emphasize that it is what has happened to the flesh—tightly
packed together or ripped apart by sea creatures—that endures in the conception of slavery and the reckoning with its reverberation. Flesh that "registered
the wounding" of the Middle Passage, according to Hortense Spillers, is the
entity acted upon and as a "primary narrative"; flesh documents through its
"seared, divided, ripped-apartness, riveted to the ship's hole."[26] Moreover, the
suffering rendered in the flesh becomes "a pivotal arena for the politics emanating" from the oppressed.[27] Skin becomes the primary document of Black suffering, the ultimate qualifier of Black raciality, authenticity, and futurity. Indeed,

"flesh [operates] as Blackness in abstraction" according to C. Riley Snorton.[28] This significance of flesh to conceptualizations of blackness appears in a bevy of cultural representations, from crude illustrations to modern pictures. Skin has served as the primary mode for realizing Black raciality, where color and then colorism have been crucial to understanding the subjugation of the Black body under racial capitalism.

Accordingly, flesh has also operated as the dominant haptic regime in the realm of Black representation. Flesh is central to how we know blackness in the world, and with regard to matters of touch, it is the fleshly encounters that seem to matter most. Flesh is the predominant human surface for thinking through questions of touch. Operating as an unnatural physical order determining protocols of feeling, the appearance of the flesh has similarly been used to read histories of suffering as recorded on the Black body—the wounds imprinted on the fugitive from slavery. Even in illustration, flesh is held as central to claims of authenticity and to modes of depiction that reinstate or reinscribe discourses of power. Along these lines, Teju Cole reads the technological limitations of photography's penchant for light (skin) against work by photographers who make productive use of darkness and shadow when shooting Black flesh to examine biases built into the photographic apparatus.[29] The treatment of the flesh becomes paramount to judging a picture and central to critiquing encounters with the Black body. But whereas "touch is the first frontier of oppression, [as] violating forms of touch [are] at the introduction of slavery," there are other surfaces on which to touch and conceptualize blackness.[30] While flesh is central to how we know blackness, there is much revealed through the exploration of hair as another human surface. Just as the "absence of the object seen" in cinema is but one scopic regime, one way to organize the viewing experience, the primacy of the flesh is *a* means for structuring the haptic.[31] Martin Jay theorizes the "cultural variability of ocular experience" by describing various scopic regimes, and while he argues that the eye is "the most expressive of the sense organs," he claims "touch" as its only competitor.[32] Issues of touch, feeling, interiority, or the historical legacy of bondage can be realized in coiffure, which is similarly marked with violence, used as a basis for political organizing, and equally capable of rendering blackness in the abstract. The feel of Black hair, feelings about Black hair, and Black hair as a collection of feeling all point to a tangled register of sentiment to which I want to attend further.

A haptic reading of an alternate human surface is significant for taking seriously the role of slavery and race in the visual sense. A gendered and racialized conception of the flesh has been central to rendering touch as uniquely feminine, and contrary to a Western "phallogocularcentrism."[33] But this approach ignores different relationships to touch and to the flesh. Indeed, the "ungen-dering" of the flesh, as slavery would have it, removes a pretense of feminine entitlement to the haptic; bondage asserts suffering and surfacism as part of the haptic and central to the production of blackness after slavery. Thus, I regard "the haptic as a feminist visual *strategy*," in keeping with Laura Marks's usage, quintessential to the representation of blackness by visual means, where the pictorial treatment of the flesh becomes the predominant point of entry for understanding issues of authenticity, realism, and the like.[34]

Such protocols of look and touch are entangled in Black hair. Most obviously, in its care and adornment, Afro-textured hair demands physical touch—to im-plement Douglass's part or to twist Johnson's locs, for example. These issues of style or the look of hair that has been manipulated into unique kinds of displays bring up issues of touch between Black people. More than this, though, Afro-textured hair has continually been subject to examination and circumspection, from slavery onward, in efforts to understand and manage its particularity: the curl and coil that make up its visual distinction. The unique way in which Afro-textured hair is said to feel, and is imagined to feel, in the hand becomes a part of understanding blackness with hair fiber serving as another surface for objec-tification. The sum of these sensuous engagements accentuates touch, and not just appearance, as a central means of engaging Black hair. Much like the pho-tographs discussed by Tina Campt, hair involves "multiple forms of touch"; and just as photographs undergo "tactile bodily interactions like touching, wearing, handling, and manipulation, as well as the varied and elaborate forms of presen-tation, display, and circulation," Black hair is similarly haptic, known to viewers through various kinds of physical contact.[35] Haptic images, those that we touch physically or emotionally, those we view up close and from afar, exist in diverse formats and interpellate viewers to see with the body as well as with the eyes. Whether three-dimensional or two-dimensional, "haptic images" solicit bodily relation between the viewer and the image, moving on the image surface; these pictures demand close contact, dissolve the viewer's subjectivity, and forge an "erotic relationship" through the experience of distance and closeness.[36] Hap-tic images hail the viewer and invite contemplation of the image surface rather than the image narrative.

Haptic visual encounters with Black hair differently frame textural distinc-tion. Thinking through texture, with no attention to qualitative distinctions about wave, curl, and kink—in *New Growth*, there is no good or bad hair—draws together the various ways of distinguishing hair into a larger position about blackness on the surface. Thus, whether describing so-called good hair in the twentieth century or utilizing the dubious "hair typing system" of the twenty-first century, qualifiers about distinction point to ways of parsing blackness for its look and feel simultaneously. These references to texture more aptly underscore the multiple subjects involved in the determination of hair's feeling, that texture does not inherently signify raciality, and that hair is not objectively "good" or "bad." The question is always "good to whom and for what?" Thus, efforts to reimagine derogatory views of Black coiffure simultaneously read together image and texture and seek to rethink subject positions around the surface of Black hair. Vernacular distinctions about the quality of hair have rendered terms such as *nappy* as pejorative and then later transformed them with the popularization of textured styles.[37] Anthropologist Ingrid Banks shows how *nappy*, a once-derogatory word reappropriated to positively describe "tightly coiled or curled black hair," became newly popular in everyday discussions as Black women began to rethink "desirable and undesirable" as racialized beauty norms.[38] Across time, *nappy* has often been read as resistant, unrefined, and in need of further management by force. In these transformations, texture is realized as a commentary on the feel of hair in the hand, not just its appearance on the individual.

Accordingly, Black hair is useful for contending with issues of feeling and interiority in addition to notions of the sensuous surface. Hapticality for people of African descent traffics in the many kinds of surfacisms brought to bear upon the Black body as a textured site of racial distinction and also in the internal sentiments associated with the exterior. Representational surfaces demand the look, a correspondence with "what is evident, perceptible, apprehensible," rather than with what is hidden.[39] Yet, to think of Black raciality as sensual, as palpable, implores us to think about mythologies of how blackness feels in the hand of the other: histories of touching Black bodies that have been used to shore up those mythologies as well as the feeling Black subject. Black hair becomes a material, visual, and symbolic site of return for contending with hapticality, materializing theories of feeling that might be broken down into interiority, touch, and texture. While hair represents a human surface, Black hair in particular has often been regarded as a site for understanding interiority— as in the psychological interior of the Black mind riddled with the legacy of colonialism and manifested in a self-hate that results in alterations to the human surface (such as skin bleaching and hair straightening). Especially after the Black Arts Movement (BAM) and the Black Power movement, textured hairstyles have been regarded as signifiers of a Black interior, a whole/healthy Black self that seeks to cast off the "shackles of the mind" imposed through enslavement. Relatedly, however, the feeling of natural hair, as in the ways that Black people have treated Black hair, and its physical handling via hot combs, chemical and mechanical straighteners, or braiding and fluffing Afros have been sites not only for moral judgment but for an enduring practice of touch as culturally and historically informed. Thus, to think of hapticality on the hair surface is to evaluate the multiple constructions of an insensate blackness, and also to take seriously those refusals of touch, such as when singer Solange Knowles croons "Don't touch my hair / When it's the feelings I wear."[40] In all of these instances the question of touch is a vehicle for engaging sentimentality and hapticality.

Afro-textured hair is an invitation to consider the ways in which Black raciality has been organized through vectors of feeling—rendered as a palpable condition, devoid of sentiment and curiously defined by the exterior. Natural hair presents fodder for thinking about the consistency of Black racial distinction in the hands—even how Black hands have been rendered with a distinct hapticity capable of wrangling Black tresses. In this way, returning to Black hair is an opportunity to sit with broader conceptions about the handling of the Black body on the long arc of racial capitalism in the United States, and in the face of persistent efforts at liberation. This interrogation of hair as an alternate human surface opens up understanding of the sensuousness of blackness by thinking beyond the flesh, and to think alongside image makers who have used the visual to shift perspectives on the sensual nature of blackness. Hair in Black visual culture forges a connection with liberation, but it is textured hair, specifically, as a haptic image that enables people of African descent to continually reengage the cultural aftermath of slavery. On the terrain of Black hair that legacy is played out not in the socio-political importance of hairstyles, but on the various hapticities embedded in Afro hair texture. Black hair is an archive of haptic encounters, calling to viewers on multiple registers of the sensory experience.

The chapters of this book explore what I describe as "haptic blackness" in an effort to better understand the physical, textural, visual, sentimental, and archival modes of constructing blackness on human and pictorial surfaces. Haptic blackness has to do with the ways in which the racial distinctions ascribed to people of African descent are rendered simultaneously visible and tactile, received with the eyes but also within the body. I read the organization of haptic blackness in the postslavery practices of race-making that were meant to maintain distinctions. Equally revealing are the resistant modes of representation that people of African descent have used to convey complex notions of feeling or to explore an interior blackness. In these, haptic blackness corresponds to the means by which Black raciality becomes simultaneously visual and palpable across surfaces and through transformations in culture and Black representation. Haptic blackness transitions conceptions of exteriority—moving the human surface from a cohesive object for embodied viewing to a textured surface constituted in habits of feeling and touch as historically informed experiences.

Iconic pictures also rely on a haptic blackness, demonstrating the manner in which the image surface produces a tangible raciality that is experienced through the eyes and within the body. Francis Harwood's eighteenth-century sculpture *Bust of a Man* employs a "haptic blackness" in textural features, which are highlighted in this *Digital Composition of "Bust of a Man"*; seen from two angles, the color and gloss of the stone are revealed as part of the sensual experience of the object (figure I.6).[41] Harwood carves definition in the lips and nose with careful detail to portray the curl of the subject's hair, creating a portrait sculpture conversant with theories of racial difference in the eighteenth century. This treatment of hair texture recurred in other three-dimensional works, as carving hair to mark the textural distinction of Black raciality in the sculpted figure helped to fashion a Black image, regardless of the stone's color. Working in the eighteenth and nineteenth centuries, artists paid careful attention to crafting tight curls on Black figures conscripted to various projects of empire. Charles-Henri-Joseph Cordier produced his *Vénus africaine* (1852), covering her breasts but deeply engaging her hair as coiled, possibly loc'd, and laid densely back and around her face (figure I.7). Jean-Baptiste Carpeaux followed with *Why Born Enslaved!* (1852), choosing to both expose her breast and reveal her hair, while Edmonia Lewis, in her *Forever Free* (1867), depicts an emancipated man in white stone, with tightly coiled curls to assert his raciality against the contrast of white marble. These works yield some of the earliest depictions of Afro-textured hair in Western art, where off-canvas artists exercised dexterity and care in trying to recreate Black coiffures. Through sculpture, these artists were explicit in their livening of the pictorial surface as reference for the human exterior.

While three-dimensional representations carry with them the opportunity to move around the object in order to take in the image, when represented on canvas by artists of European descent, Afro-textured coiffures have often received less detailed attention than white hairstyles. Whereas illustrations emphasizing hair among white subjects have used this attribute for claims about gender, sexuality, and citizenship, there has been less lore or guiding rationales for the meaning of Black hair texture in Western art. For example, Sandro Botticelli's late-fifteenth-century painting *Birth of Venus*, with her cascading locks that seem to catch wind, flowing and covering her genitals, presents an iconic treatment of hair as part of femininity and virginity for white women. Conversely, Marie-Guillemine Benoist's *Portrait d'une negresse* (1800), with her exposed breast and covered head, masks the Black subject's hair from viewers. Her nudity is an opportunity to question liberty and slavery. According to historian Robin Mitchell, the Black female body offered a vessel for reconciling the devastation of the Haitian Revolution in 1802 and the repression of a Black presence in French national identity thereafter; images of blackness supported "the development of different notions of French citizenship and subjectivity."[42] For these paintings of Black women, head coverings help to signify status; curator Denise Murrell argues, "The head scarf is particularly characteristic of typing the Black female servant: by showing it piled high on her head, and tied to the side." The headscarf references the "foulards worn in the French Antilles," and it is a reccurring sign in paintings and photographs of the late nineteenth century that illustrate Black women alongside the whites whom they serve.[43] Thus, Black hair and its covering are curiously part of the chiaroscuro described by Lorraine O'Grady, the visual implement that brings whiteness into sharper relief, whether in Édouard

1.6

Ken Gonzales-Day, *Digital Composition of "Bust of a Man,"* 2015. Courtesy of the artist and Luis de Jesus, Los Angeles. *Left*, image of Francis Harwood's *Bust of a Man*, 1758, Yale Center for British Art, New Haven, CT, 2015. *Right*, image of Francis Harwood's *Bust of a Man*, 1758, J. Paul Getty Museum, Los Angeles, 2009.

Manet's *Olympia* (1863) or in other works that construe Black hair as another marker of caste to define the Black subject as a foil for whiteness.[44]

The representation of textured hair in two dimensions largely waited for contemporary artists of African descent. Curator Kim Curry-Evans describes recurring themes around communal space, individuality, political symbolism, and "the syndrome of 'good hair/bad hair'" in the *HairStories* told by Black visual artists.[45] These include not only the modernist photographs of James VanDerZee, for example, who depicted hair among Black Americans as both part of a stylish appearance and a culture of upward mobility, but also the works by Kerry James Marshall, who has attended to Black hair in culturally specific locations. Hair is central to the private interior of Black culture, and not just its recognition in public, as portrayed in Marshall's *De Style* (1993), which locates the barbershop as a destination and not just a place used to prepare for pub-

1.7

Charles-Henri-Joseph Cordier, *Vénus africaine,* 1852. Bronze and gold, 15⁹⁄₁₆ × 8 in. (39.5 × 20.3 cm). Walters Art Museum, Baltimore, by CC01.0.

lic encounters (figure I.8). Marshall's combination of acrylic and collage puts textural variety onto the canvas in a scene that shows the care of Black hair as constitutive of community within Black life. His title offers a nod to *De Stijl* (neoplasticism), Dutch depictions emphasizing vertical and horizontal composition, while Marshall's characters reference Jacob Lawrence's *Barber Shop* (1975), riffing on Lawrence's signature angles and Black figures through Marshall's offering of a frontal view of six occupants and his play on what constitutes the subject. The climbing plant on the left side of the image duplicates the height and stature of the tall locs on the seated figure, while the mirror provides a double and a rear view for the man standing to the right, his locs pinned up into

1.8

Kerry James Marshall, *De Style*, 1993. Acrylic and collage on canvas, 109 × 120 in.
© Kerry James Marshall. Courtesy of the artist and the Jack Shainman Gallery,
New York.

a crown. Marshall extends the private/public convening around Black hair as
a destination in his *School of Beauty, School of Culture* (plate 3), portraying Afro
puffs, box braids, and locs on his signature Black subjects. Here, whiteness infil-
trates the space, revealed in the specter of dominant beauty norms as a lurking
reality; whiteness and blondness hold center space in the salon, present in the
anamorphic figure of a "Goldilocks" to mimic Hans Holbein's *The Ambassadors*
(1533). Such inclusions demand a nuanced reading of the larger image according
to Krista Thompson, where surfacism promotes a recognition of other ways of
seeing or nonnormative approaches to vision.[46] Exploring these textured inclusions, whether via paint, glitter, or found objects, *New Growth* reads such en-

gagements with visual representations for a deeper understanding of Black hair and of race as a human exterior.

Chapter Summaries

This book focuses on textured Black hair as represented in several visual medias, and it regards Black hair itself as a visual medium. In this exploration of Black visual culture, I situate hair among those practices of looking, presenting, representing, or rendering visible that are popular among people of African descent. I explore Black hair in slave narratives, abolitionist portraiture, scrapbooks, photojournalism, popular magazines, television advertisements, fiction, and documentary film, as well as in sculpture, painting, and craft and collage. By beginning with hair in the context of slavery, this book resists and rewrites conceptions of Black hair as a particularly Black preoccupation—as the source of internal ire for people of African descent exclusively. Instead, it reveals that the look, feel, and potential of Black hair has been just as relevant to public culture as other renderings of the Black body.

The first two chapters explore haptic blackness on the human surface, considering the treatment of hair fiber in slavery and in the memory of slavery. Chapter 1 begins in the nineteenth century, analyzing Black hair as an archive. Circulating throughout the Atlantic, Afro coiffure and its representation variously appear as a register of racial distinction, a chronicle of racial violence, and a record of care. This examination includes an exploration of the physical handling of Black hair, such as the cutting of Black hair to signal "slave" status, to initiate sexual violence, and to bolster academic inquiry. In this last instance, hair clippings from unfree Black people were used by early race scientists to reveal yet another site where Black bodies were consumed for the purposes of knowledge production and the generation of celebrity among nineteenth-century researchers. At the same time, however, people of African descent maintained diasporic aesthetic practices through hair. Illustrations of African peoples in the US state of Maryland and in Brazil, in lithographs and in photographs, help reveal hair grooming and styling as valuable. Together, these factors render Black hair as an archive, not simply for how it reveals information about people of African descent but also for how it records notions of feeling and practices of touch that have (otherwise) gone unexamined. Chapter 2 turns toward the issue of hair texture, where through the construction and promotion of "natural hair," people of African descent variously used texture to reorganize haptic blackness in relation to the memory of slavery. In visual and textual works, Black people intertwined the legacy of bondage and Black interiority as phenomena that revealed themselves on the human surface through hairstyles. In the twentieth century, Afro-textured hair moved into a new relationship to racial capitalism via the commodification of natural hair. A diverse collection of images, taken from Johnson Publishing Company and the marketing of cosmetics like Afro Sheen, as well as from photojournalists' portrayals of dreadlocks, underscore legibility and approachability as key frameworks for engaging the issue of texture. In these instances, hair functions like flesh in offering a material history about the production of blackness under racial capitalism.

The final two chapters of *New Growth* offer a pivot past Black hair's historical and haptic rendering alongside flesh. In chapters 3 and 4, I turn to the pictorial surface and consider cultural productions about Black hair as recuperative: as sites that reorganize notions of touching and feeling blackness, thereby complicating linear constructions of time recorded on the body. Chapter 3 attends to film and photography, analyzing the prevalence of documentary aesthetics among cultural producers who take up the camera in ways that reimagine touch and blackness. Reading the works of J. D. Ojeikere and Bill Gaskins together, I explore black-and-white photographs for how they bring the viewer closer to Black hair, fostering touch through the image surface. Similarly, I look to the body of independent documentary films on natural hair to examine how these works offer viewers new ways of touching Black hair by filming hair care. These images, I argue, laid the groundwork for new practices of touch now evolving in the twenty-first century, in our emergent visual economy. Finally, chapter 4 argues for reading blackness as a haptic inheritance conveyed through ways of creating the surface. I consider the work of Black women artists who have transformed legacies of a palpable Black raciality through contemporary artworks that reveal the surface as worked upon, hewn in ways that reference the past but link together people of African descent through what is visible and cultivated.

In this approach, I mean to take seriously Black hair as a cultural practice and as visual material, where its common rituals and representations present an opportunity to reconsider the histories of touch and feeling that have informed conceptions of texture. In veering into the haptic, I offer another mode of engaging Afro-textured hair, outside the valuations of textural quality and Black authenticity that scholars have warned against. Questioning the appearance and visual meanings attributed to textured hair offers another valence for perceiving the characteristic distinctions of blackness that have historically been viewed as biologically determined or as having a macro-level of social import. Haptic blackness, as realized in hair and images of hair, reveals touch and feeling as racialized and historically informed, and thus mutable, with a propensity for expanded conceptions of autonomy.

ARCHIVE

ONE

Ruth Cox Adams, also known as Harriet Bailey, kept a token of affection for her brother Frederick Douglass inside a small wooden sewing box (figure 1.1).[1] The feelings between these fictive kin endured a fight, a marriage, and a move, as articulated in letters they exchanged, and in a corporeal keepsake—a braid of Douglass's hair, wrapped in paper, that Adams would keep upon the green fabric inlay of her wood and mother-of-pearl box. Artist Wendel A. White's photograph *Frederick Douglass Hair* depicts these items together, as Adams might have maintained them (figure 1.2). The strands of hair that form this sentimental memento are carefully tied together by a string on one end and a knot on the other, suggesting the tender feeling with which it was given, as the hair was likely braided and then clipped to be given as a gift.[2] Identified with a note that reads, "Frederick Douglass my adopted brother Lynn Mass," this particular offering reveals the Black body in a different kind of exchange, unlike the trade of human chattel.[3] Here, hair is part of sentimental gifting between formerly

1.1

Wooden sewing box belonging to Ruth Cox Adams, ca. 1847. Nebraska State Historical Society Photograph Collections, Lincoln, NE.

• • •

1.2

Wendel A. White, *Frederick Douglass Hair*, 2012. Nebraska State Historical Society, Lincoln, NE. Courtesy of the artist.

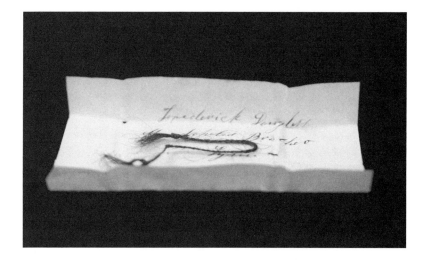

unfree African Americans, and it provides a way to register various kinds of possession—self, kin, human. Adams's keepsake pivots on multiple registers of feeling, signaling affection between a brother and a sister; touch, as indicated in the weave of the hair braid; and the material experience of the Black body, as archived in a representative artifact.

The gift of a hair clipping was not uncommon in the early part of the nineteenth century. Cut hair as a sentimental talisman fed an industry as elites embedded hair in jewelry to create mourning souvenirs, using "the cut edge of the hair" as a "medium of remembrance" to signify the body from which it came and in anticipation of its donor's absence.[4] However, by the time Douglass might have given his braid to Adams, he would have already been clear about the meanings and significations of Black hair, both in freedom and in slavery. Adams, a fugitive free woman from Easton, Maryland, lived in Lynn, Massachusetts, during the 1840s as a helper and companion to Frederick's first wife, Anna Douglass, while the abolitionist toured Great Britain. In describing the reception of his blackness in Scotland to his friend Francis Jackson, Douglass wrote: "It is quite an advantage to be a 'nigger' here. I find I am hardly black enough for british taste, but by keeping my hair as wooly as possible, I make out to pass for at least a half a negro, at any rate. . . . The people lavish nearly all their attention on the negro."[5] By this time, his hair was an increasingly prominent aspect of his appearance on the abolitionist lecture circuit, as noted in numerous portraits taken during the period; and his writing indicates that Douglass was highly aware of this. His decision to brandish his hair was also made in the face of derision. By 1847, Douglass had already published his *Narrative of the Life of Frederick Douglass* and started his *North Star* newspaper, in which he printed a scathing letter "To My Old Master," outing Thomas Auld for his brutality. Such writings inspired much ire among proslavery whites, one of whom wrote Douglass directly to explain: "As a black, your place is below the white man, as surely as your hair, and velvet like coarse skin, and smell, is inferior to his hair, and skin, and odour."[6] In this context, Douglass prized his own hair as a token of kinship to his sister, and as a sign of blackness that might be used both against him or by him in navigating the Atlantic world.

This chapter reads Black hair as an archive where, in the context of slavery, it records multiple kinds of feeling. To regard Afro-textured tresses as "repositories of feeling and emotions" is to think of their meaning as imbued through its "production and reception," and not simply as style or composition.[7] Sometimes those feelings were affection, such as those shared between Douglass and Adams. But at other times, those feelings were rage and vengeance. Because it circulates as an "enduring material," like bones, I think of hair as an archive along the lines of performance theorist Diana Taylor's description; but in its connection to rituals of care (and violence), Black hair closely aligns with the "ephemeral repertoire of embodied practice," as a way to transmit or convey knowledge or memory.[8] I begin with illustrations of Black hair, revealing how visual culture began to align hair with the head as proof of racial variety. Next, I take up efforts to intensify the scientific examination of Black hair, which focused on its tactile distinction as a way to chronicle Black raciality. The racism informing academic writing and travel illustration is an important counterpart to the physical brutality of plantation management that also utilized Black hair. I then discuss Black hair's absorption of slavery's choreography of violence. And finally, I conclude with an examination of how people of African descent organized Black hair as an archive of violent encounters and as a sign of resistance. Hair is written into the accounts of fugitive free persons who describe escape and survival, all the while inviting us to consider the role of intimate touch in their personal experiences of bondage.

In this approach, I mean to deal directly with the legacy of slavery in shaping the conception of Black coiffure. Hair is often a fleeting reference in studies of bondage, overlooked in scholarly discussions of the slavery era. Many of the more iconic images, like the cross section of the *Brookes* depicting bodies tightly packed together, do not offer much human detail about chattel cargo, and they show no specificity among individuals. When hair comes up in historical studies focused on other issues, scholars have remarked only in passing on the condition of Black hair in Atlantic transit—riddled with lice, matted with dirt and bodily fluid—but these details frequently provide only background on the conditions of travel.[9] In these studies, hair reveals or further verifies what we know about the atrocities associated with the Middle Passage—that it was inhumane with little regard for the personal care of captives. Another approach to Black hair in the context of slavery has been to use hair as evidence of race and race mixture, as in the discussion of Black hair in advertisements for Black fugitives. John Hope Franklin and Loren Schweninger discuss how "the growth of the mulatto population among runaways" made straight hair more remarked upon in advertisements, especially as "slave women of mixed origin may well have not worn the traditional head scarves in order to advertise their straight hair."[10] Collectively, then, hair was either ignored or regarded as evidence of the market conditions associated with slavery—reflecting either the totalizing extraction of transport or the means by which blackness (and whiteness) were commodified for sale.

But hair figured into the visual and affective economies that undergirded slavery, and it persisted after the point of sale. Accordingly, I turn to the visual culture of "Black hair" as constructed through slavery to think through the ways in which coiffure as a visual material absorbed chattel slavery's conscription of Black feeling. While conceptions of racial mixture helped shape ideas about the visual and textural "quality" of hair, I argue that, more importantly, Black hair archives the violence and regulation that was constitutive of racial capitalism in this context. The physical brutality of the era forces us to grapple with touch, and not just texture, as essential to slavery's imprint on Black hair. In this context, hair was essential not only to haptic blackness, to theories of palpable raciality that circulated in support of racial capitalism; it also functioned as the means by which people of African descent experienced and conveyed care to one another. The handling and representing of Black hair, whether in painting, drawing, photography, slave narratives, legal statutes, or scientific studies, from the turn of the nineteenth century to the 1850s, collectively illustrates coiffure as a means to contain and convey various notions of "black feeling."[11] Through these encounters, Black hair textures serve as another kind of archive for evidencing slavery's violence and addressing forms of Black resistance.

Witness

When British American architect Henry Benjamin Latrobe began illustrating people of African descent in the 1790s, his fixation on Black people's head coverings fit neatly with a growing investment in visual depictions of racial variety. European thinkers had been sorting humans into discrete racial categories since the seventeenth century, with details about the head becoming increasingly important to these racialized lists of characteristics. By 1775, Johann Friedrich Blumenbach had already theorized the existence of five varieties of mankind, listing Caucasians as superior, and describing the "Ethiopian variety" as the "colour black" with "hair black and curly . . . ; head narrow, compressed at the sides . . . ; forehead knotty, uneven."[12] In the decades toward the end of the eighteenth century, scientific schemata for explaining human variety were distributed across discrete (but closely related) disciplines, as physiognomists, phrenologists, and craniologists variously deployed facial traits, along with the shape and size of the head, as objective measures for understanding observable differences in people around the globe.[13] Latrobe's foray into the depiction of people emerged in a world where the head was already understood as a central means by which to understand racial distinction and human variety.

Rather than laboratory examinations, Latrobe situated his research within a framework of travel observation, as recorded in both his journal writing and watercolor illustrations. Items like his drawing *Alic, a Faithful and Humorous Servant of Bathurst Jones of Hanover* are striking for the care and detail given to the subject's face. Latrobe paid greater attention to Alic's eyelashes, and his stiff, protruding braid, than to his activities while standing at the table. These details appear in sharp relief as Alic is portrayed in profile. Likewise, with *Preparations for the Enjoyment of a Fine Sunday Evening* (figure 1.3), Latrobe's depiction of five Black people engaged in grooming also relies on profile views. Two men have their hair attended to—one by a woman standing behind him as he sits on a barrel, his hat upon his knee. Like Alic's, the woman's braids extend upward and outward, away from her head. In the foreground, a man reclines over a barrel as another man stands before him, lathering his face for a shave; a woman stands to the side to offer assistance. Shane and Graham White read these depictions for what they say about the significance of hair care among people of African descent—that even in slavery they "styled their hair," that it "was important to them as individuals, and it also played a substantial role in their communal life."[14] However, if we take seriously Latrobe's voyeuristic perspective—depicting African American grooming as if he were peering over a fence (or watching Alic work from afar)—then Latrobe's choice to disappear his own body from the scene creates distance within the image and casts an aura of observation over the depiction, making it ethnological in tone and akin to works that would come after 1800. Latrobe's profile point of view presents the entire head, illustrating the forehead and the back of the head, allowing his images to mimic the side view of skull illustrations that were increasingly popular among naturalists and ethnologists coming into the nineteenth century.

To be sure, Latrobe's depictions of African Americans were not the benign illustrations of a traveler, and his journal reveals a deep investment in racial hierarchy, not just variety. Latrobe made aesthetic judgments about people of African descent and expected congruence among characteristics of racial identity. Describing "the uncommon productions called albinos," Latrobe marveled about a man "brought from Africa—called here salt-water negroes," having "the exact features of perfect black, flat nose and thick lips, and . . . very ugly. His skin, both of his face and body, is uncommonly fair and white." Adding to his peculiarity, Latrobe explained, "his hair, or rather wool, is yellow, his eyebrows are white with a yellowish cast, and his eyelashes, which are very long and almost choke his eyes, are almost white."[15] Latrobe's emphasis on hair and skin color as features that should correspond to racial theories in academic writing of the period reveals an overt racism in his written ideas that becomes opaque in his colorful paintings of people. Nonetheless, his treatment of Black hair

1.3

Henry Benjamin Latrobe, *Preparations for the Enjoyment of a Fine Sunday Evening*, 1797. Courtesy of the Maryland Center for History and Culture, 1960.108.1.2.36.

is contextualized in larger observations about racial variety and as part of the unique cranial and cultural features supposedly prevalent among people of African descent.

Latrobe regularly used visual representations to complement his recorded observations of African American heads. In *Market Folks, New Orleans* (figure 1.4), Latrobe depicts twelve adults of Louisiana, drawn in different hues, wearing various head wraps and hats. Although the scene in which we find these subjects has to do with commerce—individuals in their diverse acts of selling, waiting, and purchasing—Latrobe takes great care to illustrate an array of hat styles and cloth head wraps. In the foreground of the image, a woman sits at the base of a tree trunk, selling fruit; she is draped in robes and adorned with a patterned headscarf and earrings. Over time, Latrobe paid less attention to the facial features of African-descended people and instead emphasized his racist judgments in his corresponding writing. In New Orleans, a place "valuable for the cultivation of sugar," he argued that Black people were essential, as "were it not for the vegetables and fowls and small marketing of all sorts, raised by the negro slaves, the city would starve." He goes on, however:

1.4

Henry Benjamin Latrobe, *Market Folks, New Orleans,* 1819. Courtesy of the Maryland Center for History and Culture, 1960.108.1.14.17.

To the negroes it is not labor, but frolic and recreation, to come to market. They have only Sunday on which to sell their truck. If more good than evil grows out of the license to these wretches to come to town and earn some comfort, some decent clothing, or even some finery for their families, by the sale of their articles, if the town is fed and the negro slave clothed thereby, it would be difficult to show how the prohibition of the practice and its consequences would be compensated by the forced idleness of these people throughout the week, as well as their idleness or forced attendance at church on Sunday.[16]

As with many other white travelers, Latrobe's illustrations reflect his written observations and ideas about his exotic subjects, a trend that persisted internationally and helped to embed political agendas into pictorial works. Depiction was a central element in the discussion of racial distinction at the turn of the nineteenth century, and writers and illustrators drew upon disciplines such as religion, botany, and physical anthropology. Drawings of different head and face shapes, or skulls with patches linked to various operations, made the work of illustrators necessary to discussions of race science. "Most artists in New York possessed some degree of familiarity with phrenology" by the end of the 1830s.[17] Improvements in visual technologies helped theories of race science proliferate, with the mass production of images supporting arguments for racial distinction. In these developments, the "vividness of wood engravings and the quasi-tactile qualities of lithographs extended the palette of scientific artists."[18] By the 1830s, Britt Rusert argues, the visual archive supporting "American racial science was largely found in popular culture"; it was not until the 1850s that "those racial typologies circulated back from popular culture to racial science."[19] Image collections of flora, fauna, birds, and people represented a transformation in illustration practices as well as in theories of polygenesis.

This penchant for representing human variety was of international interest. French traveler and artist Jean Baptiste Debret's three-volume *Voyage pittoresque et historique au Brésil* illustrates beautiful scenes of people, places, and nature in Brazil.[20] Debret was among a number of European artists visiting Brazil for inspiration.[21] In lush colors and careful detail, Debret's images depicted Africans and Afro-Brazilians (free and enslaved), white Brazilians and Portuguese, and Indigenous Brazilian people. Portraying a collection of human and natural variety, Debret's work helped audiences envision a uniquely diverse Brazil of racial multiplicity without giving away the brutality marshaled against African descendants and native peoples. Lamonte Aidoo argues that throughout the nineteenth century aristocrats promoted a notion that "Brazilian slavery was more genteel, more humane, than in other parts of the Americas," even as they actively hid cruelties of the coffle and the marketplace from European visitors.[22] Debret's romanticist illustrations align with this project of a multiracial Brazil. In his employment of "tropical romanticism," emphasizing Indigenous peoples and the natural landscape to illustrate an ambiguous Brazil for European consumption, Debret sought "to document the culture and history of Brazil from an ostensibly scientific point of view," even as he actively fabricated scenes of social interaction.[23]

Although Debret was engaged in a local project of promoting Brazilian culture, his approach to illustration fit within an international emphasis on the head as proof of racial variety. Debret represented this variety with illustrations of native Brazilians, such as portraits of *Chief Camacan Mongoyo* and *Femme Camacan Mongoyo*, alongside depictions of the Brazilian military. Here, the heads and hair of native people also served as proof of difference, as Debret illustrated *Coiffures, et suite de têtes de différentes castes sauvages* showing the heads, headdresses, and hairstyles of Indigenous Brazilians. Debret tightened his focus on the heads and hair of African peoples with his *Esclaves nègres, de différentes nations* (plate 4). This illustration of sixteen women of African descent, shown from the bust, depicts the women's clothing and distinct hairstyles. The treatment of hair ranges from an Afro-textured puff, pulled together, to rings of curls and small braids woven at the base of the head or dangling from the scalp. Some women wear flowers in their hair, or they don diverse head coverings—both decorative and functional. Debret takes care to depict the back of one woman's head to show her mix of thick, gathered curls. His fixation on the total view of Black heads extended to depictions of men as well. His *Différentes nations nègres* illustrates seven men, positioned to reveal face markings, jewelry, and hairstyles. Showing viewers an array of patterns shaved into Black coiffures, contrasted against smooth scalps, Debret also used profile views to display heads.

This set of travel illustrations included hairstyles as well as hair care to represent people of African descent and their cultural practices as examples of natural variety. For example, Debret's *Les barbiers ambulants* (plate 5) shows the practice of barbering among men of African descent. Situated near a dock, four men sit together for grooming. Reading this image from left to right, the first man lathers the face of his compatriot in preparation for a shave. Next to them, another figure sits on the ground and bows his head to have his hair clipped with scissors. Cues about the status of these men suggest different stations, as the tattered clothes of the barbers (identified as slaves in the title) commingle with conspicuous hats and gold jewelry in this scene of "barbers at work in open air."[24] Presumably, these encounters happen near the *Boutique de barbiers* (plate 6), where a boy helps a woman sharpen implements at an establishment for selling straight razors. The scene is anchored by a seated woman who darns socks and by another Black woman serving food to a lounging man of European descent. Here, profile views help suggest that people of African descent focused on their labor—sewing, sharpening, and serving—as compared to the full-frontal view of the white man who fans himself. Illustrative details such as the curve of the boy's head help give viewers a clear view of the shapes and angles of Black subjects.

The contexts for hair care among unfree Black people in these images placed the uniqueness of Black hair within particular cultural and social settings, lending a subtle but powerful pseudoscientific tone to these illustrations. By 1839, when Philadelphia physician and naturalist Samuel George Morton released his volume *Crania Americana*, theories of polygenesis had a strong foothold in the United States. Although Morton did not proclaim support for slavery, his theory of the distinct origins and purposes of distinct races proved useful for southern enslavers—a point that helped sell his pricey book amid an economic depression. Additionally, though, "illustrations also added to the book's appeal"; these included life-size lithographs of skulls depicted from various angles, along with images of Morton's instruments for measurement, which appeared throughout the text. Morton's racism employed the lens of science. His descriptions of racial variety made clear hierarchies of his observations: "The Ethiopian Race is characterized by a black complexion, and black, woolly hair; . . . in disposition, the negro is joyous, flexible, and indolent."[25] Morton had to be sure to label these "races," however, to ensure that his attempts at categorization were suggestive of science and not art.[26] In his works, the practical distinctions of hair culture fell away in his attempt at objectively portraying racial specificity through the shape and volume of the skull. But scientists and would-be scientists would only expand the varieties of evidence employed to argue for polygenesis, and hair remained a significant part of this work as viewers looked to increasingly tactile and co-present forms of material evidence.

Re/Coil

Peter Arrell Browne must have been an ardent consumer of race science illustrations. When he published his *Trichologia Mammalium; or, A Treatise on the Organization, Properties, and Uses of Hair and Wool; Together with an Essay upon the Raising and Breeding of Sheep* in 1853, he gave his readers a preview of his arguments by opening the text with a plate titled *Representing the Three Species of Mankind.* The image featured profile illustrations of an Indigenous American—his head shorn down to a mohawk and adorned with jewelry—and a white man, with his hair parted and smoothed, shaded to emphasize sheen and highlights; and both are situated above a Black man, whose mass of curls convey density but reflect no light. Although hair is the subject of the study, Browne was sure to include facial distinctions that corresponded to physiognomic characterizations of Black peoples' lips and noses, and he included variations in the slope of the foreheads among the representatives of each group. Rather than label the figures by color or race, Browne's captions describe the differences in hair specimens—in keeping with his argument that observable distinctions in coiffure were evidence of racial variety. "Pile," as he described it, was cylindrical among Indigenous people and oval among those of European descent, but "eccentrically elliptical" among descendants of Africa. While by 1850 studies of the head were regarded as scientific undertakings, Browne—a Philadelphia lawyer by occupation and naturalist by interest—planned to cut his teeth among ethnologists by using the texture of hair to prove polygenesis. His work relied on human and pictorial surfaces to distinguish blackness, in particular.

Trichology, or the scientific study of hair, offered Browne a frame of objectivity in which to situate his hobby and from which to participate in ethnological studies of the human species. His major work, *Trichologia Mammalium*, offers 179 pages on the subject, supported by ten pages of illustrations on hair follicles and shafts with numerous charts and graphs about measurement. While Browne's volume offered a comparative study of pile, his central argument was that people of African descent had wool, not hair, thus proving a closer relation to animals than to whites or Indigenous persons. Browne used eleven measures to make his determinations on the qualities of Black hair, ranging from observations of the shape of the filament, the direction of growth, the color of strand, and the length. In a category unto itself, "eccentrically elliptical or ellipsoidal wool," as Browne described it, "is crisped and frizzled, and sometimes spirally curled; black; short; pierces the epidermis at right angles; has the coloring matter disseminated in the cortex and fibers, and the scales numerous; sharp at the anterior extremity, and not investing so closely the shaft."[27] The illustrations and figures included in the text serve to corroborate the scientific nature of his method, demonstrating that Browne subjected hair samples to meticulous examination. He goes on to explain that in "pile that is eccentrically elliptical," when examined closely, "between two pieces of glass, and moderately pressed, a part of it will exhibit, under the microscope, the thin edge of the ellipse, and another portion will represent one of the flattened sides."[28] Browne acknowledged distinct aesthetic variations in the practice of Black hair care, citing that "negroes shave their heads in figures; at one time in stars, at another in the manner of friars; and still more commonly in alternate stripes; and their little boys are shaved in the same manner."[29] The goal of this text was to demonstrate the scientific method as central to claims "that the negro and the European are separate species of beings," with visual evidence to support its claims of rigor.[30]

Proving polygenesis, however, was Browne's larger interest, which he built upon across multiple projects. Even at professional organizations, Browne took up his mantle—arguing that people of African descent possessed wool, making for a close alignment with sheep due to the matting capabilities of each kind of pile, which also make it fit for haberdashery. On November 3, 1849, Browne delivered a paper on "the classification of mankind, by the hair and wool of their heads," to the American Ethnological Society. He was not alone in his examination of Black hair texture as a route by which to understand racial distinction; his presentation was meant to counter the work of a Dr. Prichard, who argued that Black hair was not in fact wool. The haptic racism latent in such debates and explorations was commonplace by the 1850s.[31] Central to slavery's haptic racism was the idea that Black hair *appeared* to *feel* different from the hair of whites. Slaving whites frequently described the texture of Black hair as coarse and hard, or as "wool," likening its thickness and curl to that of animals.[32] Historian Winthrop Jordan explains that these sorts of concepts highlight texture as well as appearance as a means of diminishing Black hair. As they did with skin, race thinkers theorized "woolly" hair as both an outcome of environmental conditions and a defense against the elements.[33] Labeling Black hair as "wool" signaled a harshness that justified abusive forms of touch. Browne and others took what was meant as a euphemism at the time and used it as the basis for investigation. Accordingly, not simply in the microscopic examination of Black hair, but also in the social significance of its unique characteristics—its growth, its care, its textural possibility—Browne saw proof of racial distinction. He went on to publish this paper before writing *Trichologia Mammalium.*

Although Browne's public-facing work emphasized the "scientific" exploration of pile, his private collection of hair samples was steeped in the sentimentality of album culture, situating this fascination within the practice of scrapbooking.[34] Amid papers bordered with elaborate designs, Browne displayed hair samples from his three racial groupings, with an emphasis on samples from notable white men and former presidents of the United States, as well as those from persons of African descent and animals. Tufts of hair gathered together with ribbon are pasted to the pages of Browne's albums and appear alongside his handwritten notes about how the hair was obtained. United States presidents and white men of high regard get the most careful attention in Browne's collection, revealing the archive as a sentimental pastime as well as a scientific pursuit. For example, an especially ornate page is dedicated to hair belonging to George Washington (plate 7). Framed with blue flowers and a decorative border, Washington's portrait headlines the page, and below it a sparse collection of hair is adhered with a blue ribbon. A news clipping is included at the bottom, along with a few lines of poetry:

Fame spread her wings and with her trumpet blew,
Great WASHINGTON is come, what praise is due—
What titles shall he have? She paus'd and said,
Not one—his *name alone* strikes every title dead.[35]

Similar care is given to the other presidents in Browne's volumes, all of whom have pages with portraits and hair samples; and their names are displayed in a formal manner, such as "His Excellency Gen. Andrew Jackson" and "His Excellency, John Q. Adams." Touch is conveyed not simply in the handling that was required for Browne to keep the hair together, tighten the ribbon, and attach all the elements to the page, but also in the touching sentiment that is apparent in his respect for the distinguished persons included among his ten-volume archive. White men are denoted not just in the represented tresses of hair, but also in the care given to saving their pile and the amount of information collected about the samples.

Care is absent, however, in Browne's treatment of Indigenous and African persons. Overwhelmingly, these samples appear on otherwise blank or basic pages that name them as part of "P. A. BROWNE'S COLLECTION OF PILE," framed by a repeating (rather than a unique) border. Likewise, the hair sections are gathered and taped directly to the pages of the scrapbook, giving them no special care to indicate them as mementos. Although most of the presidential hair samples that Browne cataloged were given to him by people related to the subjects, such as a barber or a widow, the pile attributed to people of African descent was sent to Browne by slavers, medical professionals, and missionaries. A frequent note accompanying Black hair samples reads "no letter of provenance," illustrating the lack of personal accounting to describe the hair and casual handling around obtaining the material that shapes the collection. Samples from whites often include accompanying communication, especially those accompanying presidential hair samples. In addition to the portraits, entries from George Washington, James Monroe, and John Quincy Adams include the hair sample, a letter describing how it was obtained, and documentation of a willingness to share the material. Conversely, no portraits accompany the Black hair samples, and without correspondence from the subjects, these items are part of an archival collection where Browne's voice and his views of the hair constitute the only representation of Black subjects.

Browne's claims for differences in the quality and character of Black coiffure are structured into this approach. Although his collection includes some sixty examples attributed to people who are "African" or "Mulattin" of African descent, in no instance does the contribution appear voluntary, as Browne was committed to excluding free persons of African descent. This page from his scrapbook, *A Slave of Mr. Jm. H. Hundley had three children at a birth, 2 black & one white* (plate 8), features four hair samples taped to the page. Organized to illustrate heredity, Browne lists "Father & Mother: pure negroes" at the top sample and beside two specimens of curly black hair. Below them, he lists the "Black Child. Pure negro" next to a similar case; and finally, there is a "White Child. Black Albinos" to describe a tuft of coiled blond hair. In these inclusions, Browne's collection portrays his outright refusal to include consenting people of African descent—and not for lack of opportunity. In the 1840s in Philadelphia there was a robust Black population, including African Americans doing professional work related to medicine and the provision of mortuary services. However, Browne justifies their exclusion from his scholarly writing, noting his quest for purity. He explains that "it might easily be supposed that in a city like Philadelphia, abounding in black faces, no difficulty would be encountered in procuring *pure* negro hair. It is quite the contrary."[36] His catalog goes on to list "the wool of Congo Billy, a pure negro, and will be seen to be furcated" along with nine others, citing his commitment to purloining hair samples from African-born and enslaved people of African descent. Browne's *Eccentrically elliptical pile. African*, a page that describes "Congo Billy, the manumitted slave of Col. L. B. Davis, Wilmington, Delaware," includes a sample of Afro-textured curls tied together with string (plate 9).

Common to these notes and descriptors are that they present people of African descent as identified by the whites who enslaved them. Individual identities would have been irrelevant for Browne's purposes anyway, as his focus was on amassing "bodily 'proof' of black inferiority," as C. Riley Snorton describes. "Enslavement was a necessary condition" among science and medical researchers who used unfree Black people for study because their consent and their suffering were irrelevant; enslaved status made them "inexhaustibly available through their interchangeability."[37] As with many other forms of scientific research of the period, the people of African descent in Browne's collection lacked opportunities for "consent"—their hair is described as "extracted" and taken by authority for Browne's personal benefit.[38] The lack of care expressed in ascertaining the origin of Black hair samples is replicated on the page of the archive, indicated only in short, disconnected patches of curl taped to the scrapbook.

Browne's curious collection of hair as proof of racial distinction falls between other more notable efforts to theorize and visualize racial difference, such as Joseph T. Zealy's photos (1850) and Arthur de Gobineau's writing (1853). Whether rendered via textual, visual, or material form, these endeavors reflect a demand for multimodal sense-making about blackness and constitute a call for seeing and feeling. Such complex, affective engagement underscores touch and "not just vision or color" as essential "to the very construction of the idea of 'race' in the modern world." Historian Mark Michael Smith argues that slavers construed blackness as a "tactile condition" that rendered Black skin as "thicker and tougher than white skin and, ergo, much better suited to hard manual labor."[39] Touch, along with the visual, helped to maintain racial boundaries. Haptic theories of racial distinction justified the conditions of slavery, projecting "black skin as thick and insensitive," suitable for both hard work and physical brutality; the extraordinarily thick and harsh Black skin demanded the brutality of the lash.[40] Thus, haptic racism in slavery set the course for imagining an inherently insensate and insensitive Black body, a notion that proliferated well into the twenty-first century.[41] This same notion of harshness around Black physicality also appears in conceptions of Black hair, where white onlookers perceived Black hair textures as coarse compared to the hair of Europeans. Haptic blackness constructed through slavery resulted in a fixation on touching as a means of understanding blackness, while also furthering theories about the abrasive feel of blackness.

But the construction of Black raciality as palpable on the human surface—in skin and hair—is also repressive to the conception of Black feeling. The idea that one might sense blackness with the hand also assumes an unfeeling Black subject, where touch and the visual combine and the affective register for blackness is "thick-skinned." The infamous carte de visite of Peter Gordon and his scourged back underscores the point (figures 1.5 and 1.6), providing a reference for Gordon's singular suffering but also for the collective character of Black flesh as observed among other fugitive people.[42] Photographed in the spring of 1863 in order to depict the whipping scars, the skin on Gordon's back emphasizes the haptic exterior, a palpable indication of violence observed among numerous African Americans who fled slavery during the Civil War. This photo, made popular at the time through its reprinting as an Independence Day feature in *Harper's Weekly*, brings the viewer up close to Gordon's torn flesh, never properly healed, ripped apart by the lash. It is through engagements with Gordon's images that viewers are to consider his pain, the blood that must have accompanied the open wounds, the suffering he must have endured while waiting for them to scab and heal. A runaway by the time his photo was taken at a Union camp for soldiers along the Mississippi River, Gordon likely survived the harshest of conditions, both in his life under slavery and in his fugitive flight as contraband. Yet in this image, the flesh alone does not fully disclose "hapticality" as an interior; it only partially conveys the diverse vectors of feeling central to Gordon's experience. It is the full image, which gives us a clear view of his head *and* his hair, which also bears a story of his living conditions, the lack of leisure or personal time—perhaps even exclusion from a community of other Black people that might have helped him care for his body or barber his hair. Even with such visual evidence, the stories one might share about Gordon are unclear. His scourged back could indicate whippings due to a lack of productivity or motivation to maintain a high yield of productivity.[43] Read against his flesh, matted and tangled, Gordon's hair corresponds to his back. Together, the two invite touching for sense-making: to look and feel at once. Gordon's photograph conjures the haptic in both its content and circulation. Measuring less than 11 × 7 cm when mounted, Gordon's photograph put his body in the hands

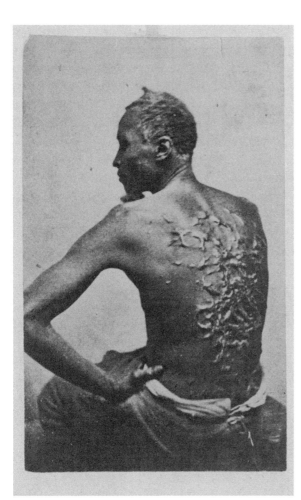

1.5

McPherson and Oliver, *Escaped Slave Gordon, Also Known as "Whipped Peter," Showing His Scarred Back at a Medical Examination, Baton Rouge, Louisiana* (front), 1863. Mount 11 × 7 cm (carte de visite format). Library of Congress, Prints and Photographs Division, 2018648117. https://www.loc.gov /item/2018648117/.

• • •

1.6

Escaped Slave Gordon, Also Known as "Whipped Peter" (verso), 1863

FROM LIFE, *Taken at Baton Rouge, La. April 2.ᵈ 1863.*

Camp Parapet, La.
Aug.ᵗ 4ᵗʰ 1863.

Colonel.
I have found a large number of the four hundred contrabands examined by me to be as badly lacerated as the specimen represented in the enclosed photograph.
Very respectfully
yours.
J. W. Mercer.
Asst. Surgeon 47ᵗʰ M. V.

Fac-Simile
of Original Official Report
to Col L. B. Marsh.

of an antislavery sympathizer, while the photographic reproduction invites the viewer to rub the surface. The textures of Gordon's suffering provide a canvas for visually sorting through the feelings of the viewer who holds Gordon's image, which is a stand-in for Gordon's body. Whereas abolitionists intended this image (and others like it) to conjure sympathy, Gordon's photograph was meant for touch. The archive of his suffering came to represent a Middle Passage iconography of lacerated backs and torn flesh, in part, through hailing the viewer to rub the image and sense the texture of abuse in the viewer's own body, without providing a deepened insight into Gordon's sentiments.

Human surfaces draw in touch and feeling in ways that conjure but diverge from the pictorial surface. While the haptic engagement of human surfaces is riddled by theories of the subject's hold on sentiment—Gordon's ability to feel as a racially inflected idea, for example—haptic images almost always foreground the feelings of the viewer over the affect of the individual in the illustration. Tina Campt describes how "the materiality of the image as a photoobject of bodily interaction" can be known to viewers through seeing as well as through "tactile bodily interactions like touching, wearing, handling, and manipulation," so that the viewer's haptic engagement with the visual object is key for consideration among the sites of feeling.[44] But where Campt reminds us that "the reading of surfaces, particularly of flesh and skin, is profoundly implicated in the pernicious role photography has played in the history of racial formation,"[45] we are reminded that pictorial surfaces have been helpful in supplanting human feeling(s) by distancing viewers from suffering, while also fabricating closeness. Accordingly, Gordon's carte de visite reveals (and replays) the maiming written on his body as a human surface, just as his hair also provides a record of atrocities, though viewers might differently engage with or ignore coiffure as material for a focus on the flesh.

Marked with Mistreatment

The abundance of illustrations of Black hair, as well as its importance to scientists, suggests a peculiar value for Black coiffure that does not easily factor into theories of value under slavery's capitalism. Parsing "capitalist slavery," or the "modernizing" of the peculiar institution, which often entails a focus on wage labor, markets, contracts, credit, rules of law, and the maximization of human freedom, yields no clear value for Black hair as a salable item like cotton, for example.[46] Even the "commodification and collateralization of the slaves themselves" and the commercial linkages that joined disparate places in the Atlantic world do not openly point to Black hair as particularly notable in these exchanges.[47] Indeed, flesh is key. To think of Black value in this economy is to think of the "flesh as a prime commodity of exchange," according to Hortense Spillers.[48] This commoditization of the body is manifested in the womb, with speculations about Black women's fecundity, and up to and including death, in the market for Black corpses and body parts. As historian Daina Ramey Berry states, "The act of being treated as a commodity . . . touched every facet of enslaved people's births, lives, and afterlives."[49] This commoditization extended to the entire Black body, treating an unfree Black person "as [a] stand-in for actual currency" when settling debts or bequeathing economic assets.[50] Black hair was not given an exchange value in the manner of flesh at the marketplace; but after sale and through interpersonal interactions, hair remained part of the experience and demonstration of ownership. Violence used as a tool of productivity and wielded to meet the demands of the plantation, as an evolving site of manufacture, was meted out through the fiber of Black hair. A violent touch specifically directed toward the handling of Black hair was a prominent part of Black people's experiences and is documented in various accountings of life under slavery. Scenes in life stories of unfree people recount a fit of jealousy by an enslaver—man or woman—who, in an effort to control their chattels and control perceptions of their appearance, forcibly cut Black hair. One often ignored incident is that described by Harriet Jacobs in her *Incidents in the Life of a Slave Girl*. She recalls Dr. Flint cutting her hair as a punishment. Jacobs explains the double bind in which she existed, facing the threat of sexual violence from her enslaver and the jealous rage of his wife, especially after the birth of her child. Flint threatens to sell her child when she rebuffs his sexual advances, and he then proposes head-shaving with the hope "that will humble you"—a threat Jacobs finds absurd. "Humble *me*! Was I not already in the dust?" Flint's notion to "humble" Jacobs is carried out however, in the cutting. She goes on to describe the episode:

> When Dr. Flint learned that I was again to be a mother, he was exasperated beyond measure. He rushed from the house, and returned with a pair of shears. I had a fine head of hair; and he often railed about my pride of arranging it nicely. He cut every hair close to my head, storming and swearing all the time. I replied to some of his abuse, and he struck me.[51]

Jacobs locates the forcible cutting of her hair alongside other brutality, such as when Flint "pitched [her] down stairs in a fit of passion." Removing her hair, however, presents a unique mode of abuse, one meant to humble her against the pride that allowed her to refuse his sexual advances, but also intended to punish her for appearing attractive to other suitors, such as the father of her children,

Samuel Sawyer. These scenes of "extreme violence and humiliation" asserted a "psychological component" to the punishment, according to Kali Gross, where enslavers aimed "to break slaves in total submission."[52] Jacobs's experience reveals that qualitative conceptions of texture or attractiveness had little bearing on the experience of brutality, and that styling oneself or care of coiffure could hasten rebuke.

Jacobs's experience complicates facile descriptions of "good hair" as a symbolic capital in the context of slavery.[53] The significance of Black hair was not limited to "symbolic potency," as Orlando Patterson might have it, where the occurrence of Afro-textured coiffure operated as "a powerful badge of status" in and of itself, with the shaved head functioning as "symbolic of castration—loss of manliness, power, and 'freedom.'"[54] The forcible cutting of Black hair was not simply about symbolism, and hair texture was not limited to the figurative. Hair was embroiled in expressions of force and the legislation of violence against people of African descent in the United States and the Caribbean. Black hair was worked on, by Blacks and by whites; Black hair conveyed information about the Black subject and the conditions under which an individual lived. The appearance of Black hair certainly mattered at the market, where traders "blackened" the coiffure of bondspersons as part of improving their appearance for sale. Likewise, where hair texture figured into a taxonomy of racial makeup, signs of "mixture," as evidenced by a loose curl pattern, would have mattered in *conjunction* with skin color; hair mattered when skin color was deemed significant. "Whiteness was doubly sold in the slave market," according to Walter Johnson, "packaged and measured by the traders and imagined into meaning by the buyers: into delicacy and modesty, interiority and intelligence, beauty, bearing, and vulnerability."[55] Signs of race mixture factored into the labor stolen from and assigned to people of African descent—a fact that would not guarantee an improved quality of life, however. Hair also provided a mark of distinction when Jacobs ran away, as her enslaver emphasized when advertising for her recapture: "Black hair inclined to curl; but it can be made straight."[56] Here, fear of her "discursive mobility" guides her description.[57] The notice uses her hair to forward, and discount, Jacobs's presumed efforts to pass for white.

But texture placed no limit on the affective use value of Black hair. After market, the material of Black hair provided fodder for the expression of white violence and white ownership of the Black body as property. Although Black hair did not represent a commodity in the form of salable goods, subjection in the form described by Jacobs reveals hair as imbricated in immaterial, emotional work, or "labor in the bodily mode."[58] Affective labor, "the labor of human contact and interaction, which involves the production and manipulation of affects," yields "relationships and emotional responses" rather than possessions.[59] Ironically, however, that yielding is thus uniquely complicated by slavery's blurred lines of humanness, commoditization, and work. As an "abstraction" the Black body is fit for the projection of white "desires, feelings, and ideas."[60] Jacobs's story is one of many in which Black women discuss forced shearing in the context of sexual violence, thus placing forcible cutting as a counterpart to sexual violence.

Such encounters meant that Black hair straddled private/public distinctions in its affective use value to white property owners. Euripe Dupuis birthed Victor Duhon, who had been fathered by her enslaver, Lucien Duhon; Victor Duhon explained his mother's sexual assault on the Duhon plantation in Lafayette Parish, Louisiana: "I didn't have brothers or sisters, except half ones. It is like this, my mama was a house servant in the Duhon family. She was the hairdresser. One day she barbered master's son, who was Lucien. He says that he'll shave her head if she won't do what he likes. After that she his woman till he marries a white lady."[61] Although Dupuis was forced to care for Lucien, including providing hair care, he used her hair to threaten violence and abused her until he decided to marry another woman. Hair cutting figured into intimate violence against Black women, but it was also used by white women to suppress sexual encounters between white men and Black women. Art historian Charmaine Nelson describes James Brittian, who "recalled . . . the beauty of his African-born grandmother, who had hair 'fine as silk and [that] hung down below her waist,'" and who suffered under a jealous mistress. The mistress, out of rage, ordered Brittian's grandmother "whipped" and her hair cut off, and subsequently "ordered that his grandmother henceforth wear it shaved to the scalp."[62] Thus, the incorporation of Black hair in white violence knew no gender distinction. "Mistresses were principal perpetrators of violence" in the plantation household, according to Thavolia Glymph, a primary scene for abuse as "the control and management of slaves required white women's active participation and authorized the exercise of brute or sadistic force."[63] Black women would have their hair forcibly shaved as part of the intimate violence that suppressed notions of privacy—the private space of the home and private space of the discrete body.

Beyond the domestic realm, however, the forcible cutting of Black hair was also public and state sanctioned, enforced in prisons and spaces of punishment. Thomas Cobb's *An Inquiry into the Law of Negro Slavery in the United States of America* explains that "long hair, being the badge of a freeman, was prohibited to slaves. Hence, one that permitted a fugitive's hair to grow long, was subject to a fine."[64] In Virginia in October 1670, the General Assembly revised a law from the previous year establishing a large reward for anyone who captured a runaway or servant. A reward of a thousand pounds of tobacco was reduced to two hundred pounds. Repeat offenders were directed to keep their "haire close cut," whereas freepersons, including runaways, were permitted to keep their long hair. Cutting Black hair close to the scalp was used to signify people as property. These laws were, in part, also about removing Black people's individuality, as might be accentuated through hairstyling, and they rendered hair fiber part of the management of chattel persons. This regulation extended to people who were free "on paper," such as Black women in eighteenth-century New Orleans, for example, whom Governor Miró "prohibited from wearing feathers and jewelry, ordering them to bind their hair in a kerchief." Miró's goal was to "prevent them from dressing above their station or like white women."[65] In these dictates, whites used Black hair to control appearances, to ensure that Black visibility conveyed social status beyond the flesh, and thus these regulations revealed the need for more than skin color in ordering social stratification.

No idiom exemplifies hair cutting as a source of terror more than the treadmill. "Devised in England in 1818 as a form of 'hard labor' for prisoners," this wide wheel with steps contained prisoners who "turned the wheel by walking or running while gripping a bar to keep from slipping and being mangled by the steps."[66] In the image *An Interior View of a Jamaica House of Correction* (figure 1.7), the scissors used to cut a woman's hair while she is forcibly held down are an instrument of terror used alongside the treadmill and the cat-o'-nine-tails. In Jamaica, prison environments were also places for cropping hair, removing a sign of individuality, and taking away self-expression. Diana Paton explains an instance of hair cutting done "because it is the greatest annoyance they find they can inflict on the women [who] with great trouble get their hair into little plats" before having it forcibly cut.[67] Hair cutting as a form of punishment continued in the apprenticeship period in the British West Indies, even as British officials debated the practice.[68] This image of the treadmill features a caption drawing attention to "THE WHIPPING OF FEMALES," which Governor Lionel Smith called "conduct so repugnant to humanity, and SO CONTRARY TO LAW" that he wanted it stopped immediately. He goes on to cite "the injustice of cutting off the hair of females in the House of Correction, previous to trial," a claim that underscores the central scene in the image. At the lower center, a woman is held down by one man, as another applies a straight razor to her scalp. Alongside them, another woman sits with her head covered—perhaps waiting for her turn.

1.7

An Interior View of a Jamaica House of Correction, ca. 1834. Steel engraving, 12.2 cm ×
17.4 cm. © National Maritime Museum, Greenwich, London. Michael Graham-Stewart
Slavery Collection. Acquired with the assistance of the Heritage Lottery Fund.

Visually, then, a shaved head indicated the complicated relationship between the corporeal and the symbolic under capitalist slavery. On the one
hand, Black coiffure had no exchange value on the market, even as the appearance of hair mattered to the price of the Black body as commodity. Once a person was enslaved, however, the "value" associated with hair increased, having
affective worth in the expression of power, control, and ownership. In these
encounters, Black hair further complicates the significance of the visual as relevant to racial capitalism. It is not simply the fact of the Black body as available
for extraction—exchanged in sum or in part for monetary gain—but also that
what remains presents ongoing opportunities for *new* transactions, fitting into
visual and affective economies that signify on behalf of the enslaver. The Black
body is subject to extraction in subsidiary exchanges, where demonstrations
of getting one's "money's worth" is ongoing, rendering humans as ampoules
for anger or emblems of ownership. Slavery, colonialism, and whiteness acted
upon the Black body in ways that were recorded or that became written on the

body. Referencing the sexual violence of slavery, historian Jennifer Morgan locates "childbirth" among "the scars from whippings or brandings [that] stood as a visible 'advertisement' that slave owners equated human beings with chattel."[69] The image and condition of Black hair in the context of slavery did similar work to convey status upon Blacks and whites. Thus, before emancipation there already existed a conception of "looking free" versus "looking slave," and in keeping with capitalism's penchant for the rule of law, the management of Black hair became legislated to support this structure. Long hair as a "province" of free persons made short hair not just a punishment but also a requirement.

Hairbreadth Escapes

Notions about looking free would have certainly undergirded Frederick Douglass's choices about self-presentation. More than viewing it as a spectacle, Douglass might have regarded his hair as a sign of autonomy, especially as measured against legal statutes about the cropping of Black hair. Douglass and other fugitive free people discussing coiffure in the context of slavery provide a window onto the ways in which the experience of Black hair and the representation of Black hair might be disaggregated. They remind us of the *interiority* of the human archive, where hair did not simply document the violence meted out against people of African descent—the grabbing, the pulling out, the forcible cutting—but also addressed the sentiments overlooked in conceptions of blackness as ready for touch. Unlike the scrapbooks of the naturalist or the paintings of the traveler, the archive of the human surface, indeed, entails multisided sensation.

Although Douglass was public in his critique of phrenology and race scientists, he found his own value in the racial meanings attributed to Black hair. Piecing together elements of Douglass's life through speeches and letters, Frederic May Holland included an interesting incident, excerpted from a contributor's letter, in his *Frederick Douglass: The Colored Orator*. Douglass is said to have recounted a scene where his blackness could not deter a presumably white passenger from electing to sit beside him.

> I have heard Mr. Douglass tell a story in which his color was no longer of any use. Said he, "I used to find myself favored with a double seat in the cars, very convenient when one is traveling at night; but recently I had an all-night ride before me, and prepared my bag for a pillow, covered my head with my shawl, and was about falling to sleep; when someone shook me, saying at the same time, 'Move along and give me a seat.' I roused myself, took my cap as well as my shawl from my head, so that my hair would

be observable, thinking that would be sufficient to insure me my resting place; but a more severe shaking came and a peremptory command to move and give up one seat. Then I said very meekly 'I am a nigger.' 'Go to—with your nigger, move along and give me a seat!' 'So,' said he, 'My color is no longer of any use.'"[70]

Relying on a different use value than that employed by race scientists and sadistic enslavers, Douglass attempted to utilize texture as a deterrent, as a means to signal his blackness and thereby secure his own comfort. As with the use of his hair texture in Scotland, Douglass found flashing his coif carried material gain, whether for the production of celebrity abroad or for personal space on domestic transport.

But the look and texture of Douglass's hair mattered to sympathetic audiences, including African Americans, even as those significations were both separate from and coterminous with the associations ascribed by whites. Douglass's hair was an oft-cited element of his striking appearance in person. His hair was a key feature of Douglass's spectacular public persona—thick, long, and graying as he aged. Douglass's hair was no afterthought, as indicated by the way his style changed over time. Black writers intrigued by the abolitionist addressed his image in published discussions of his appearance. Author Charles Waddell Chesnutt commented on Douglass's appearance in his *Frederick Douglass* (1899), writing that "Douglass possessed, in large measure, the physical equipment most impressive in an orator. He was a man of magnificent figure, tall, strong, his head crowned with a mass of hair which made a striking element of his appearance."[71] Taking his frontispiece from the Cornelius Battey portrait of Douglass at the 1893 World's Fair in Chicago, Chesnutt explained that Douglass's "stately figure, which age had not bowed, his strong dark face, and his head of thick white hair made him one of the conspicuous features of the Exposition."[72] Booker T. Washington similarly marveled at Douglass's appearance, praising the icon in his *Frederick Douglass* (1906): "His bearing was singularly impressive. His head was not large, but compact and high. His hair was coarse, his strong spare mouth supported by a broad and prominent chin. His eyes were bluish gray, and in conversation they were full of light and fire."[73] Discussing Douglass's ability to attract a crowd, particularly late in life, Washington wrote, "He was over six feet in height, broad-shouldered, well-proportioned, and his movements had all the directness and grace of a man who had been bred a prince rather than a slave." Washington found him "strong, and impressive. His complexion was that of a mulatto. His head was strikingly large and crowned with an abundant crop of white hair of almost silken fineness."[74]

These descriptions reveal that as Douglass aged, and as his hair lengthened, it became part of his captivating appearance. Late in his life, Douglass's hair appears thick and eventually white in a full bush, complemented by his similarly full white beard (facial hair is absent in his earlier pictures). Its graying, but also its fullness, were part of showing the esteem in which Douglass was held and conveyed wisdom to the people he addressed. This notable head of hair might have helped compel abolitionists' fascination with the image of the activist. Douglass had his portrait circulated in books and daguerreotypes and was the most photographed American of the nineteenth century.[75] A cursory glance at the images taken between 1848 and 1860 reveals that his hair is shown prominently as a significant aspect of the photographs, much like his clothing and his pose. Early images of a young Douglass show his hair dark in color, rippled in texture, and combed over to reveal "the prominent side part of the hair [which] was the accepted gentlemanly fashion," according to Ginger Hill.[76] As Douglass aged, the part disappeared from the hairstyle, and his hair grew in length. Thus, the visual significance of Douglass's hair is preserved in an array of records, not least of which is his collection of portraits.

Alongside these images, however, Douglass also represented his coiffure through his life writing, layering the internal and external feelings of nineteenth-century blackness with sentiments known to the fugitive free. Across four titles, Douglass offered four different frontispieces, capturing the evolution of his hairstyle. *Narrative of the Life of Frederick Douglass* (1845) and *My Bondage and My Freedom* (1855) feature portraits of a younger Douglass. These images, together with those in his *Life and Times of Frederick Douglass* (1881), show the lengthening and graying over time. However, these evolutions in Douglass's style may also point to his changing relationship to his hair fiber itself. More than indicating a changing conception of fashion and appearance, Douglass's hair evolution also tracks his changing condition—his access to personal care in freedom, and his record of survival.

Textually, Douglass locates his hair at a brutal turning point during his bondage. Douglass cites his coiffure as proof of his confrontation with Edward Covey, which was first recounted in his *Narrative of the Life of Frederick Douglass* (1845). He describes running toward the woods after a bloody beating, explaining that Covey "gave me a heavy blow upon the head, making a large wound, and the blood ran freely." Douglass finds the brutality of this incident so severe that he sets out for St. Michael's, Maryland, to report the overseer's abuse to Hugh Auld, Douglass's enslaver, aiming to use his appearance as proof of the attack. Debilitated by the assault, Douglass falls in the woods "and lay for a considerable time." He goes on: "The blood was yet oozing from the wound on my head. For a time

I thought I should bleed to death; and think now that I should have done so, but that the blood so matted my hair as to stop the wound."[77] Douglass presents his matted hair, marked with blood and dirt, to Auld and to the reader. Here, coiffure documents the strife he endured to get away from Covey; his hair archives the beating and the blood, like the flesh; the texture of the hair helps stop the bleeding but also captures the evidence of the brutality by retaining the blood that would have dripped down were it not for the density of Douglass's locks. Upon arrival, "I then presented an appearance enough to affect any but a heart of iron. From the crown of my head to my feet, I was covered with blood. My hair was all clotted with dust and blood; my shirt was stiff with blood"—all indicators to verify the confrontation with Covey. However, while Douglass offers up his hair as a different kind of racial proof, different from the taxonomies of racial science, his appearance fails to solicit sympathy from Auld. The would-be fugitive's bloody coiffure, here, signifies white brutality and not Black interiority. In the face of this alternate proof, Auld castigates Douglass as "deserving" of the beating and says he should return to Covey, who is reputed as a "good man."[78]

While the length of his hair grew in photographs, Douglass also transformed this particular aspect of his narrative in subsequent versions of his autobiography. The archive of Black hair is rendered differently in later iterations of Douglass's life. By 1855, Douglass took more creative license in describing his escape from Covey—"the thought of dying all alone in the woods, and of being torn in pieces by the buzzards, had not yet been rendered tolerable by my many troubles and hardships"—but more importantly, Douglass shifted his description of the condition of his hair. Rather than describing his curls as tangled *by* the blood, Douglass explained: "I was glad when the shade of the trees and the cool evening breeze combined with my matted hair to stop the flow of blood."[79] This small change in description, from his hair matting from Covey's attack to its having already been matted when the bleeding commenced, is significant for how it portrays his physical condition in the context of slavery. When Douglass took increased authorial control over his life writing, removing abolitionist William Lloyd Garrison from the text and adding the voices of other Black authors—James McCune Smith and George L. Ruffin—his visage comes closer to that of Gordon, with matted hair and a scourged back.[80] Douglass's matted hair suggests a lack of touch, or care, that he may have also attempted to transform in portraits of his parted and combed coiffure.

Harriet Tubman similarly filed the absence of physical touch in the archive of her hair, in addition to evidence of the supernatural. In recounting her life to Emma Telford, Tubman's friend and biographer, Tubman intertwines thoughts on her appearance and the absence of intimate touch. Recounting an instance of life-changing brutality, having been hired out to "'de wust man in de neighborhood'" to cover the costs of her living expenses, Tubman describes a visit to a local store. Concerned about her appearance, "'I had a shoulder shawl of the mistress over my head and when I got to the store I was ashamed to go in.'" Tubman's concern for her appearance had to do with the fact that in slavery, "my hair had never been combed and it stood out like a bushel basket." She explained that "when I'd get through eatin' I'd wipe the grease off my fingers on my hair and I expect that thar hair saved my life."[81] Although she managed hair care with no cosmetics, the fact that she states her hair "had never been combed," as if by someone else, points to the absence of touch by another as impactful on her facade and on her feelings about her presentation. Nevertheless, despite its appearance, Tubman ascribes significant power to her hair as she suffered a near-fatal blow that day. Observing a scuffle and refusing to help an overseer re-enslave a fugitive person, Tubman recalled seeing the overseer "raising up his arm to throw an iron weight at one of the slaves [and] that was the last thing I knew." Instead, the weight hit Tubman and "broke my skull and cut a piece of that shawl clean off and drove it into my head." This violent encounter transformed Tubman, resulting in her visions or spells, what we now refer to as epilepsy, which she believed would have been worse were it not for the texture and thickness of her hair.[82] Tubman ascribed to her hair the power to protect her from death but also to contain within it evidence of the violence she faced in the context of slavery. Alongside these spiritual and evidentiary values attributed to her hair, Tubman viewed coiffure as relevant to her appearance, to her idea about her own presentability in public. Tubman describes her hair in terms of the lack of personal care—the absence of physical touch—that might have helped improve her appearance and self-confidence.

Coiffure as an archive of haptic encounters recedes from the photographic surface, however, secondary to the sentiments evoked by the image. Portraits such as Tubman's 1868 carte de visite (figure 1.8), showing her in a full, patterned gingham skirt with her textured hair parted down the middle, twisted around the edge to smooth her hairs in place, represent a free woman and offer a different haptic engagement. Tubman's image appears in the album of Emily Howland, a white abolitionist and teacher, whose photograph collection includes respectable-looking African American teachers, veterans, and politicians.[83] While the checkered flecks of her skirt draw attention, in this instance, it is her hair and not just her clothing that help Tubman signal her freedom. Tubman's hair is parted down the middle, like Ruth Adams's (figure 1.9) and that of many other African American women photographed during this period. The care given to hair in these images portrays the presence of touch in the lives of

1.8

Benjamin F. Powelson,
*Portrait of Harriet
Tubman*, 1868. Mount
10 × 6 cm (carte de
visite format). Library
of Congress, Prints and
Photographs Division,
2018645050. https://
www.loc.gov/item
/2018645050/.

free people and offers up tender feelings or affection as another haptic record written on the body.

This combination of touch and feeling imbues the memento. The touch signaled in the braid that Douglass gifts to his sister, as well as the style of his hair as a freedman, refuted the abusive touch of slavery and the violence that made his hair into a swab for blood. A caring kind of touch gets registered not only in photographs of the activist with his hair parted, but also in the braiding of his lock as a sentimental token. These items signal affective connection between fictive kin, an "enacted" bond.[84] Such signification, like much of the relation-

1.9

Portrait of Ruth Cox Adams, ca. 1870. Nebraska State Historical Society Photograph Collections, Lincoln, NE.

ship between Douglass and Adams, refuted slavery's "destruction of kinship and friendship ties."[85] Douglass's braid offered a keepsake of the body as a sign of love and connection to his sister with whom he shared affection but also the common experience of enslavement and fugitivity. In such a gift, hair is indicated not as a scientific proof of Black raciality but as an affective proof of Black raciality marked by the exigencies of survival and the expression of sentimentality in life under slavery.

These multiple registers of feeling indicated by hair mark the material as a record but in ways that function unlike Browne's collection of pile and in ways that differ from the travel illustrations of Black people's grooming. While those other examples emphasize touching of the human surface, Douglass's braid conveys affective touch, or touching the interior. Whereas violence and regulation under slavery construed Black hair texture in line with a larger haptic racism—as harsh and wool-like—the regard for hair among fugitive free people like Douglass, Adams, Jacobs, and Tubman reveals an entirely other framework for coiffure. Hair provides a record of feelings and the possibility of rewriting contemptuous forms of touch.

TEXTURE

TWO

Frederick Douglass the icon loomed large into the twentieth century, decades after his death, and the face of the late abolitionist served as a symbol of liberation. Appearing in a television ad for hair products, the fictional Douglass stands in a doorway (figure 2.1), wearing a black suit and bow tie, his thick white hair combed over to connect with a full beard and white mustache. Douglass enters the room and speaks to a student who is dressing for school. He asks, "Haven't you forgotten something?" Recognizing the fugitive icon, the student (played by actor Stanley Bennett Clay) responds, "Hey, aren't you Frederick Douglass? Yeah, we studied about you in school yesterday. About how you were a slave and took your own freedom, and then began to fight for freedom and dignity for all our people. Say, but what did I forget?" Douglass quickly asks, "Are you going to go out into the world with your hair looking like that?" referring to the student's unpicked Afro. Clay explains, "Mr. Douglass, times have

2.1

"Frederick Douglass" enters the doorway. Still from a commercial for Afro Sheen hair products, 1970s. https://www.youtube.com/watch?v=g8ffzI2czHs.

changed. We wear the natural now." As he moves farther into the young man's bedroom, Douglass interjects, "You call that a natural? That's a mess! I've been watching the progress of our people and I'm quite familiar with the natural, and I'm also aware that it is worn as an expression of pride and dignity." The young man begins to agree, as Douglass queries: "So haven't you forgotten . . . ," reminding the young man to use his "Afro Sheen comb easy and hair spray for sheen." As the product line appears in the foreground, on the dresser and ready for use, the background reveals a host of university paraphernalia; flags representing the University of Illinois, the University of Iowa, and the University of Minnesota adorn the wall of the teen's bedroom. The spray of product over his head produces a blur that ends the dream sequence, with the young man explaining, while picking and patting out his hair, "I can really dig this getting my 'fro together." Douglass fades to a voice-over—"my sentiments exactly"— and when the view clears, the young man's hair is groomed, rounded, and smoothed. Clay looks around for Douglass, who is nowhere in sight, then faces

2.2

Clay examines cosmetics. Still from a commercial for Afro Sheen hair products, 1970s. https://www.youtube.com/watch?v=g8ffzI2czHs.

the camera as the shot zooms out to show the Afro Sheen products; the actor's voice-over exclaims, "Man, ain't nobody gonna believe this!"

This seventy-five-second spot placed Frederick Douglass in conversation with a new generation of Black people, who emphasized racial pride and who engaged the visual to consider the long Black freedom struggle.[1] This single still of the commercial (figure 2.2) positions Douglass in the background, standing behind the specter of Black male youth activists, represented in Clay, with the Afro Sheen product in the foreground. Douglass's hair and body serve multiple vectors in a phantasmagoria of Black social progress, perpetuating a myth of the Black freedom struggle as led by men, bequeathed to men. Whereas the struggle for Black freedom sought to "end American apartheid, to achieve economic justice, and to foster the liberation of oppressed peoples throughout the world," according to Jeanne Theoharis, this advertisement used keywords such as "pride and dignity" as shorthand for Black liberation, made attainable through self-care.[2] The single picture portrays a legacy of Black resistance from the nineteenth century to the 1970s that begins with fighting slavery and ends with Black consumerism, obscuring contemporary activism signified in the college flags blurred in the background.[3] Such visual symbols indicate the active embrace of that "emergent courtship between hegemonic institutions and minority difference," which Roderick Ferguson explains helped to co-opt student protests and divert radical politics toward the promotion of Black capitalism.[4] Slavery, as a memory and a visual sign, is made to fit among other cultural shifts associated with civil rights activism: Black Power activism, anti-apartheid movements, and decolonization. By the seventies, after the boycotts, riots, and student protests of the sixties, packaged and condensed symbols of Black resistance would come to undergird divergent attitudes about blackness and racial capitalism.

Black visual culture formed a crossroads on the terrain of "natural hair," entertaining both capitalist and anticapitalist approaches to haptic blackness. Afro Sheen products, a well-known line of hair care from George E. Johnson Sr.'s Johnson Products Company,[5] began by offering Ultra Sheen products for straightened styles, but "capitalized on the growing Afro-centric 'Black is Beautiful' ideology" of the 1970s "by offering Afro Sheen to customers preferring 'natural' hairstyles."[6] Advertisements for the products reveal that by the 1970s, the promotion of natural hair was imagistic as much as it was ideological. Spectacular campaigns for hair products fit neatly among pro-Black illustrations created by Black artists associated with collectives like AFRICOBRA, the printmakers of independent materials issued by the Black Panther Party, as well as the complex but vivid array of Black programs on television, all depicting textured hair as popular and political. Connections between images of beauty and images of protest coalesced, as reflected in the work of photographer Kwame Brathwaite, helping the idea of Black Is Beautiful take on new visibility.[7] Unique unto itself, and yet part of a larger cultural transformation, the marketing of natural hair as a commodity spoke to diverse audiences and used texture to engage Black liberation in the mid- to late twentieth century.

By the 1970s, Afro-textured hair had become the focus of a new point of view. Noliwe Rooks reveals that hair straightening long held a controversial place in African American media and culture from the nineteenth century onward; it was debated among intellectuals and entrepreneurs, with Black newspapers sometimes banning advertisements for hot combs and pomades that promoted smooth or straightened hair.[8] Later in the twentieth century, however, when "natural" emerged as an identifier for an array of styles emphasizing the coils and curls visible among people of African descent, a number of products for textured hair also emerged, helping to entangle Afro texture with consumerism and middle-class identity. Styles such as the "au naturel" that first appeared during the 1950s in "bourgeois high-fashion circles" were increasingly incorporated by the beauty industry in its representations, even as these styles eventually gave way during the 1960s to the political associations with the Black Power movement.[9] At the same time, the shape and texture of the Afro became synonymous with the term *natural*. Tanisha Ford explains that "'natural' was shorthand for the concept of racial purity," and the Afro, with its rounded shape, "became symbolic of one's black consciousness."[10] By 1968, the natural came to serve as a visible marker of a new sentiment. Cultural nationalism "demanded that race pride not only be expressed through activism but also be embodied in one's personal style and appearance."[11] Styles that embraced the textured coifs of African descendants were linked to an embrace of Black racial distinction and supported a robust image culture.

This chapter explores the textural means by which people of African descent revisited and revised haptic blackness. I argue that through the construction of "natural hair," Black cultural producers restructured theories and approaches to a palpable raciality after slavery, rewriting notions of interiority, legibility, and normativity as indicated in the consistency of the human surface. Again, hair in addition to the flesh presents a way to rethink blackness as organized around sensation, in addition to history and culture. Whereas new ways of engaging the texture of coiffure were frequently associated with proclamations about the right to the city and the nation, haptic blackness took a new shape around the ways in which people of African descent transformed material relations to both human surfaces and social spaces under the violence of racial capitalism.

Among people of African descent, reimagining the texture of Black raciality frequently meant revisiting the precolonial past. Cultural producers taking up the texture of blackness and Black life in the mid- to late twentieth century often (re)turned to Africa and the Middle Passage as sites for reckoning. Functional yet imaginary reliance on "Africa" and "slavery" as "common possession[s]," according to David Scott, supported "the ideological production" of community.[12] Among purveyors of US popular culture, constructing a "Motherland" and revisiting the abuses of slavery through visual culture were conversant with literary and theatrical works across the arts meant to engage a pro-Black identity construction.[13] Such representations typically viewed slavery as a process of thefts—stealing people, stealing land, stealing kinship communities, and stealing culture. Within this framework, the embrace of natural hair was frequently framed as a refusal of slavery's attempts at cultural annihilation, as a reclamation of the Black self as it was in spite of, if not before, the Middle Passage. Thus, the invocation of "'nature' to inscribe 'Africa' as the symbol of personal and political opposition" to Western hegemony, such as in the wearing of Afros and dreadlocks, according to Kobena Mercer, not only inverted "aesthetic oppression" in their refutation of antiblackness.[14] These styles also proposed a distinct look and feel to racial distinction, promoting and publicizing a textural quality to blackness. These efforts embraced, rather than repelled, conceptions of a texturally distinct, or haptic, blackness. But whereas such configurations elicited different relationships to markets, different experiences associated with natural hair reveal the means by which racial capitalism not only organizes social structures but also seeks to form the body and its spatial interactions, with and through the visual.

Entanglements

Although debates about hair straightening appeared in African American printed matter of the nineteenth century, mid-twentieth-century print materials presented a shift, as African diasporic people pronounced Afro-textured hair as a surface for reconsidering the Black interior. Popular musicians added both visibility and political salience to the wearing of natural hair, such as soul singers Miriam Makeba and Odetta, women whose "natural hair was a political symbol of the emerging Black Freedom movement" even as their hairstyles originated from personal rather than political preferences.[15] Part of this association had to do with the international confrontations with imperialism, realized in the tide of independence from European colonialism sweeping the continent in "the year of Africa," 1960.[16] In the face of a rising Africa that faced suppression by Western governments, the embrace of Black features and African aesthetics carried increasing symbolic significance. Personal style—dress and hair—functioned as a demonstration of attitude, but also signified internal reassessment of the value of blackness.

Reading the human surface as a discursive marker of a Black interior was a pervasive practice in the mid-twentieth century, with a common emphasis on questions about how to repair a damaged Black interior. During the 1960s, Black psychologists interested in the impact of racism on Black people's self-concepts explored "self-hatred," or the ways in which African Americans dissociated from conceptions of blackness. This body of literature explored various tropes to get at an internalized "abhorrence for being black and acceptance of contemptuous characterizations about blacks as a group," where "social discrimination and negative reflected appraisals and low levels of self-esteem" were examined together.[17] Heightened around bulwarks of desegregation—the integration of the military, housing, and schools—scholarship examined the ways in which African Americans internalized white perceptions of people of African descent.[18] Working, living, and learning in close physical proximity to whites were thought to have a causal relationship to the internalized distaste for one's own blackness, as well as to the development of negative beliefs and attitudes about Black racial distinction. Such an approach to Black raciality prioritized resistant expressiveness, as opposed to the "quiet" and "inner life" of Black peoples, which Kevin Quashie describes.[19] In this conception of the Black interior, of both those who internalized racism and those who resisted it, outward appearances offer sites of refutation—whether through the distaste of, or the embrace of, supposedly "black" characteristics, as realized in hair texture but also in language and social comportment.

Slavery became central to interrogations of the human exterior. Historically based and fictionalized visual portrayals of slavery in the mid- to late twentieth century attempted to show the cultural, social, and psychological impact of bondage on people of African descent. New films deviated from Hollywood's mainstay treatment, as reflected in films such as D. W. Griffith's *Birth of a Nation* (1915) and the nationally acclaimed *Gone with the Wind* (1939). Later works resisted the "key stock characters and melodramatic tropes: a pure, virtuous white girl who dies an untimely death, a belle who becomes the object of a dashing cavalier's affection, and a romance played out against the backdrop of a gracious plantation estate filled with black 'servants.'"[20] Rather than place slavery in the background, new films added greater depth to slavery, with key Black actors performing significant roles as bondspersons. Ossie Davis portrayed the witty "Joseph Lee" in *Scalphunters* (1968), a western about a revenge-seeking fur trapper, before expanding his performance of bondage as "Luke" in *Slaves* (1969), a film about a cruel Kentucky master. The Black figure as "slave" showed up with a vengeance in films like *The Legend of Nigger Charley* (1972) and *The Soul of Nigger Charley* (1973), in which actor Fred Williamson kills his master in pursuit of freedom and then suppresses a white uprising at the end of the Civil War. Blaxploitation films focusing on slavery made overtures toward distinguishing the abuse of the bodily exterior from Black people's internal thoughts and realities. For example, a willingness to fight drives lead actor Ken Norton in a double feature as a "slave" forced into pit fighting and sex with the mistress in *Mandingo* (1975) and *Drum* (1976). Fight scenes among bondspersons, such as Drum's bloody battle with Blaise (played by Yaphet Kotto), portray the physical abuse of the Black body as delightful to white onlookers, in contrast to the internal desire for peace and collaboration among unfree Blacks. New films engaged Black interiority by highlighting for viewers the internal ruminations on resistance, such as hidden plans to revolt, disguised by a smiling face or quiet demeanor.

Resistance aside, however, these films also took seriously the handling of the Black exterior. New motion pictures were sure to place the physical brutality of slavery before the viewer, alongside suggestions that this system stripped people of African descent of their culture and pride. Visions of slavery's impact on the human surface included scenes of physical brutality, implements of torture, and close-up shots of glistening bare skin, portrayed as sweating from fear or harsh labor. Portrayals of the suffering Black body subjected to a brutalizing touch draw together diverse depictions of slavery, such as the bizarre pseudo-documentary *Goodbye Uncle Tom* (1971), which spends almost three minutes on the viciousness of the hold, with close-up shots of whites harshly handling Black people—checking teeth, forced-feeding, and fondling genitals. Likewise, actress Cicely Tyson became iconic in her ability to represent Black women's suffering, first in her Emmy Award–winning role in *The Autobiography of Miss Jane Pittman* (1974), and then going on to star as Harriet Tubman in *A Woman Called Moses* (1978), in which misery included Tubman's performance at a "darky pageant" for white amusement, with her being forced to act as a mule pulling a wagon, leaving her dazed and dirty with tattered clothes.

Revisiting the hold, then, as a route toward understanding the suffering surface and the altered interior helped to make films such as Alex Haley's *Roots* into essential viewing. After the publication of *Roots: The Saga of an American Family* in 1976, the groundbreaking *Roots* miniseries emerged in 1977, followed by *Roots: The Next Generation* in 1979 and *Roots: The Gift* in 1988. Across almost ten hours, *Roots* put viewers *in touch* with a valuable African past but also up close to the physical brutality of slavery and the New World of African Americans in the US South. Iconic scenes such as the whipping of Kunta Kinte, played by LeVar Burton, for refusing to accept "Toby" as his new name assigned in slavery, portrayed Black suffering as a consequence, in part, of whites' demands to consume the entirety of the Black person, to make the interior consciousness acquiesce to the exterior of the captive body. *Roots* even offered "the Middle Passage scene" to show viewers "the transition between freedom in Africa and slavery in the new world," a representation seen "rarely in films and never on television," according to Matthew Delmont.[21] He describes these inclusions as part of the means by which *Roots* sought to add to the public's understanding of the "human cost" of slavery, which pervaded college-campus discussions after the Black freedom struggle but had not circulated more broadly.[22] Ideas about the appearance and the consistency of blackness as shaped by the Middle Passage and the brutal touches imposed in slavery were contrasted by the history and material culture of a precolonial Africa. Haley's *Roots* attempted to show Africa as a wellspring for Black aesthetics, where practices like naming and lineage were of deep importance to people. Here, too, Cicely Tyson appeared, locating pride and tradition in Ghana, her hair styled in Bantu knots as part of her depiction of Binta, mother to lead character Kunta Kinte. These inclusions helped make *Roots* a hit, garnering a record-breaking number of viewers during its premiere. "By the end of 'Roots Week,' ABC announced that a record 130 million Americans, representing eighty-five percent of all TV-equipped homes, had watched at least part of the series."[23] The suggestion of historical expertise added value to *Roots*, along with its immense production costs, yielding an "investment" in unearthing more truths about US slavery for viewing audiences.[24]

Thus, when entrepreneur Willie Morrow argued that Black hair, too, suffered the Middle Passage, his work was in line with both scholarly arguments about Black interiority and popular portrayals of slavery as a pivot point in Black culture. An Alabama migrant, Morrow moved to San Diego, California, in 1958, where he began his life's work as a barber but also as a collector, inventor, and cultural producer of all things related to Black hair care.[25] He authored more than twenty books and pamphlets, including an illustrated book, *400 Years without a Comb* (hereafter, *400 Years*) in 1966, which he would later transform into a film, *400 Years without a Comb: The Inferior Seed*.[26] Morrow's book *400 Years* draws in part from his own collection of ephemera about Black hair—a collection that has grown to include "more than 250 paintings, sculptures, drawings, photographs, historic artifacts, styling implements and documents that trace America's Black hair culture to its roots in Africa four centuries ago," hair picks, and hair products from the early twentieth century, as well as devices such as hair irons, pressing combs, tongs, and dryers.[27] Depicting transformations in style alongside an exploration of Black hair during slavery, Morrow made the case for new and revised modes of care, promoting his own products through a Black nationalist lens. His primary claim: the habits of personal care practiced in the Americas were contrary to the art and history of Black hair in precolonial Africa.

In Morrow's *400 Years*, slavery serves two functions. The first is to illustrate the Middle Passage as a disruption to African cultural practices. In just over one hundred pages, Morrow describes Afro hair textures as repulsive to whites in the context of slavery; he argues that the texture of Black hair was suited for pulling and mishandling as part of a general mishandling of Black bodies. Morrow details this process along a time line: "The Comb, Hair, and Africa (c. 1600)"; "Hair in Bondage (c. 1700)"; "Hair Care Revolution (c. 1800)." Across eight chapters and more than 140 illustrations, Morrow walks readers through the ways in which slavery unsettled Black hair cultures and, summarily, Black consciousness. Morrow argues that precolonial Africans "knew of no other skin color or type of hair than that of their own," with physical characteristics such as "the wide nose, thick lips, ebony skin, [and] curly hair . . . [viewed as] elements of beauty." Morrow describes a Black world with intraracial diversity distinguished by tribal designation, but with visual homogeneity. Like writers contemplating the impact of social contact amid desegregation, Morrow framed the closing of social distance between Europeans and Africans as having a deleterious impact on the Black psyche. Although the question of bodily aesthetics was central to explorations of internalized racism, most frequently referenced in the meanings associated with "skin color and racial identity among black Americans," some more controversial texts underscored the importance of hair, as reflected in Morrow's work.[28] For example, William Grier and Price Cobbs's 1969 book *Black Rage* paid considerable attention to self-hatred organized around Black hair, focusing on both texture and touch. They trace a self-hating sentiment running through the painful grooming practices inflicted on children by mothers, but also present the suffering that Black men and women endure to straighten their hair. While these practices do not yield a white resemblance, according to Grier and Cobbs, hair straightening marks the surface of self-hating Blacks, creating congruence with the interior as a "psychologically 'white' position" and revealing that one "turns on black people with aggression and hostility and hates blacks and, among the blacks, himself."[29] Morrow uses slavery to historicize this supposition, proposing bondage as the means by which Black hair culture came to participate in such a project.

Central to each of these notions is a hypermasculine conception of black racial identity. These approaches to blackness as a surface emphasize a concept of native Africanness that gets disturbed by a feminine presence. Each author presumes a masculine Black subject battling self-loathing that is first instilled through the abusive touch of the Black mother. Grier and Cobbs "trace this sentiment through painful grooming practices inflicted on children by mothers" as an initiation into a bruised interior.[30] Relatedly, Morrow's illustrations depict Black women as the locus for transferring slavery's aesthetic devaluation from one generation to the next. In *400 Years*, Black women are chief perpetrators of self-hatred, causing pain through the use of improper combs and solvents for hair care. Moreover, while men are depicted as early innovators in slavery, experimenting with axle grease and lye to produce straighteners, Black women are shown as fixated on white beauty norms as they pinch the noses of infants to narrow the profile or examine the ears of newborns for signs of an emergent dark complexion. Like other Black cultural nationalists who locate women's value in the domestic realm, *400 Years* circumscribes Black women's importance while also constructing them as perpetuators of slavery's vices.

Black women become the vessels for slavery's culture of abuse and destitution. In this line of thinking, liberation would result from the work of Black men as innovators or entrepreneurs, such as Morrow himself. In this context, selling hair products, as well as selling "the natural," intertwines the embrace of texture and the refutation of a feminine influence.

For cultural producers like Morrow, texture presents a way to reflect on slavery's impact on the Black surface. Morrow uses the contemporary style and habit of handling Afro-textured hair as a way to comment on the permanent transformation of Black cultural practices. He contends with touch but also with material culture as a way to speak about the enduring hapticities of the hold. In *400 Years*, both Black hair and the comb attain "psychological importance," as each succumbed in slavery. "Freedom, dignity, and a sense of self-worth were lost when the comb was lost," and "without the comb, the hair was nothing, and when hair became nothing, the individual became nothing as well." The loss of material culture and proper practices of touch impacted the valuation of texture, according to Morrow, and this loss initiated four hundred years of suffering. Precolonial Africa represents a place and time in which people of African descent had a sense of beauty, and in which hair was a part, involving its own material culture that Morrow represents through the illustration of African combs. These "beauty-enhancing instruments," designed for curly and coiled hair, were a material form of culture left behind "when the African was snatched from his homeland," and thus "his heritage and part of the beauty that he knew was left behind," exchanged for crude combing implements like the forks used in the context of US slavery.[31] With the Middle Passage, not only were people of African descent taken away from the continent, they were taken away from their culture, material and symbolic, rendering the comb as a link between the Black surface and the Black interior.

Revisiting the comb put Morrow in step with a number of other cultural producers of the period. Historian Robin Kelley locates Morrow's work among other "counterhegemonic" productions that "re-wrote the history of the Afro"; Kelley argues that "like the drum, the African comb or pick was an essential part of African culture," such that the loss of this tool was a loss of art and history that devolved into "black self-hatred."[32] Morrow offered the comb as a totem around which people of African descent organized an aesthetic practice that was obliterated through slavery. He argued that through the loss of the comb, Black people lost the corresponding aesthetic practices it accompanied. The idea of the comb as a way of touching precolonial Africa's histories and cultures was pervasive throughout the twentieth century and suffused with a heightened sense of cultural reclamation amid the transformations of the 1960s and 1970s. Investigations of African combs as archaeological artifacts and aesthetic devices offered ways for academics to understand diverse cultures and countries across the continent. Combs were located among the "the pervasive influence of aesthetic considerations" in every aspect of life, from cooking to artistic activities to self-styling.[33] The care taken to design such implements also symbolized a similar degree of care in the finished products of the object's use—design in a cake pan yielding a decorated cake, and the intricate design of the comb used for creating careful designs in coiffure. Comb designs changed over time, for reasons beyond purposes of utility, and combs were frequently regarded as beautiful objects to possess in and of themselves.[34] Varying in the number and size of teeth, but also in height and design of the handle, "combs exemplify the African fusion of art and utility," with handle designs that reflect religious denominations, common proverbs, and popular phrases.[35] The aesthetic variety and historical significance observed in African combs found cultural significance among consumers of Black fashion and style who saw in them a correspondence to the new Black consciousness. Curator Carol Tulloch argues that "the Afro comb has had a particular cultural resonance on an equal footing with the hairstyle it was used to create," making the implement and the Afro a signifying pair.[36] In the radical parlance of the period, the Afro comb presented an alternative to the hot comb used for straightening. Its function as a signal of Black value would be similarly anchored in language, cited as a barometer for sexual choice—"if she can't use your comb, don't bring her home."[37] Like much of the Black fashion associated with radical politics of the period, Afro combs also quickly found the market. The wooden Afro combs and other kinds of Black kitsch sold in *Ebony* magazine were in rapid production, with "thirteen Afro combs designed" and patented between 1970 and 1980.[38] On this trajectory, the cultural transit of combs for Black hair have rendered the object as both archaeological artifact and commodified symbol of Black consciousness.

Illustrations of combs, grooming practices, and hairstyles helped Morrow evidence slavery's cultivation of Black hair in the United States. Drawings helped Morrow portray the hair surface and the sentiments associated with slavery. In lieu of traditional citations, he provides immensely detailed drawings of people, hairstyles, combs, and social settings for hair care, as well as two photographs, including one of himself. The illustrations tell a story about the evolution of Black hair, moving the reader from depictions of the intricate braids and coifs worn by women of the Congo and Simbo Island, for example, up through depictions of Sojourner Truth's and Phillis Wheatley's covered heads (figure 2.3). Morrow makes interesting visual connections, placing Frances Ellen Watkins Harper's textured bun in line with "African Women's head dress," framed

2.3

Hairstyles of four
women, 1966.
Illustration from
Morrow, *400 Years
without a Comb*, 9.

Frances E. W. Harper, style of the 1850's

African Women's head dress

by three women whose head wraps emulate the shape of Harper's style. He also
references facts such as the suppression of long hair in slavery, writing that
"many Blacks grew beards and long hair like their white counterparts, [but]
they were looked upon by white society as being trouble makers"; yet he also
offers a portrait of Frederick Douglass who, Morrow believes, was "never auto-
matically classed with troublemakers" (figure 2.4).[39] Such assertations contra-
dict the historical evidence of people of African descent cutting and shaving
Black hair with scissors and razors throughout slavery. Slavers educated "black
personal servants" on wielding such implements, finding their own whiteness

2.4
Frederick Douglass portrait, 1966. Illustration from Morrow, *400 Years without a Comb*, 71.

enlarged through the employ of Black barbers. Moreover, in the North and South, in freedom and in slavery, "Black barbers negotiated their position as captive capitalists" in shaving white men, in particular.[40] Yet, in Morrow's body of work, such claims appear to be serviceable to his larger thesis—that slavery was a system of destitution and cultural annihilation—and figured into popular notions about the Black interior as revealed on the Black exterior. His extensive inclusion of drawings helps the reader to visualize Black hair's transformation through slavery and to recognize familiar cultural practices like braiding, pulling, and the rough handling of Black hair as grounded in this legacy. The images enable Morrow to reveal a history by aesthetic association, using images of fugitive free people like Douglass and Tubman to show readers examples of hair among iconic Black freedom fighters who were similarly embroiled in these cultural dynamics.

Joining other visual representations of slavery, Morrow eventually transformed his *400 Years* into a film, titled *400 Years without a Comb: The Inferior Seed*.[41] Released in 1989, Morrow's sixty-minute film continues his discussion on the enslavement of Black hair through the deprivation of proper combs and opportunities for good hygiene. Although Morrow's film largely duplicates the book, moving images highlight his arguments from the written text, opening his narrative in "Africa," illustrated with sounds and images of drumming, alongside Black women braiding and picking textured hair with an Afro comb. Quickly, the camera cuts to bare-chested Black men hidden in a haystack before being "captured" by whites. One white man, dressed in a three-cornered hat and a leather jacket, holds a shirtless and glistening Black captive in a headlock, while tugging at his hair. The camera jumps again to undressed Black men swaying in a wave-like motion to signal the Atlantic crossing, presumably on a ship, before Black men and women appear in "America," grooming animals with combs and pinching the noses of newborn babies. A final introductory scene displays Black people grooming one another's hair with dinner forks while humming about a return to "home," where the proper comb has been left. This introduction to slavery as the eradication of Black hair (culture) concludes with an African pick located in a body of water, floating toward the left side of the screen, ostensibly "up the river." Filmic images help Morrow add more context to human suffering in his arguments about hair under slavery. For example, in the book Morrow explains that "the only means of cutting the hair was with the big, awkward shears used to trim the domestic animals of the plantation or farm," but on screen he depicts Black men turning to animal grooming tools for personal care, showing the odd coupling of humans and implements for husbandry.[42] Moving images of animate, suffering, and sweating bodies become the visual contexts for harmful cultural practices, pulled into Morrow's project of rethinking the suffering Black body under slavery.

Textured Blackness

Radical and mainstream forms of visual culture, alongside literature and performance, provided important sites for celebrating Black hair in the 1960s and 1970s. Although the images included a variety of textured styles, the Afro circulated as the most iconic natural hairstyle of the era and was represented in art, music, and politics. In a period punctuated by the images and activities associated with the Black Power movement, the Black Panthers, and the Black Arts Movement, this era of "Modern Black Nationalism" paid greater attention to "mass culture and Black working-class life," according to GerShun Avilez, resulting in an "aesthetic radicalism" that tethered together diverse cultural producers who were and were not formally associated with political organizations.[43]

Among political groups, the representational heft of the Black Panthers was essential to portraying natural hair in spectacular fashion. Emory Douglas, artist, printmaker, activist, and minister of culture for the Black Panther Party, created the iconic artwork for the organization that appeared in the *Black Panther* newspaper. Although his subjects varied widely—from the Vietnam War to police brutality—Douglas's illustrations of Panther men, women, and children helped to solidify and publicize the aesthetics of the movement. This "Revolutionary Art," which the paper began printing in 1967, was meant to "represent the black condition and to visually theorize black liberation," offering "imagistic lessons designed to instruct readership on the 'correct' way to embody and enact their ideological and programmatic directives."[44] Douglas employed a bevy of artistic strategies, such as "distinctive illustration styles, cartooning skills, and resourceful collage and image recycling," to make impactful visual statements in the *Black Panther*.[45] Using bold lines and bright colors, text, and images, Douglas provided an explicit picture of Black freedom as a posture in the face of clearly delineated adversaries—the police, the government, capitalism, and imperialism. Promotional posters such as his 1969 *Afro-American Solidarity with the Oppressed People of the World* (figure 2.5) feature a Panther woman, armed and adorned. Although she is ready to fight, with a gun strapped to her back and a spear in her hand, she also wears hoop earrings and a short natural style, represented in the rippled margin of her Black coif. With such inclusions, Douglas portrayed personal aesthetic choices as measured and connected to the commitment of radical resistance, making natural hair part of an attitude, not the entirety of the politics. His posters, along with the images printed in the pe-

Afro-American solidarity
with the oppressed
People of the world

2.5

Emory Douglas, *Afro-American Solidarity with the Oppressed People of the World*, 1969. Offset lithograph on paper, 22 ⅞ × 15 in. Collection of the Oakland Museum of California, All of Us or None Archive. Gift of the Rossman Family. © 2021 Emory Douglas / Artists Rights Society (ARS), New York.

riodical, were representative of how the Black Panthers disseminated their own images to further their fight against social injustice and inequality, even in the face of negative external portrayals of the organization.[46]

But textured hair inspired artists of varying political sentiments. Fine artists working in paint were also depicting the Afro or textured styles in works portraying people of African descent. For example, Philadelphia-born portrait artist Barkley L. Hendricks took up the Afro in ways that emphasized its round shape and textured surface to comment on the practice of painting. His most notable treatment of hair, the 1969 portrait *Lawdy Mama* (plate 10), features a solitary Black woman, facing forward, demarcated with a double halo—her large gold-tinged Afro, set against the gold leaf background as reference to the halos in Byzantine icons. Art historian Richard Powell locates the timing of this portrait as fit for reading in association with the Black Arts Movement, even as "Hendricks clearly raised the ante on what 'black art' could be" through simultaneously exploring realism, minimalism, and "a form of cultural portraiture."[47] A number of Hendricks's subjects don naturals throughout the seventies, but their hair becomes part of an overall style (and attitude) about portraiture, often coupled with sunglasses, for example, masking the gaze of a sitter even as she or he confronts the viewer. Such treatment of the Afro functioned differently from that of the natural in Wadsworth Jarrell's *Revolutionary (Angela Davis)* in 1971 (plate 11), a work that suggests the hair and the activist are each of cultural significance. Painted in the signature bright colors of AFRICOBRA works, along with a collection of Black Power slogans, Jarrell's treatment of hair more explicitly associates itself with the Black freedom struggle. He argues that the organization's intention was to explicitly engage the movement's aesthetic philosophies, in this instance using the letter *B* "to represent only the profound statement of praise extolling our people at that time—'Black is Beautiful.'"[48] The Afro, then, as a bodily aesthetic and a representational object, figured into art exhibitions for diverse publics.

But the most enduring and spectacular promotion of natural hair was served up through an image-laden advertising and media culture that was procapitalist rather than anticapitalist. Although the associations between natural hair and Black liberation were represented in music and politics, some of the most enduring images of the Afro come from advertisements in print magazines and television, which aimed to market products for textured hair to everyday people, activists, and artists alike. Product manufacturers and media entities cocreated images of natural hair, situating textured coiffure among other consumerist illustrations. Through simple photographs of the textured hair of Black people, advertisers helped to popularize, again, synergies between the natural and the middle-class lifestyle, but without clear political commitments, all while drawing on subtle tropes of radical activism to maintain a vague connection to Black liberation.

A consumerist commitment to "buying Black" as a political philosophy was essentially combining politics, aesthetics, and commodification; this sentiment gestured toward the anticapitalist concerns of the Black Panthers, but also devolved quickly into a procapitalist philosophy. Manning Marable asserts his suspicion of this ethos, describing Black businesspersons as "the linchpin of underdevelopment and capital accumulation within the Black community" in their commitment to profit without regard for social change on a grand scale. Complicit with the state, Marable argues, Black entrepreneurs, by pursuing profits and "exhorting black consumers via black nationalist appeals to 'buy

Black,'" and by organizing campaigns against "the white private sector to subcontract goods, services or advertising through Black-owned firms," advanced ideas about proper civic conduct for the masses at the expense of liberation.[49] Black capitalism focused on accumulation, and "control over the Black consumer market in the U.S.," enabling Black entrepreneurs to pursue wealth without engaging with US capitalism as "structurally racist" or contending with its "devastation" of Black communities that would not be eradicated or undone by a wealthy elite.[50] Support from the thirty-seventh US president, Richard Nixon, helped to solidify Black capitalism as problematic. Nixon promoted the notion as a ploy to quell antigovernment protests while ultimately aiming to suppress an increased interest in communism and to expand the number of African American Republicans. While selectively parroting philosophies of the Black Power movement with calls for "dignity" and "self-determination," Nixon instead embraced "voluntary segregation, self-reliance, and private enterprise."[51] The promotion of Black capitalism within Black consumer culture thus trafficked in the words and images of Black liberation, all while maintaining a perpetual commitment to the state.

Chicago-based entrepreneurs George E. Johnson Sr. and John H. Johnson collaborated to forge the most visible promotion of natural hair within this Black consumerist framework. Together, their companies defined visual representations of Black hair in the mid- to late twentieth century. George Johnson marketed his hair products in the pages of *Ebony* magazine (the flagship periodical) and *Jet* magazine, published by Johnson Publishing Company.[52] Primarily with his *Ebony* magazine, John H. Johnson promoted a strategy he termed "enlightened self-interest," putting Black consumers on the radar of white corporate entities and enticing them to include Black models in more ads in order to attract Black consumers. This strategy helped *Ebony* as "the magazine's advertising revenue nearly tripled between 1962 and 1969."[53] Robert Weems argues that in the late 1960s, corporations sought "to exploit blacks' growing sense of racial pride" by creating a "'soul market,'" which offered a way to transform Black politics into revenue.[54] Over time, the visual tactics employed for the promotion of natural hair under this model suggested that a pro-Black cultural consciousness could be achieved via consumption and not just political activism.

Ebony's version of politics linked to natural hair an amorphous image of "black leadership," spearheaded by Black men in particular. Beginning with a six-page spread and cover feature for the December 1967 issue (plate 12), *Ebony* aligned natural hair with social uplift and self-improvement. A brightly colored cover with photographs of celebrity entertainer Sammy Davis Jr., actor Harry Belafonte, football player Jim Brown, comedian Bill Cosby, actor Sidney Poitier, and basketball player Lew Alcindor (who eventually became Kareem Abdul-Jabbar) showed that texture had a specific connotation: "Natural Hair—New symbol of race pride."[55] Against an orange background, the nine oval-framed headshots of Black men wearing natural hairstyles were.meant to represent dignity for this group of elite artists, athletes, and actors. This promotion of a male-centered Black aesthetics ignored popular sentiments of the period, where natural hair was prevalent across genders and ignited by the style choices of Black women. But gendering natural hair as masculine served a larger strategy of national advancement led by "race men," as Hazel Carby terms them, through the conflation of the Black male body and "the state of the national soul."[56] This approach to "black manhood [as] the privileged site of political subjectivity and activism," or what Erica Edwards terms "black charismatic leadership," meant to confront and defend blackness "against dehumanization and white supremacist terror."[57] In this approach, the monthly periodical introduced the fictions of political culture to popular culture, pretending a male-centered pursuit of African American ascendancy that ignored women like singer Abbey Lincoln or the fact that "prior to the mid-1960s, natural hairstyles were worn almost exclusively by black women."[58] *Ebony* organized a cadre of Black men wearing natural hair around other politically charged scenes of the period but did not promote a particular alignment with an organization or an explicit notion of the Black freedom movement.

Natural hair in *Ebony's* introductory spread appeared among a constellation of images and commentary about the value of textured hair to Black men from different walks of life. For instance, inside the cover readers found a mix of professional color headshots as well as candid black-and-white photos, all situating natural hair in various locales. The images of natural hair observed at the 1967 Watts Festival convened in Los Angeles and on SNCC activists Stokely Carmichael and Cleveland Sellers, featured at an Atlanta draft protest, acknowledge the presence of textured hair at political activities without explicit support from *Ebony*. Instead, these depictions have a documentary feel, as if to illustrate the direct experiences of "natural-wearers," a framing that is further supported with quotes from a street interview. One respondent explained to *Ebony*:

> I used to be middle-class looking. I looked like a nice Negro. White people on buses and in other public places would often start conversations with me. They would ask me questions. It would usually end with their telling me how much they like Negroes. It was sickening. Now, since I started wearing my hair long and nappy, white folks don't bother me anymore.

But alongside these inclusions, journalist David Llorens defined natural hair around "wearing one's hair in its natural state; giving it no treatment that would disguise its authentic character or texture," and in association with "the movement towards blackness" after the March on Washington.[59] Llorens does not name groups such as the Black Panthers or the Black Power movement, but he does denote the bevy of transitions associated with wearing Afro textures, ranging from an embrace of an African past to renewed psychological foundations. Llorens is cautious, however, noting that "many black people in America have a texture of hair that cannot be worn in an Afro (or a Natural with the capital *N*), but they do nevertheless wear their hair—witness Adam Clayton Powell—natural."[60] Signifying on charismatic Black men in leadership and the March on Washington, without naming grassroots and radical political organizations, Llorens distinguished natural hair from a radical political posture, arguing that protests have "not positively altered such things as the income gap between whites and blacks" but have instead "opened new channels of communication in America's black communities."[61] *Ebony's* editorial treatment of natural hair sidestepped the valorization of cultural nationalism even as it endorsed the embrace of Black aesthetics to locate a new appreciation for texture amid other values promulgated in the magazine.

Instead, natural hair offered a route toward advocating for a particular notion of masculinity. *Ebony* proposed textured hair as part of the ideal, successful Black man, one who achieved both self-pride and sex appeal through hair. When Llorens finally turns his attention to "the sisters," his focus is the desirability of men with natural hair: "There is little evidence of their turning the 'drummer' down *because* he wears a Natural." He cites women who believe that longer locks add "strength to the man's appearance—which is reminiscent of the Biblical character Samson."[62] Llorens argues that for "both the black man and woman, the move to the Natural is often a rejection of not simply the white beauty standard, but in fact a way of reflecting a whole set of attitudes (and values) that are usually associated with White America." He goes on to assert that the Black man could find a renewed concept of masculinity in natural hair, while "the black woman has not been free to doubt the pervasiveness of the blond-haired, blue-eyed white woman as a sex symbol."[63] Textured hair marked sexual potency and financial success as values exclusively available to Black men at this time and rendered these characteristics as part of a masculine leadership potential.

Conceptions of success were essential to the mainstreaming of natural hair in *Ebony* magazine. Such a stance helped the periodical generate an audience for advertisements selling natural hair products like Afro Sheen, which the

2.6

"Raveen Au Naturelle
Spray 'n' Glow."
Advertisement, *Ebony*,
December 1967.

magazine embraced alongside its formal discussion of hair texture. Images for
"Raveen Au Naturelle Spray 'n' Glow" (figure 2.6), promising to leave hair "soft,
manageable," letting "you glide a comb through your hair quickly, easily," appeared along with promotions for "Duke Natural Easy Comb" and "Duke Natural Spray Sheen," which vowed to leave men's hair "looking soft, well-groomed
with a vital, alive-looking lustre." Using actor Richard Roundtree's face on
cans of Duke capitalized on an increasingly popular brand of masculinity, as
Roundtree was already appearing on television programs by the late sixties even
though he would not star in his breakout role in *Shaft*, the iconic film about
a Black private detective, until 1971. Such ads were important despite their
simplicity as they marked the "diversification of the black image presented
in *Ebony* magazine from 1957 to 1989," a period when there was a noticeable
transformation in hairstyles, "particularly the increase in natural hair styles in
advertisements."[64] Pride and achievement were nebulous values that seem di-

rected toward the specific race politics of the period but also toward a general public.

Over time, ads for natural hair products became more complex, promoting natural hair through detailed narratives about texture in pictures about community and race pride. In a full-page ad in the January 1969 issue of *Ebony*, "Afro Sheen Stays on the Case" (figure 2.7), a Black man faces forward to eye the camera, while a woman stands before him, in profile. Against a blue background, standing together, roundness and fullness are the defining features of their Afros. Black cosmetic containers for Afro Sheen products are central in the ad, appearing above the tagline " . . . with a New Conditioner and Shampoo just for your Natural"; the fine print explains, "Mother Nature doesn't care. She rains. She blows. She dries out hair." The feminine antagonist—"Mother Nature"—creates the conditions that Afro Sheen helps fight against, accentu-

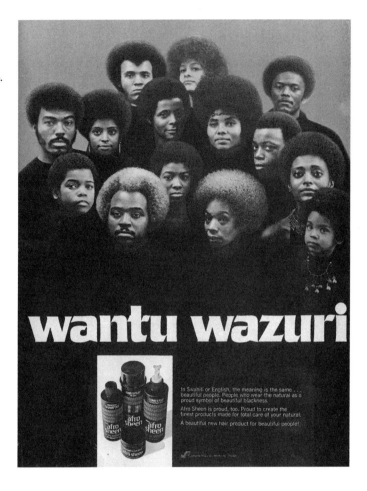

ating masculinity in the achievement of a successful Natural. "Four easy steps to complete hair care" are then listed in order of use: shampoo, conditioner, comb, and hair spray.[65] Afro Sheen print ads reiterated many of these tropes, showing the physical embrace between Black people as a rhetorical embrace of Africanness. In March 1970, *Ebony* ran one such ad, "Wantu Wazuri" (figure 2.8).[66] Set against an orange background, fourteen Black people face the camera to proudly display their Afros; they range in age from children to adults with gray hair. While they are adorned in beads, they wear all-black clothing, and the colors of the image work together to highlight the hair and one Afro set against another. Beneath the title caption, a small photo of Afro Sheen products is supported with text: "In Swahili or English, the meaning is the same . . . beautiful people. People who wear the natural as a proud symbol of beautiful blackness.

2.9

"Afro Sheen Blowout Kit for the Natural," late 1960s. Division of Medicine and Science, National Museum of American History, Smithsonian Institution, Washington, DC.

Afro Sheen is proud, too. Proud to create the finest products made for total care of your natural. A beautiful new hair product for beautiful people!" Here, the Afro is part of a prideful blackness, and users of Afro Sheen value togetherness.

The spectacular importance of the Afro in selling goods meant that Afro-textured hair would become a commodity detached from any notions of biological determinism. A large and fluffy Afro could be enjoyed by an expansive audience once Johnson Products produced its Afro Sheen Blowout Kit for the Natural (figure 2.9). While the images on the box emphasize the texture of Black hair—an Afro-clad man, replete with textured muttonchops, caressing the face of an Afro-wearing woman—the product seems contrary to the image. The fine print explains the kit contains "crème relaxer" and "shampoo neutralizer," as well as gloves for application; the chemicals inside include an activator to ignite the "straightening" properties. Users of chemical straightening products will recognize that Johnson Products' Blowout Kit is not unlike any other chemical process used to permanently straighten the coiled textures of Black hair. Conversely, television commercials for the Blowout Kit literally animate the hair, showing Afros growing in size through this chemical process, promising to get rid of "tangles, for a fluffier and easier to comb" hairstyle. The Blowout Kit is an example of the ways in which the market for "natural hair" involved selling products and selling images, which did not in fact coincide with one another philosophically. The nature of artifice in "natural" hair was not simply about the combing and patting we see in commercials but also the chemical alteration of untreated hair into a permanent transformation; "natural hair" was a chemical and commercial production. Similarly advertised in *Jet* magazine, the Blowout Kit promised a "Natural Explosion," combining slang—"if the Fluffy Blowout is your thing, then do it with our thing"—and directions to consume more imagery via a compound ad promoting both the Afro Sheen product and the television program *Soul Train* by featuring the tagline: "Climb aboard the 'Soul Train' every week. It's the hippest TV trip in America."[67]

Television greatly expanded the visual impact of Afro Sheen. *Soul Train* (a weekly music program that rivaled *American Bandstand*), hosted by Don Cornelius and shot in Chicago beginning in 1971, was central to the spectacular importance of this cosmetic line. *Soul Train* put forth a visual aesthetic that emblematized the period's conception of Black appreciation, as participants' hair and clothing featured popular fashion. Drawing on "black Nationalism" and its emphasis on "black self-sufficiency, especially blacks' ownership of their own businesses," Cornelius remained at the helm as the conceptual person but also "staffed the program with a black technical and production staff," in addition to targeting a Black audience.[68] This partnership helped expand *Soul Train* from a local show in Chicago to one that was "broadcast in seven other cities—Philadelphia, Atlanta, Detroit, Cleveland, Houston, San Francisco, and Los Angeles."[69] *Soul Train* worked for George Johnson, who did not need the show to sell his products but who could count it among his many business ventures. "Johnson and Cornelius jointly pioneered African American television advertising. The former made commercials starring African Americans, and the latter aired them during commercial breaks."[70] Johnson funded the show, promoted it in the *Chicago Defender*, and made appearances to introduce the syndicated episodes; his professional persona was part of the visual story that was *Soul Train*. Together, *Ebony*—along with Johnson Publishing Company's weekly digest, *Jet*—and *Soul Train* were part of an institutional pastiche of Black male media partnerships. Relatedly, the *Soul Train* and Afro Sheen partnership was the public-facing element of a masculinist-oriented Black enterprise not just in sound and image but in structure. The Afro Sheen marketing package was authored by Emmett McBain, an African American advertising executive "who worked for Vince Cullers and associates, the first Black-owned full-service advertising agency," before moving on to cofound "Burrell-McBain advertising with Tom Burrell."[71] Importantly, the collaboration between *Soul Train* and

Johnson Products would "mark the first time that a black advertiser sponsored a nationally syndicated show"; the selling of pro-Black symbolism propelled Johnson Products to become the first Black business to trade on the American Stock Exchange and helped *Soul Train* operate within an unforeseen level of "autonomy."[72] While Afro Sheen was not dependent upon *Soul Train* to sell its products, the partnership did expand the visibility of Afro Sheen's narrative about Black hair. Television spots were more dynamic, calling on music, fashion, and dialogue to weave together a story about who wears natural hair and what kind of products naturals should purchase.

Television advertisements promoting Black hair products drew upon a popular and televisual blackness taking shape in the 1970s. *Soul Train* kept music at the forefront of this approach. In particular, Afro Sheen television commercials added music to the "new Afrocentric sentiment," again using the phrase "Wantu Wazuri," sung in Kiswahili and translated to "Beautiful people use Afro Sheen," and performed by "Donny Hathaway and his wife Eulaulah Hathaway, with music from the Chicago ensemble the Pharaohs (precursor to Earth, Wind and Fire, featuring Louis Satterfield, Don Myrick, and Ben Israel)."[73] However, viewers of the period were also seeing a number of programs on television that addressed Black issues and put race men at the helm. Serious shows such as *Tony Brown's Journal* talked openly about electoral politics and socioeconomics; but even situation comedies such as *Sanford and Son* or *Good Times* added texture and visual variety to a television landscape portraying Black voices. Television spots for Afro Sheen referenced blackness through the use of Black vernacular and fashion, while still shying away from an emphasis on economic struggle. Instead, commercials for products construed a notion of modern Black people situated in diverse settings: at work, around town, at theater performances, at Black protest rallies, and at home, preparing to enter the world.[74] Settings for models who wore and discussed Afro Sheen products included tap dancing on Broadway, standing at an office water cooler, and walking the streets of an unnamed windy city. One commercial depicts a Black woman described as the "Queen of Sheba" by a voice-over. At the opening, she wears an unfluffed 'fro before a dream sequence introduces the Afro Sheen product line that transforms her into "today's queen." Another ad features teenagers clad in dashikis and wearing Afros as they recite a rally cry about natural hair as "a symbol of responsibility to black people," mimicking the vision of youth activists of the previous decade but attaching their image to hair products. Television ads for Afro Sheen expanded the appeal of textured hair as part of a respectable appearance, but with fuller narratives acted out in commercials that circulated to wider audiences than those reached through print alone.[75]

Dread

Unlike the Afro, dreaded hair represented the embrace of nonnormative sensualities and defiance of material dictates on Black bodies in space. Sections of hair twisted, matted, and knotted together, dreadlocks entail a textured surface of individual strands joined together and crafted by hand rather than with implements, such as an Afro comb. In the absence of manufactured products for loc'd hair or the involvement of corporate interests, dreads and dread wearers have historically lacked the kind of image culture that supported the mainstreaming of the Afro. Instead, the mass portrayal of dreads would first be disseminated through news media, as international stories featuring dreads often framed the locs as a discursive sign of an anticapitalist fringe. Whereas the Afro quickly became imbricated in a consumer culture, dreads were repeatedly associated with conflict, both through the everyday experiences of dread wearers and in the international news images that depicted spectacular conflict between the state and wearers of loc'd hairstyles.

A diverse cadre of diasporic people with locs can be organized around adverse and often violent struggles with state and local governments, where these spectacularly deadly confrontations reveal sedimented postslavery regimes of haptic blackness. Loc'd hair marked the movement that came to be called "Mau Mau," or freedom fighters who also identified as the "Kenya Land and Freedom Army," and who were committed to "armed struggle should decolonization fail to give them free land."[76] This group of radicals, variously "defined as a movement, a war, a revolt, a revolution, a rebellion, a freedom struggle, a liberation movement, and a nationalist struggle," fought for actual territory in Kenya, between 1952 and 1956.[77] The Mau Mau resisted settler colonialism and disenfranchisement at the hands of the British, while the British feared the loss of a prized colony. Activists took to the forest to live and to strategize against the British land grab and the suppression of Kenyan farmers. Mau Mau were actively fighting against colonialism that "denied access to education, land, state institutions, and public services" and ensured that "Kenya's African communities were socially alienated, economically marginalized, and politically disenfranchised."[78] Although the issue of land had material significance in the lives of Kenyan farmers relegated to diminished parcels of space and made subservient to British outsiders, Mau Mau resistance also posed a discursive question—"To whom does Kenya belong?"

However, the international image of the Mau Mau was filtered through the framing of British print news, which focused less on the goals of removing British settlers or the establishment of an independent Kenya in 1963. Instead, Britain's "influence on the press during the state of emergency allowed the government to dictate the image of the Mau Mau," casting them as a senseless fringe element focused on random violence and brutal terrorism.[79] But while the Mau Mau were described as vicious and brutal for their resistance to colonialism, they were in fact subject to a greater degree of abuse from the British, both before and during the conflict. Historian Daniel Branch enumerates the killing of Mau Mau, citing "the anti-colonial rebellion and civil war claimed the lives of approximately 25,000 Kenyan Africans" as distinct from the "32 European settlers [who] were murdered, and a further 63 European combatants [who] were killed during the war."[80] Headlines like "Mau Mau Massacres 150 Natives in Night Raid near Kenya Capital" and "Soviet-Trained Mau Mau Terrorist Is Sentenced to 7 Years' Hard Labor" focused on Mau Mau violence rather than on the sadism of colonial occupation.[81] The corresponding imagistic narrative of the Mau Mau during the early 1950s included simple maps of the region to illustrate the Kenyan terrain in question and photos of leaders including Jomo Kenyatta and General China (née Waruhiu Itote). The press switched to more staged and spectacular images of the resistance moving into the 1960s.

In these portrayals, the image of dreads added another texture to the dissent presented by the Mau Mau. Loc'd hair was a key element of Dedan Kimathi's image. He was a leader of the insurgency who was targeted by the British military for directing "attacks on settler farms, arson, and political murders," which was the version circulated internationally by the British press.[82] After he was captured on October 21, 1956, a picture of Kimathi showed him wounded from a gunshot to the thigh, stripped of his robes, and with his dreadlocks wound tightly atop his head as he lay on a stretcher. Illustrating Kimathi as a feeble captive was an important element in the British assertion of victory over the Mau Mau and in discouraging uprising in other colonies. Another portrait of Kimathi at his trial, with his dreadlocks parted in half and twisted together, circulated without attachment to his political concerns, functioning as a portrait study in racial distinction (figure 2.10).[83] While Kimathi's depiction with locs appeared within stories of his being subdued and brought to justice—photos of him captured or seated in the courtroom—Mau Mau leader Field Marshal Mwariama's locs were part of contrasting Kenya's fringe element against credible leadership. A story about Independence Day celebrations in Kenya, with now Prime Minister Jomo Kenyatta, claimed that Mwariama "embarrassed" the political official with his embrace, as Mwariama represented the group of "terrorists still lurking in the Mount Kenya forests" (figure 2.11).[84] Here, the visual contrast between Kenyatta, dressed in a collared shirt and kufi hat, and Mwariama, in a denim and patchwork jacket along with his loc'd hair, is part of presenting a choice between civilized and uncivilized Kenya. By the early sixties, more than ten years

2.10

Dedan Kimathi Waciuri at His Trial in Nyeri, 1956. Authenticated News. Photograph from via Getty Images.

• • •

2.11

Kenyatta and Mwariama, 1963. Central Press. Photograph from Getty Images.

after the emergency, dreadlocks and Mau Mau sentiments were represented as extremist, distant from Kenyatta, and counter to the new direction of the country.

Tension around the Black body and national space similarly punctuated conceptions of Rastafarians; textured hair also marked Rastas as radical outsiders. Emerging in the 1930s, Rastafarianism similarly proclaimed "Africa" as essential to the Rasta's identity, embracing the ascendancy of Haile Selassie of Ethiopia and the "back to Africa" moorings of Marcus Garvey as a means of connecting diverse orders or mansions of Rastafarianism.[85] A "liberating religious and spiritual philosophy," Rastafarianism mixed Pan-Africanism, Garveyism, and Christianity to argue for "the exodus of the Rasta from the corruption of mainstream Jamaican society," the refusal of "participation in the plantation economy," and the promotion of "counterhegemonic eating, language, behavior and lifestyle practices."[86] For Rastafari, the rejection of the present conditions in the slums and the embrace of Africa marked a revolutionary awareness and a desire to escape out of Babylon.

Loc texture embraced a racial blackness rooted in a historical and religious past. For a Rasta, dreadlocks suggest "that despite enslavement and oppression he belongs to a princely race with a glorious past," where this hairstyle promoted "a greater self-awareness, a deeper consciousness of the Rasta's origins, and also of his present condition."[87] Dreadlocks were part of an intricate belief system. Biblical references served a theology of "'Black supremacy,'" making "the royalty of Black skin, hair and culture" valuable, while the wearing of locs "and the untrimmed beard" indicated a "divinely mandated act with spiritual, political and cultural pragmatic realities" dating back to an African-descended biblical Black lineage initiated with King Solomon.[88] Such thinking deepened conceptions of dreadlocks as counterhegemonic, as this hairstyle resisted a biblically informed promotion of Black valuelessness steeped in Christianity that had circulated since the Middle Passage.[89]

But textural distinction and the associated lifestyle were imbricated in violence *against* Rastas. Anthropologist Deborah Thomas argues "Rastafarians' radicalism evoked fear—indeed, dread," because in the first thirty years of their emergence, "Rastafarians were seen as a threat to the consolidation of the Jamaican state."[90] She cites the reoccurrence of forced shaving as police terrorized Rastafarians into the 1970s, when the image of "bearded Rasta men were used during target practice" by law enforcement, while children wearing locs were "removed from prestigious schools because they refused to trim their hair," and elders were denied entrance to establishments.[91] Such rehearsals of slavery's haptic engagement with Black bodies informed the physical encounters between Jamaicans of different political positions but also dispersed into a global media environment that used hair texture to further promote hostile haptic encounters. In New York in particular, during the 1970s, news accounts framed dreadlocks as the prevalent style of Rastafarians, whom the paper described as murderous drug dealers. Drawing connections between "poverty, ganja, the original outcast status and the fact that some criminals have grown dread locks and moved into Rasta communities for sanctuary," the media produced an image of a people that justified violence against them, suggesting the group's chosen identity ultimately "brought Rastafarians and the law into conflict."[92] Newspapers in the United States deployed the smoking of herb and the wearing of long, uncut hair—parts of the Rastafarian belief system—to demonize Rastas. However, a "common political anguish" attributed to Rastas and to reggae reverberated with the concerns of Black Power activism and fostered diverse cultural productions born of "protest against the economic and political situation" in Jamaica.[93] These conflicting yet popular conceptions of dreadlocks have helped to further obscure the persistent violence against Rastafarians.

Governmental efforts to destroy MOVE were similarly spectacular and were known to many after 1985, when Philadelphia mayor Wilson Goode, in consultation with the Federal Bureau of Investigation, dropped a bomb on the MOVE house at 6221 Osage Avenue, killing eleven people including five children, and destroying some sixty-five homes in the neighborhood. But MOVE had a lengthy engagement with local police and employed its own media strategies separate from and against the mainstream news portrayals of them. Founded in Philadelphia during the early 1970s by John Africa (née Vincent Leaphart), this independent community focused on rights for all living things—plants, animals, and people (figure 2.12). Although the group was primarily made up of African Americans, MOVE did not exclude non-Black persons from membership but insisted on members taking the last name *Africa* to signal the continent as the origin from which all human life sprang. Central to MOVE's philosophy was an anticapitalist sentiment, observable in their lifestyle: "MOVE members washed cars, walked dogs, and chopped firewood for money"; their political philosophy focused on animal rights, vegetarianism, and a hostility toward technology. They "eschewed middle-class modes of dress and wore their hair in dreadlocks," as their concept of "back-to-nature" meant eating only raw fruits and vegetables, refusing to diaper children, and bathing without soap/deodorant.[94] Their anticapitalist sentiment was not just visible but also philosophical, recorded in "The Guidelines," an unpublished manual on how to live the life of a MOVE member. "The Guidelines of John Africa" describe the "'the System,' borrowing a phrase that New Left radicals made popular in the 1960s to describe capital-

1

Rashid Johnson, *Self-Portrait with My Hair Parted like Frederick Douglass*, 2003. 45³⁄₁₆ × 57¼ in. (114.8 × 145.4 cm). Museum of Contemporary Art, Chicago. Photograph by Nathan Keay. © MCA Chicago.

2

Andy Warhol, *Portrait of Jean-Michel Basquiat*, 1982. Dye diffusion print. Image:
3¾ × 2⅞ in. (9.5 × 7.3 cm). Sheet: 4¼ × 3⅜ in. (10.8 × 8.6 cm). J. Paul Getty Museum,
Los Angeles. © 2021 The Andy Warhol Foundation for the Visual Arts, Inc./Licensed
by Artists Rights Society (ARS), New York.

3

Kerry James Marshall, *School of Beauty, School of Culture*, 2012. Acrylic and glitter on unstretched canvas, 108 × 158 in. © Kerry James Marshall. Courtesy of the artist and the Jack Shainman Gallery, New York.

J.B.Debret. del.ᵗ   Lith. de Thierry Frères, Sucr.ˢ de Engelmann &Cⁱᵉ

ESCLAVES NÈGRES, DE DIFFÉRENTES NATIONS.

4

Jean Baptiste Debret, *Esclaves nègres, de différentes nations*, 1834–39. Source: New York Public Library. https://digitalcollections.nypl.org/items/510d47df-7983-a3d9-e040 -e00a18064a99.

LES BARBIERS AMBULANTS

5

Jean Baptiste Debret, *Les barbiers ambulants*, 1834–39. Source: New York Public Library.
https://digitalcollections.nypl.org/items/510d47df-7983-a3d9-e040-e00a18064a99.

6

Jean Baptiste Debret, *Boutique de barbiers*, 1834–39. Source: New York Public Library.
https://digitalcollections.nypl.org/items/510d47df-7983-a3d9-e040-e00a18064a99.

7

Peter Arrell Browne, *George Washington Hair Sample*, *Peter Arrell Browne Papers* (1762–1860), vol. 1 of 10, leaf 1. ANSP Archives Collection 756.

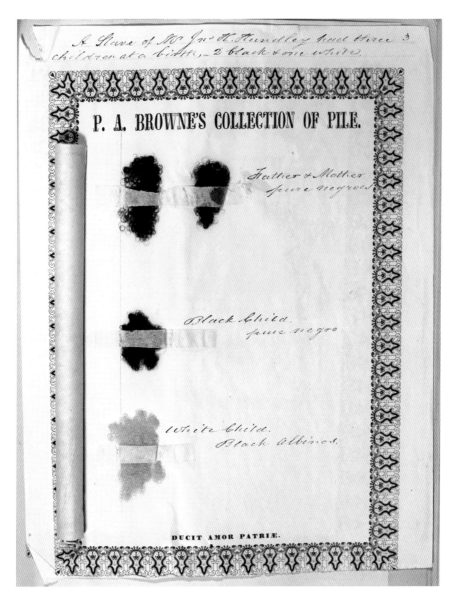

8

Peter Arrell Browne, *A Slave of Mr. Jm. H. Hundley Had Three Children at a Birth, 2 Black &
One White*, *Peter Arrell Browne Papers* (1762–1860), vol. 8 of 10, leaf 42a. ANSP Archives
Collection 756.

• • •

9

Peter Arrell Browne, *Eccentrically Elliptical Pile*. African. *Peter Arrell Browne Papers*
(1762–1860), vol. 6 of 10, leaf 75. ANSP Archives Collection 756.

Eccentrically elliptical pile. African.

P. A. BROWNE'S COLLECTION OF PILE.

*Congo Billy. The manu-
mitted Slave of Col. S. B. Davis,
Wilmington, Delaware.*

DUCIT AMOR PATRIÆ.

10

Barkley L. Hendricks, *Lawdy Mama*, 1969. Oil and gold leaf on canvas, 53¾ × 36¼ in.
© Barkley L. Hendricks. Courtesy of the artist's estate and the Jack Shainman Gallery,
New York.

11

Wadsworth Jarrell, *Revolutionary (Angela Davis)*, 1971. Acrylic and mixed media on canvas, 64 × 51 in. (162.6 × 129.5 cm). © Wadsworth Jarrell. In the collection of the Brooklyn Museum, New York.

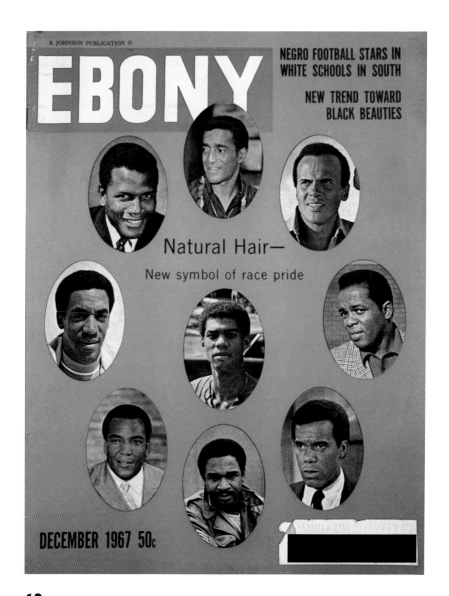

12

David Llorens, "Natural Hair—New Symbol of Race Pride." *Ebony*, December 1967.

13

Ellen Gallagher, *Afrylic*, 2004. Plasticine, ink, and paper on canvas. 243.8 × 487.7 cm (unframed). © ELLEN GALLAGHER. COURTESY OF GAGOSIAN.

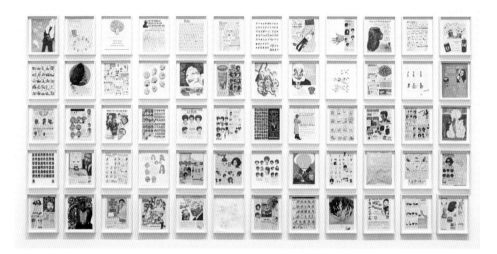

14

Ellen Gallagher, *DeLuxe*, 2004–5. Grid of sixty photogravure, etching, aquatint, and drypoints prints with lithography, screen print, embossing, and tattoo-machine engraving; some with additions of Plasticine, watercolor, pomade, and toy eyeballs. Each: 33 × 26.5 cm. Each framed: 39 × 32.6 × 4.6 cm. Total: 215.26 × 447.04 cm.
© ELLEN GALLAGHER. COURTESY OF GAGOSIAN.

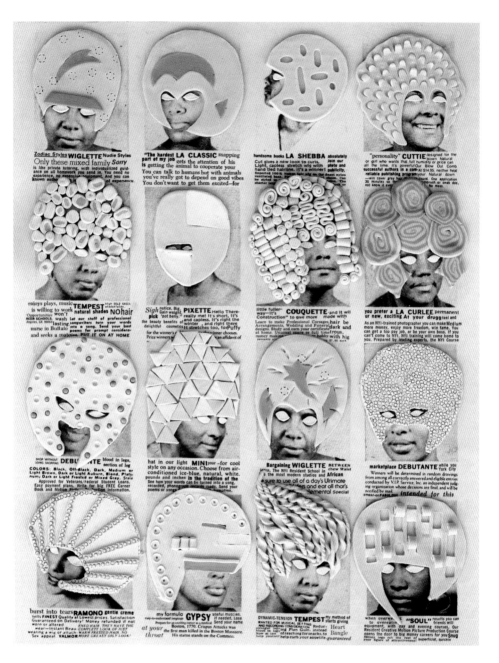

15

Ellen Gallagher, *Wiglette* (detail of *DeLuxe*), 2004–5. Unframed: 33 × 26.5 cm. Framed: 39 × 32.6 × 4.6 cm. Total: 215.26 × 447.04 cm. © ELLEN GALLAGHER. COURTESY OF GAGOSIAN.

16

Lorna Simpson, *Earth & Sky #24*, 2016. Collage on paper, 11 × 8½ in. (27.9 × 21.6 cm). Framed: 12½ × 10 × 1½ in. (31.75 × 25.4 × 3.8 cm). Photograph by James Wang. © Lorna Simpson. Courtesy of the artist and Hauser & Wirth.

17

Lorna Simpson, *Phenomena* (detail), 2016–17. Collage on paper, nine framed collages. Unique. Installation dimensions variable. Each: 11 × 8½ in. (27.9 × 21.6 cm). Photograph by James Wang. © Lorna Simpson. Courtesy of the artist and Hauser & Wirth.

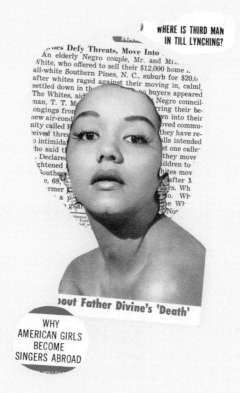

18

Lorna Simpson, *Jet #21, '55*, 2012. Collage and ink on paper, 11¼ × 8½ in. (28.6 × 21.6 cm).
© Lorna Simpson. Courtesy of the artist and Hauser & Wirth.

19

Lorna Simpson, *Completing the Analogy*, 1987. Silver gelatin print, engraved plastic plaque. Overall: 36 × 48 × 2 in. (91.4 × 121.9 × 5.1 cm). Plaque diameter: 10 in. (25.4 cm). © Lorna Simpson. Courtesy of the artist and Hauser & Wirth.

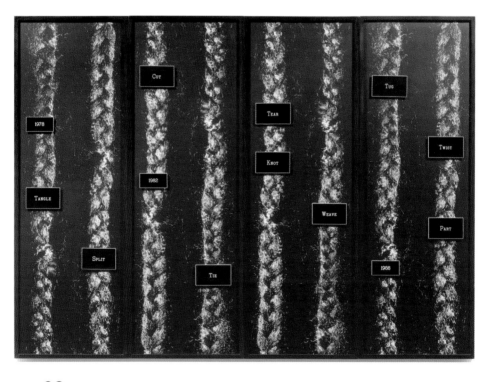

20

Lorna Simpson, *1978-1988*, 1991. Four silver gelatin prints, thirteen engraved
plastic plaques. Overall: 48¾ × 67½ × 1⅝ in. (123.8 × 171.5 × 4.1 cm). Each framed
print: 48¾ × 16¾ × 1⅝ in. (123.8 × 42.5 × 4.1 cm). Photograph by James Wang.
© Lorna Simpson. Courtesy of the artist and Hauser & Wirth.

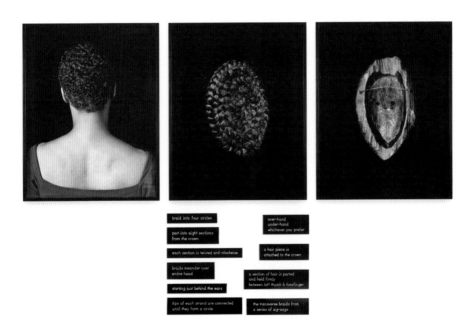

21

Lorna Simpson, *Coiffure*, 1991. Three silver gelatin prints, ten engraved plastic plaques. Overall: 72½ × 106 × 1⅞ in. (184.2 × 269.2 × 4.8 cm). Each framed print: 43 × 34 × 1⅞ in. (109.2 × 96.4 × 4.8 cm). Photography by James Wang. © Lorna Simpson. Courtesy of the artist and Hauser & Wirth.

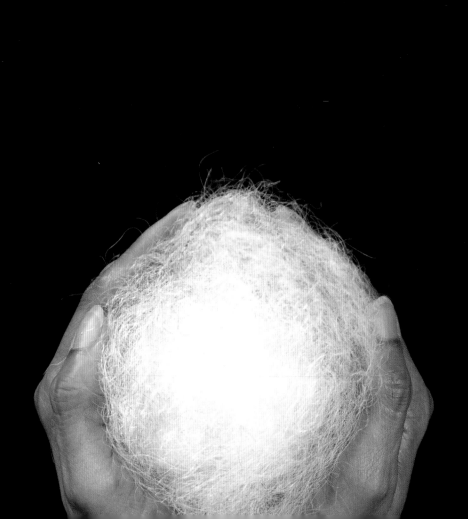

22
Sonya Clark, *Mother's Wisdom or Cotton Candy*, 2011. Courtesy of the artist.

23

Sonya Clark, *Hair Craft Project*, 2015. Silk thread on canvas. Participating stylists (*left to right, top to bottom*): Kamala Bhagat, Dionne James Eggleston, Marsha Johnson, Chaunda King, Anita Hill Moses, Nasirah Muhammad, Jameika and Jasmine Pollard, Ingrid Riley, Ife Robinson, Natasha Superville, and Jamilah Williams. Courtesy of the artist.

24

Sonya Clark, *Hair Craft Project*, 2015. Photographs. Participating stylists (*left to right, top to bottom*): Kamala Bhagat, Dionne James Eggleston, Marsha Johnson, Chaunda King, Anita Hill Moses, Nasirah Muhammad, Jameika and Jasmine Pollard, Ingrid Riley, Ife Robinson, Natasha Superville, and Jamilah Williams. Courtesy of the artist.

25

Alison Saar, *Nappy Head Blues*, 1997. Wood, paint, found objects, 19½ × 13¼ × 12¼ in. © Alison Saar. Courtesy of L. A. Louver, Venice, CA.

26

Alison Saar, *Delta Doo*, 2002. Monoprint/woodcut and Chine collé, 33⅞ × 24⅜ in. (86 × 61.9 cm). © Alison Saar. Courtesy of L.A. Louver, Venice, CA.

27

Alison Saar, *Compton Nocturne*, 1999. Wood, tin, bottles, paint, and tar, 33 × 80 × 28 in.
Weatherspoon Art Museum, University of North Carolina at Greensboro. Museum
purchase with funds from the Benefactors Fund, 1999.38. Photo courtesy of the
Weatherspoon Art Museum, University of North Carolina at Greensboro.

28

Alison Saar, *Compton Nocturne*, 2012. Lithograph, 19¼ × 25¼ in. (48.9 × 64.1 cm).
© Alison Saar. Courtesy of L. A. Louver, Venice, CA.

29

Alison Saar, *High Cotton*, 2017. Linocut and monotype on Korean chiri kozo paper,
21⅛ × 14 in. (53.7 × 35.6 cm). © Alison Saar. Courtesy of L.A. Louver, Venice, CA.

30

Alison Saar, *White Guise*, 2019. Woodcut, relief, shellac-stained paper, hand-tinted iron on Mulberry non-bleached, natural deckled edge (BlueHeron Arts), 55 × 27½ in. (139.7 × 69.9 cm). © Alison Saar. Courtesy of L. A. Louver, Venice, CA.

31

Alison Saar, *White Guise*,
2018. Wood, copper,
ceiling tin, bronze, and
tar, 91 × 40 × 30 in.
(231.1 × 101.6 × 76.2 cm).
© Alison Saar. Courtesy of
L.A. Louver, Venice, CA.

32

Alison Saar, Installation photograph from *Topsy Turvy*, L.A. Louver, Venice, CA. March 28–May 25, 2018. © Alison Saar. Courtesy of L.A. Louver.

2.12

"MOVE Watch," *Philadelphia Evening Bulletin*, May 4, 1978. Members of MOVE watch another member surrender to "Philadelphia police Thursday afternoon on the city's west side. Police had set up barricades to starve them out of their house. Special Collections Research Center, Temple University Libraries, Philadelphia, PA.

ism, political corruption, and the emerging neoliberal order."[95] In sharing excerpts of the document, Louise Africa cites the text:

> Economic depression is the deceptive exploitation of political distribution, it is the penalty of overabundance, massive indulgence, lawless accumulation, inflative excessiveness. World politics that encourages the distortion of sales, the deceptive prosperity of jobs and spending, goods and services, the illusion of balanced economy. Politics that will promote the manufacture of accessories, stimulate spending, run into a depression and complain about excessiveness, tell you that you are overindulging, wasteful, reckless, the same reform world system that is recklessly pushing the inflationary contraband of accessory, waste, overindulgence.[96]

Its anticapitalist politics made MOVE known throughout the city of Philadelphia, although attitudes varied about the sect. On the one hand, MOVE was not unilaterally regarded as problematic since the organization maintained the support of many Black Philadelphians who were not affiliated with the organization and who helped to advocate for their right to exist (figure 2.13), as indicated in this photo of Pennsylvania State Senator Roxanne Jones exiting court with Pam Africa (née Jeanette Knighton). At the same time, however, bodily practices and lifestyle habits among MOVE members fueled stories about the group as a sensual and financial nuisance. Public complaints about the group referenced the smell emanating from the house, attributed to animals and outdoor defecation, but also the loud cursing over bullhorns, which MOVE members used to address passersby and during various demonstrations around the city. Distaste for the body politics associated with MOVE were well known, and MOVE acknowledged and refuted the narrative of its members as unkempt or filthy radicals. Beginning her first newspaper column on June 28, 1975, Louise Africa addressed hostile attitudes about the group with the headline "ON THE MOVE: From the Writings of John Africa." On the question of hair, she wrote explicitly, "We of MOVE are not oblivious to the fact that we are called 'dirty and uncombed.' We make no concession to being fashionable—we ain't never led nobody to believe we're out to win no 'best dressed' contest—and we ain't interested in 'fronting' for no Afro-Sheen Products." She went on to say that "Blacks are still warring with blacks. Capitalism is still running rampant in this country."[97]

L. Africa's critique of MOVE detractors did not negate MOVE's aesthetics altogether so much as it refuted the mainstreaming of an approachable idea of natural or textured hair as represented on the packaging of Afro Sheen. Moreover, in turning the discussion toward the impact of capitalism as more important than an amicable texture—an acceptable haptic blackness—her column connected MOVE's style choice with a focus on other ways of existing that were outside of, or less concerned with, dominant notions of hard work and middle-class striving. This position corresponded to the organization's regular activities; MOVE's financial self-sufficiency meant they evaded poverty framing in local news, even as they refused to abide by class norms of "hard work" and bill payment. Accordingly, members of MOVE were in regular confrontation with city government, with both the courts and the police. Although most crimes were misdemeanors, "in a single seven-month period spanning the winter and spring of 1973–74, some forty different MOVE people were arrested one hundred-fifty times, fined approximately $15,000, and sentenced for up to several years in jail each."[98] The group was castigated as a financial burden to the city, with "unpaid gas and water bills, back taxes, and police overtime being the most promi-

2.13

"MOVE Supporters Leave Court," *Philadelphia Evening Bulletin*, March 16, 1978. Pennsylvania State Senator Roxanne Jones and Pam Africa (née Jeanette Knighton) exit together. Photograph by Don Camp. Special Collections Research Center, Temple University Libraries, Philadelphia, PA.

nent costs," totaling "two hundred-fifty thousand dollars, at a minimum."[99] Although these costs stemmed from the state's harassment of MOVE, the notion that the organization pestered the city helped justify MOVE's eradication.

Loc'd hair became a visual signifier of MOVE as nonnormative and problematic. While the city government demonized the group, the local news media followed along with images that helped criminalize MOVE members. A published police information sheet on MOVE members (figure 2.14) shows individuals with cropped, tight headshots that emphasized loc'd hair as part of each suspect's visage. Dreadlocks were not simply a feature of MOVE's self-styling; they were actively incorporated into hostility against the group. Black Philadelphians reported harassment for wearing locs even without membership in the organization, and MOVE members reported having dreads yanked from their heads and having their hair mentioned in verbal abuse by the police. In one of the first notable confrontations with the police, the MOVE home on Thirty-Third Street in Philadelphia was the scene of a police shoot-out following days of verbal altercation and after the city cut off food and water to the

INFORMATION

Arrest warrants are outstanding charging the following persons with:

Riot and Contempt of Court

PAGE ONE

2.14

"Police Information Sheet on MOVE Members," *Philadelphia Evening Bulletin*, August 26, 1978. Special Collections Research Center, Temple University Libraries, Philadelphia, PA.

SPORTS FINAL

The Philadelphia Inquirer

Vol. 299, No. 38 — Wednesday, August 9, 1978 — 15 CENTS

MOVE Routed in Gunfight; Officer Killed, House Leveled

First shot fired from basement, witnesses say

By Murray Dubin

James J. Ramp, slain in shootout

Officer Ramp lies fatally wounded (left) as a policeman (right) begins to drag another wounded officer to safety

The mayor: Grief filled with rage

By Rob Fiverg

Delbert Africa, covered by a police officer, climbs out of a basement window after the shootout; police beat him before he was handcuffed and led away

Sadat, Begin to meet Carter at Camp David

By Saundra Saperstein and Nicholas P. Yates

WASHINGTON—President Carter has invited Egyptian President Anwar Sadat and Israeli Prime Minister Menachem Begin to Camp David for a head-to-head summit, the White House announced yesterday.

Weather & Index

Their pain becomes anger for the death of a colleague

By Dick Cooper

2.16

Delbert Africa dragged by police. "MOVE Routed in Gun Battle with Police," *Philadelphia Inquirer*, August 9, 1978. Photographs by J. G. Domke.

MOVE routed in gun battle with police . . .

residents. A full-page spread of images from the *Philadelphia Inquirer* (figures 2.15 and 2.16) shows loc'd hair being used to assist in administering physical abuse as well: when police apprehended Delbert Africa from the Thirty-Third Street house, an officer grabbed his hair and used it to pull D. Africa to the ground before kicking and hitting him with a gun. The scene shows D. Africa's hair used against him, as a tool used by the officer to assault and abuse him. After this encounter in the Powelton Village neighborhood, the city "proceeded to demolish the house completely. Every brick and scrap of wood was torn down and the property was turned into a vacant lot," an act that also destroyed physical evidence relevant to a police shooting at the scene.[100] Hair provided a way to single out and harass people of African descent and, much like the Afro decades earlier, it could be weaponized and used against individuals in their clashes with authorities.

Collectively, dread wearers with anticapitalist politics in fraught relationships with the state often organized around the ways in which people of African descent occupied social space. In Kenya, Jamaica, and the United States, in the late twentieth century, dreads in particular appeared at the center of news stories about unruly people who posed threats not just to the nation, but also to other people of African descent. In these encounters, dreadlocks have been viewed as markers of a differently textured sociality. This natural hairstyle has served as shorthand for values that run counter to the strictures of citizenship, particularly as defined for Black peoples. Mau Mau leaders were uninterested in a secondary citizenship—in being a lower caste to British settlers who would control Kenyan farms. Rastas refuted "loyalty to an independent Jamaican state" as well as involvement "as wage laborers in a capitalist economy"; they were demonized and brutalized in the United States and in Jamaica for "their rejection of the modernist model of development [that] placed them outside the boundaries of citizenship."[101] The visual and narrative constructions of people who wore dreadlocks enabled state violence against them, intensifying conceptions of violence as inherent to blackness. The nonnormative sensuality of dreaded hair was used to construe radicals in the wilderness, herb-smoking recluses, and lewd city dwellers. Hair as an aesthetic means of reinvigorating hapticality for revolutionary purposes figured into a global "Black radicalism," or what Cedric Robinson argues was "a specifically African response to an oppression emergent from the immediate determinants of European development in the modern era."[102] All of these ideas enabled violent forms of touch as a means for handling the textural dissent of African-descended people whose bodies and material realities rejected the rationales underpinning accumulation as a value.

Conclusion

The twentieth-century construction and embrace of natural hair represents a turn toward the human surface as a reformation of haptic blackness, a way of revising the valuation of racial distinction visually and granularly. Textured hair represents a way to rethink interiority, material relations, and the legibility of blackness as a surface. Revisiting hapticality after the hold, and in the midst of decolonization movements, came to signify liberation through efforts to clinch a differently textured Black experience. At the site of the body, this new approach to consistency not only meant the texture of coiffure, but the ways in which Black bodies inhabited spaces. These endeavors refuted the extracting impulse of racial capitalism. The embrace of Afrocentric hairstyles at once represented shifts toward a racially distinct national identity and a permanent status as resistant outsider, refusing Western norms and capitalist ascendancy.

In other instances, natural hair served a larger media narrative about Black consumerism as another avenue for advancement or "liberation," without making stringent demands on government entities. Discourses of Black economic self-determination were diffused in visual representations as a sufficient form of politics. The market for "natural hair" produced Black entrepreneurs in cosmetics and media, with the commodification of the Afro helping to buttress Black-owned media institutions and product manufacturers. Through the commodification of texture and the mass mediation of radical Black aesthetics, routes toward liberation split along lines that either submitted to or renounced the strictures geared toward accumulation. Where "neoliberalism" pivoted, or "changed the distribution of respectability" as Grace Hong theorizes, Black image producers constructed an acceptable approach to textured difference as a way to both embrace blackness and promote middle-class striving.[103] Johnson Publishing Company was one of the lead image purveyors at the forefront of this project. "Natural hair" became "fetishized and folded into the broader process of institutionalizing dominant hegemonic understandings," as Richard Iton describes, through the periodical's advertising and editorials.[104] Expounding on the value of blackness in visual culture and the role of mass mediation, the artists and images I discuss in the remaining chapters propose another valence for thinking about liberation—experimenting with freedom on pictorial surfaces in order to propose new engagements with the Black exterior.

TOUCH

THREE

In the previous two chapters I explored hair as an archive of feelings among fugitive free people of African descent, as well as a record of the affective labor in which Black peoples were engaged as part of the experience of enslavement. Along these lines, I have tried to illustrate that violence was central to the meaning and value associated with the visual and material qualities of Black hair, so that when people of African descent embraced texture in the twentieth century, their efforts reflect their attempts to reorganize the Black body in space after slavery and after colonization. These dynamics underscore haptic blackness as construed on the human surface, with hair operating much like the flesh in the context of slavery; but, over time, hair evolved in line with Black radicalism, making the mutability of this human surface unique unto itself. In the remaining chapters I explore haptic blackness on the pictorial surface. Images foster sensuous engagements with blackness, as depiction helps to fix feelings in time, to make permanent the touch created in embodied viewership.

The smooth surface of a film or a photograph as well as the coarse exterior of assemblage interpellates viewers in ways that collapse efforts to distance and objectify blackness. Images combine historic experiences of feeling and various notions of Black exteriority. Those images that objectify touch—that actualize the experience of contact—render Afro-textured hair as the means by which haptic blackness functions as a code rather than as a condition.

Touch holds the center of the frame in Carrie Mae Weems's 1990 photo-graph *Untitled (Woman Brushing Hair)* from her *Kitchen Table* series (figure 3.1). As in other images in her collection, Weems sits at the head of the table. This time her head is tilted to the side, pressed against the woman who brushes her hair. The overhead light starkly illuminates the mostly bare table but casts a shadow on the wall, revealing the woman focused on brushing and the hanging textile decor that appears on the back wall. These points of physical contact at the center of the image—the subject's head leaning against the woman brushing her hair, the brush sweeping through the hair, and the woman's hand resting on the subject's head—help accentuate that contact is at the center of the story. Physical touch between women, ignited by hair care, becomes a pivot for affec-tive relations in this scene; the care and caress are the only points of certainty in the image. Weems stages an encounter that is suggestive of both comfort and distress, depicting the subject with eyes closed along with the two packs of cigarettes and two drinks on the table. As the wall decor changes from image to image, reflecting the mood in the room—whether in a photograph of Malcom X when the artist converses with a male guest in one scene, or the blank wall that appears in tense moments with others, or as Weems appears alone—Weems's choice of decor for the hair brushing scene is also a tell. The hanging textile is present only in scenes with other women, so that the background wall centers craft and feminine artmaking, such as the art of hair care. Touch is at the cen-ter of this particular story, as Weems reveals physical contact and affective en-gagement through hair without regard for a final presentation of style. Her use of black-and-white photography employs light and shadow in ways conversant with other Afro-diasporic photographers who have similarly used gray scale and the camera, with its legacy as a documenting apparatus, to complicate proxim-ity and contact with photographic representations.

Black and white is also the medium used by conceptual artist Lorraine O'Grady in her *Landscape (Western Hemisphere)*, an eighteen-minute video that provides viewers with a close encounter with an indiscernible visual material (figure 3.2). In single-channel format, O'Grady suggests both day and night, as viewers hear the sounds of birds chirping, a train arriving, a thunderstorm, and cicadas. The black-and-white screen image portrays material blowing in the

3.1

Carrie Mae Weems, *Untitled (Woman Brushing Hair)*, *Kitchen Table* series, 1990. Photographic print, 28 ¼ × 28 ¼ in. © Carrie Mae Weems. Courtesy of the artist and the Jack Shainman Gallery, New York.

wind, revealing patterns of waves and glints of light, only to be uncovered as a head of blowing curls when a large lamp illuminates the material before, finally, the entire screen fades to black. O'Grady's depictions of curl clusters and loose strands of black and silver hair employ a continuous close-up shot that brings the viewer in intimate relation to the subject's hair, too close to recognize the image of curl pattern—a mixture of waves, twists, and near corkscrews. "Black" as the latent character of the curls gives way to black on the screen as O'Grady presents intimate closeness to hair. Sometimes the screen shows almost total darkness and at others, the light reflects off the subject's strands, adding a visual texture through contrast with hair that is graying. Although the camera operates as a tool of indexicality, O'Grady wields it in a manner that produces intimate relation, bringing the viewer seemingly "inside" the subject's mane without revealing her body. The resulting image refuses indication, offers no visual sense-making. This proximity enables the camera to trick the eye by obscuring for viewers that they have been watching hair and not some other earthly material, such as trees. O'Grady's abstraction of Black hair in *Landscape (Western Hemisphere)* renders textured coiffure unrecognizable and unfamiliar. In effect, the artist presents hair and the camera as foreign objects, at once producing an experience of closeness and distance, indexicality and a subjectivity. O'Grady's obfuscation of raciality presents an exploration of the "use of blackness," while at the same time playing with motion conveyed through video.[1] According to curator Adrienne Edwards, O'Grady "transforms her hair into a moving abstract landscape" wherein "we locate the remains of enslavement" and "the pathways to transgressive resistance embedded in the heights, depths, and expanse of the waves of her hair."[2] Even in abstraction Black hair is read as a representation of slavery, even in absence of the physical body. The movement in O'Grady's coif is part of the story, and that her hair blows in the wind but does not blow away suggests a racialized history as essential to the visual quality of Black hair. "Landscape," as a description for landforms occurring in "nature" but also for the purposeful cultivation or modification of "nature" for visual appreciation, asserts a legacy of racial contact in O'Grady's depiction, especially as the term is modified "Western Hemisphere." Black materiality is the landscape of the Western Hemisphere but it is also cultivated or transformed through its existence within the Western Hemisphere. Proximity to Afro-textured hair presents viewers with a conundrum: an abstraction of the body that is meant to transcend an emphasis on the corporeal of Black raciality for a focus on Black visual material, which is similarly grounded in historical referents to a racialized past. The film surface provides a screen for an obscured human surface, producing touch through disrupting a reliance on the eyes alone.

3.2
Lorraine O'Grady, *Still #01*, from *Landscape (Western Hemisphere)*, 2010–12.
Courtesy of the artist.

This chapter considers film and photography on Black hair for their haptic qualities, limning the manner in which artists and cultural producers have used documentary aesthetics to recuperate touch as associated with the haptic Blackness of Afro-textured hair. Contact between women in Weems's image reveals that skin is not the only "canvas upon which touch and its cultural associations are represented," because hair is also an affective and perceptive terrain.[3] Likewise, O'Grady's video presents a "cinema of the senses," employing techniques such as "blurring overload of photographic precision, extreme close-ups," and "variations in sound pitch and intensities" to establish an "ebb and flow between the figurative and the abstract," defamiliarizing the human form and collapsing distance with the viewer.[4] One image relies on narrative and the depiction of touch; the other plays with the image surface to hail the body of the viewer. Each employs the camera's penchant for objectivity to elicit the subjective. Although each image incorporates hair, each depiction also relies on the camera to contend with touch and the haptic qualities of blackness. Laura Marks, a theorist of intercultural cinema, similarly regards the centrality of the camera in her exploration of video among filmmakers who appeal to the senses as a means to excavate memory and contend with displacement; she considers especially Arab and Arab-diaspora filmmakers, for example, who conjure intimate sensory experiences through which "knowledge is transmitted tactilely rather than visually," and in which skin has the propensity to "distinguish, know, and remember."[5] Appeals to touch or the invitation to embodied viewing is particularly important for artists working cross-culturally and in the wake of exigencies unique to diaspora and dislocation. Works such as *Landscape (Western Hemisphere)* and an array of Afro-diasporic camera images engage memories of intimacy, touch, and embodied viewing, utilizing hair to contend with touch more broadly. These works rely on the subjective experiences produced by intimate relation, with hair and with the image. Although these artists employ the photographic apparatus, they consistently complicate its claims to objective knowledge production by exposing the body as a site of comprehension. These artists meld the camera's authority and the viewer's subjectivity by engaging haptic blackness with a documentary aesthetic, using black-and-white images, affective modes of evidence, and vernacular portrayals while asserting the presence of the camera.

Although images having to do with people of African descent do not monopolize haptic representations, the histories informing the haptic construction of blackness are distinct, as I have discussed in chapters 1 and 2. On the basis of the tactile and visual constitution of blackness, representations of uniquely sensuous materials such as Afro-textured hair become relevant to a larger conception of slavery's cultural legacy. Efforts to address touch in the narrative and on the surface contend with longer histories of intimate contact, such as those that lacked "consent," as described by Saidiya Hartman.[6] I explore how haptic images of an always already textured material signify on practices of touching blackness, and the ways that image makers contend with histories of contact. Such representations deploy the camera against a legacy of film and photography as central to objectifying Black raciality, while also denying those same practices of indexicality in favor of the embodied and the sensuous.

I begin by thinking about Afro-diasporic photographers who collapsed the distance between the viewer and coiffure surface through producing black-and-white photographs of textured hair. Gray-scale prints occur in representations of people of African descent and are variously associated with images aiming at straightforward and accurate storytelling, such as those attributed to reportage and ethnographic documentation. Newsprint's reliance on the absence of color differentiates its photographs from the color employed in magazines, such as those appearing in *Ebony*, for example. But beyond photojournalism, photographers taking images of serious matters, such as political conflict, have also relied upon black-and-white depiction, as in SNCC's own documentation of its preparation for civil disobedience. Similarly, "struggle photography" representing conflict surrounding anti-apartheid activism in South Africa that circulated to news sources and to NGOs employed "clear, easily decipherable narratives of oppression and resistance," depicting "protest rallies, police brutality, and victims of violence and poverty," and magnified distinctions of scale or violent confrontations through the use of gray scale.[7] This color choice aligned with print news representations that were unsympathetic to the fight against apartheid, but photographers announced their "subversive intentions" through framing and various inclusions.[8] Black-and-white photography thus represents an important representational choice conversant with a bastion of sobering illustrations, even when it is used for the appreciation of beauty. Next, I consider "natural hair documentaries" that educated viewers and advocated for textured hair through the treatment of touch in their narratives and in their representational techniques. Along with photography, documentary film has provided an important rejoinder to institutional and anthropological approaches to Black subjectivity. In these documentary accounts, notions of beauty, pride, shame, and history are often contextualized within practices of touch motivated by hair care and personal hygiene, where the story line reiterates concerns from the sixties about slavery as having produced a cultural residue. These ideas are shared across age and gender as film subjects reflect on the meanings attributed to their hair, largely in Black communities but also in society at large. Beginning in the late 1980s and growing in prominence into the twenty-first century, "natural hair documentaries" mark some generic distinctions that I outline below; but they should also be read against the climate of Black screen portrayals of the 1990s, when Black visibility carried intensified relevance in a transforming visual climate. The penchant for documenting Black hair culture persisted into the early twenty-first century as producers moved their video content to online venues. Individuals interested in using video as a format for engaging Black hair documentaries and tutorials could upload their work to sites like YouTube and Vimeo, while still producing feature-length works to show at film festivals. These short videos feature the talking-head format so prominent in traditional documentary films, showing individuals answering questions about products, or sharing personal experiences around hair, while shifting conceptions of "expertise." Such camera images become central to the twenty-first century landscape of representations, wherein the vernacular presents another approach to the documentary aesthetic, suggesting the photographic capture of the everyday as if it "naturally" occurred, without cultivation. In these portrayals, creatives seeking to commodify the resistance read into Afro-textured hair also rely on the production of the ordinary and voluminous depiction to challenge former modes of handling blackness.

Photographing Black Hair

Black-and-white photographs predominate *Hair in African Art and Culture*, which opened in February 2000 at New York's Museum for African Art.[9] Curator and art historian Roy Sieber, along with Director of Exhibitions Frank Herreman, presented photographs and objects meant to reveal and highlight Afro-textured hair as an aesthetic practice. Comprising "field photographs and traditional sculptures," their exhibition presented "the wide variety of coiffures worn by peoples throughout the continent" with the aim "to offer a glimpse of African-inspired hairstyles worn by African Americans."[10] Juxtaposing diverse objects of material culture such as handcrafted razors, the curators tell a story about Black hair as an artistic substance, showing the synergies between art objects and African hairstyles. Images of hairstyles in 1940s Namibia and 1950s Tanzania are juxtaposed with various sculptures so that photographs do the work of documenting hairstyles among people across the continent of Africa—the coif of a heeler in Côte d'Ivoire, a portrait of girls in a coming-of-age ceremony in Ghana. There are also images such as the face-forward headshot of a bare-breasted woman in Ghana and the tetraptych *Stages of Coiffure-Making* that are used to comment on the process of Black hair and to show its resonance with Ghanaian wood sculpture. Similarly, *Child with Partially Shaved Head*, a 1950 photograph from Cameroon, is paired with a Makonde wooden head adorned with human hair from Tanzania. In this coupling, the curators accentuate the reoccurrence of hairstyles in disparate locales on the continent of Africa. Although the image reiterates the shape and style of hair in the sculpture, as a stand-alone photograph it also tells the story of an intrusive camera and the photographer, at the edge of the frame, as the child considers taking a banana. This camera-person interrupts the encounter between a child and an adult. In these encounters, anthropologist Deborah Poole argues, "the photograph also contain[s] within it the possibility of authenticating the presence that constitute[s] the basis of the ethnographer's scientific method," garnering the need for the photographer's attendance at the scene to capture the interaction.[11] Not just any photographs, but black-and-white photographs in particular, render the camera an implement used to document exotic cultural activities of which hair is a central part. Alongside the camera, black-and-white prints verify the seriousness of the documentary work taking place at the scene, with these particular photographs offering records of hair and hair culture in Africa as premodern. This style of photograph, situated with a story about art and aesthetics, treats Black hair as part of "a transparently representable past," in keeping with the "ideological assumptions of anthropologists working on the African diaspora,"

3.3

Malick Sidibé, *Soirée familiale*, 1966. Gelatin silver print, 8 ¼ × 8 ¼ in. © Malick Sidibé. Courtesy of the artist and the Jack Shainman Gallery, New York.

and lending a salvage element to art history of the diaspora.[12] Documentary photographs locate coiffure in the everyday, capturing the context in which Black hair customs exist.

Eliding this framework, Afro-diasporic photographers have also used black-and-white images to foster intimacy, employing these tones to capture the events around them and to locate photography in the formation of new subjectivities. Photographers Seydou Keita and Malick Sidibé, for example, use black-and-white photography to create images that indicate intimacy and portray Malian subjects as fashionable. Their works are central to a "post-colonial photographic production." Not only are these works created by and for Africans, but "the relationship between the photographer and the subject matter is that of great familiarity," observable in "a look of complicity" between the subject and the photographer.[13] Their photographs chronicle transformations in attitudes toward studio photography and independence, and in so doing, they reveal hair as an evolving time line within those transformations. For example, Keita frequently depicts women with their hair covered throughout the 1950s. These give way to social scenes of glee and textured hair in Sidibé's 1960s scenes, captured in photographs like *Soirée familiale* (figure 3.3). In these distinctions, Manthia Diawara designates hair as a point of connection and departure in the photographic works of Malian photographers, citing Keita's distaste for women with Afros that morphs into the undeniable "diaspora aesthetics" captured in Sidibé's images of a transformed and "common habitus of black pride, civil rights, and self-determination," promoted through global flows of popular music, political activism, and forced head shaving to remove Afros in the mid-1960s.[14] Black-and-white depiction helps to illustrate a sharp contrast among colors and makes patterns stand out, whether in Keita's backdrops or in the patterned clothing worn by Sidibé's partygoers. The resulting "vernacular modernism," as Christopher Pinney describes it, serves "to consolidate the intimate space between viewer and image" and is partially a production of the black-and-white photographic surface.[15] In this choice of depiction, artists forge community between the viewer and the image, inviting "tactile looking" that engages the "touching" aspect of the photograph as object, and not simply as an objective window into an interaction.[16] In their use of black-and-white photography, Afro-diasporic photographers collapse the distance between the viewer and the image subject; these artists refuse the distance imposed by regimes of evidence and verification and instead cultivate intimacy with this same medium.

A black-and-white schema creates closeness in Nigerian-born J. D. Ojeikere's iconic *Hairstyles*.[17] Snapping photos in Lagos, Ibadan, Kaduna, and Ilorin, Ojeikere treated hair with exaltation by organizing the models and the camera to emphasize the form and structure of a diverse array of styles. Heads appear as platforms or "pedestals for the hair."[18] Framing his subjects at eye level or slightly above the camera adds to the sense of admiration, as the figure appears greater than the camera and the only information given is about the coiffed hair. Taking multiple photographs of each example, "most often from the back, sometimes in profile and less often from the front," Ojeikere aimed to illustrate the "sculptural aspect" of textured styles and to abstract the form from the individual wearer.[19] Images of cornrow plaits radiating from a center point emphasize the precise lines of hair parts and the symmetry created by braiding. *Untitled (Modern Suku)* shows height and structure (figure 3.4), combining flat braids against the scalp with taller braids that employ artifice to build a dense dark mound. Alternatively, the reflective sheen of wrapped coils portrays smoothness for *Untitled (Agaracha)*, where light helps to emphasize the firmness of each distinct hair cord (figure 3.5). In these photographs, Ojeikere's proximity to the style as well as his camera's point of view is underscored by his use of gray scale, revealing the refractive quality of Afro-textured hair even in the simply sectioned puffs in *Untitled (Mkpuk Eba)*, shown as one of many similar heads (figure 3.6).

Ojeikere's hair photographs at once refute indexicality and embrace the documentary. Despite capturing numerous styles to create a visual catalog of coiffures, his images provide no identifying information. In interviews Ojeikere clarifies some of their characteristics, explaining, for example, that "the style Kiko takes more time than the style Didi." But more generally he insists that his focus is on what he calls "quotidian hairstyles," as distinct from those for special ceremonies that "are determined by the type of ceremony, the social position of the family or of the woman and artistic talent of the hairstylist," such as wedding ceremonies attended by Efik women.[20] The lack of labels to offer any identifying information for the hairstyles requires that the viewer simply appreciate the image: "I preferred not giving them any title. The context and the names of the hairstyles aren't important and don't influence our enjoyment."[21] At the same time, Ojeikere commits to the value of documentary, in fact, arguing the camera enables him "to record knowledge and moments in history and culture."[22] Many of his images portray the cultural practice of hairstyling as significant and changing, and the photographs position Ojeikere as both inside a culture in flux and outside it, behind the camera hoping to salvage proof of its existence. Refusing the index puts Ojeikere in conversation with other photographers of African descent who have similarly elided the authenticating impulse of the camera's complicated history around depictions of Black people.

3.4

J. D. 'Okhai Ojeikere, *Untitled (Modern Suku)*, *Hairstyles*, 1979. Reproduced by permission of the estate of J. D. 'Okhai Ojeikere/Foto Ojeikere.

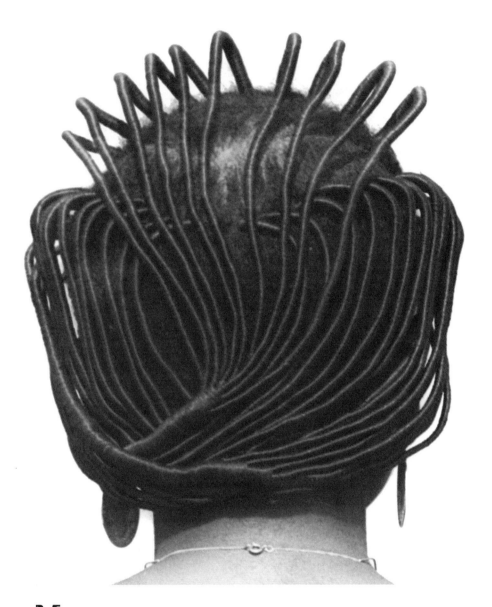

3.5

J. D. 'Okhai Ojeikere, *Untitled (Agaracha)*, *Hairstyles*, 1974. Reproduced by permission of the estate of J. D. 'Okhai Ojeikere/Foto Ojeikere.

3.6

J. D. 'Okhai Ojeikere, *Untitled (Mkpuk Eba)*, *Hairstyles*, 1979. Reproduced by permission of the estate of J. D. 'Okhai Ojeikere/Foto Ojeikere.

For example, US photographer Charles "Teenie" Harris refuted photography's racializing strictures, "refusing labels and titles" on his images of Black Pittsburgh.[23] In the face of a Western photographic practice that objectified people of African descent, these artists utilize the camera in ways that emphasize a "requisite ambivalence," according to Olu Oguibe, maintaining "a fundamental distrust of the photographic medium" through lighting, camera positioning, and printing techniques that delegitimize its clinical intentions.[24] Ojeikere's dedication to recording and celebrating Nigerian hairstyles figures into an emergent cultural nationalism intended to visualize, log, and "inventory for future generations" transformations in everyday life.[25] Some of those changes impacted all representations, such as in the mixed art scene of 1960s Nigeria described by art historian Chika Okeke-Agulu, where the government sought to establish national cultural institutions while artists faced "the sobering realities of the unraveling postcolonial body politic" with art that was not simply dedicated to praising the new nation.[26] *Hairstyles* speaks to the transitional impact of Nigerian independence, the rethinking of old and new traditions represented in customary and modern designs.[27] A regard for documenting and the use of black-and-white prints helped *Hairstyles* circulate as a record of transformation, making it among Ojeikere's most popular works, "exhibited in European and American museums, where they have become a shorthand for a kind of primary subjectivity of African photography."[28] But those same aesthetic choices, including his way of creating photographs to convey cultural appreciation, not only rebuff the stereotypical photographic treatment of peoples on the African continent; they also speak to other Afro-diasporic photographers. Such choices shift presumptions about the value of the photographic subject—the hair—and in the absence of textual information, Ojeikere's photographs reveal only the texture, structure, and aesthetic project that constitute the style.

Black-and-white photographs also present shadow as a means by which to generate intimate proximity, such as in photographer Bill Gaskins's *Good and Bad Hair*. A collection of images about hairstyles and hair culture of the 1990s United States, Gaskins's images depict a variety of Black hair textures, showing both straightened and textured hairstyles. Shadow forges contact in Gaskins's images, such as in *Scarlet, Columbus, Ohio* (1991; figure 3.7). Here, the subject appears at the forefront of the image, her gaze cast into the distance, with a shadow line across her body that leads the viewer's eye to the light box and shadow on the wall, where Scarlet's double is cast against the background. The texture of her hair causes a ripple in the silhouette, making the textural distinction palpable to the viewer. Similarly, light cuts across the subject's face in *Red, World African Hair Care, Braid, and Trade Show, Atlanta, Georgia* (1997), on an

3.7

Bill Gaskins, *Scarlet, Columbus, Ohio*, 1991. Reproduced by permission of the artist.

angle, to feature the textural variety of the subject's brightly colored locs. Such instances of casting shadows on Afro-textured hair emphasize its distinct look and feel. As a technique, it can accentuate the portrayal of surface variety in the linearity of a dreadlock updo on a city street in Brooklyn, New York, or of box braids in Baltimore, Maryland.

Like Ojeikere, Gaskins presents a recuperative project, depicting hair in ways that not only valorize the texture but make its physicality tangible on the picture plane. Although he describes never learning an explicit definition for bad hair, Gaskins recalls that together with family conversation and "television commercials, the concept of good hair was firmly set in my mind"; moreover, "good hair was hair that was not curly or coarse in texture. Good hair was not difficult to comb." Based on these experiences, he believed that "anybody's hair that was naturally curly, naturally thick—essentially African—was bad hair."[29] His photographs challenge the binaries of good and bad as values and also confront a conceptual duality about the varieties of texture by showing diversity. Gaskins's black-and-white images not only depict hairstyles but also reveal the underexplored world of hair shows, making the viewer witness to drama and artifice, where participants purchase hair products or watch fashion shows that

3.8

Bill Gaskins, *Carolyn, World African Hair Care, Braid, and Trade Show, Atlanta, Georgia,* 1997. Reproduced by permission of the artist.

feature garments created from synthetic hair tracks. In a collection that depicts Black hair on city streets as well as at public gatherings, Gaskins interrupts ideas of hairstyling as a private matter. *Carolyn, World African Hair Care, Braid, and Trade Show, Atlanta, Georgia* (1997; figure 3.8) shows the viewer Black hair in process, with the braided style draping along the subject's face and her unbraided "natural" forming a rounded crown above her head, invoking a hair halo in its density. Gaskins's photograph employs gray scale to not only present the granular distinction of hairstyles but also explore the visual experience of texture, realized in the coiffure as well as in the paisley printed dress.

Documenting Black Hair

The reimagination of touch is among the key interventions tackled in documentary films on natural hair. Filmmakers confront the issue of physical contact in ways that help recalibrate haptic conceptions of blackness through filming demonstrations of hairstyling, as well as through asking participants to recount memories of hair care. Combining narrative and illustration, these films portray personal and social histories of grooming. Natural hair documentaries take up the shared "doing" of hair and not just the final appearance of a style. Emerging in the 1990s, these films focused specifically on the treatment of Afro-textured hair and frequently offered explicit discussion of "natural hair" as an idea and a politically informed choice about self-representation. The journey, or transition, from straightened to textured styles is central to this storytelling, as shown through firsthand testimony from hair care experts and laypersons discussing their personal experiences. Film subjects share first-person accounts about childhood experiences with hair straightening, about the impact of straightening on self-concepts, and about the role of family values in shaping sentiments about personal appearance. Treating appearance as the crux of a larger transformation, these works present viewers with Afro-textured styles as opportunities for political activism, for education, and for appreciation. Most commonly, film participants wear their hair in textured or "natural" styles, which provide a contrasting image to the recounting of their experiences around straightening with heat or with chemicals. In their emphasis on the "back to natural" journey, whereby participants discuss returning their hair to its "original" textured state, women, the primary discussants in these films, share experiences with beauty regimens that refuse the straightening techniques that began in childhood. In stories of this personal evolution, participants hark back to the interiority concerns of the 1960s, making the transition to "natural" central to the process of overcoming an internalized self-hatred. Much like documentary film more generally, these films employ solo shots of experts and textural distinction between camera interviews and the addition of archival evidence, or B-roll, all deployed to assert the veracity of storytelling. Natural hair documentaries utilize these same filmic tropes but in ways that historicize, illustrate, and reimagine the role of touch in the visual construction of Black hair.

By the 1990s, Afro-textured hairstyles became popular once again, both in everyday life and in media representations. Textured hair punctuated a larger embrace of upward mobility during this period, entangled in representations of the Black middle class and scholarly examination of the Black past. Not just Afros, but hairstyles including braids extended with synthetic hair, locs, and twists were highly visible in diverse media portrayals. According to historians Robin Kelley and Earl Lewis, such styles were part of the work of "revisiting stereotypes, exploring diversity within black communities and turning to the interior" as part of a new appreciation for "black nationalism" as visualized in Malcolm X hats and kente cloth, which were prevalent alongside the dreadlocks seen among students "on many college campuses."[30] On screen as well as in everyday life, natural hairstyles were increasingly visible and part of the racial pastiche of prime-time television programs. *The Cosby Show* of NBC included dread-locks for Lisa Bonet's "Denise," and Tempestt Bledsoe's character "Vanessa" also wore a variety of textured styles, in addition to the Afro-textured pony-tail worn by Keshia Knight Pulliam as "Rudy." Natural hairstyles were woven into the middle-class lifestyles of characters on shows like Fox's *Living Single*—where attorney "Maxine Shaw" wore braids, and her love interest "Kyle Barker" wore short locs—as the show confronted the political significance of Black hair in the workplace. Natural hair functioned as one of many "cultural signifiers," along with "historically Black college/university paraphernalia, jazz albums, [and] Black art."[31] Thus, the look and treatment of Black hair was summarily woven into the economic imperatives of media representation. According to sociologist Herman Gray, "a discursive space was opened in commercial net-work television" coming out of the 1980s, in which Black actors and Black audi-ences "figured more centrally" in the "economic viability and aesthetic vitality of commercial television," diminishing the popularity and profitability of pro-grams that refused to acknowledge the "cultural force of women and African Americans."[32] Once again, and not unlike the turn toward Black representa-tions in the 1970s, Black visibility carried overt capitalist imperatives. The leg-acy of natural hair as a sign of cultural nationalism maintained a multifaceted and lucrative significance.

The valuation of Black representation in the 1990s also played out against a pointed disappointment with the socioeconomic suppression of Black people, as revealed through a bevy of more cynical images. These portrayals showed Black life hamstrung by a complicated relationship to accumulation and to structures of governance. Film scholar Ed Guerrero describes this decade as revealing "a renewed sense of racial oppression and foreclosure, pessimism, and sinking social expectations" compared to the 1960s, as African Americans faced an "intense period of nihilism, fragmentation, and self-doubt" made manifest on film screens with movies like *Deep Cover*, in which actor Laurence Fishburne plays a cop turned drug dealer in an undercover sting operation.[33] Some of the most popular Black films of the period emphasized the pangs of capitalism at the root of their stories, but in ways that were digestible to mainstream audi-ences. Legible blackness portrayed through crime and drugs, observed in films like *Menace II Society*, put social realism at the forefront of what was deemed the "explosion" of Black images in the nineties. The popularity of such films offered immense "crossover appeal" to mainstream audiences, "but only by a dubious logic to account for the *black* of 'black film,'" according to Michael Gillespie.[34] In this context, Regina King's box braids in *Boyz n the Hood* (figure 3.9), by John Singleton, and Ice-T's dreadlocks in *New Jack City*, by Mario Van Peebles, are

3.9

Still from *Boyz n the Hood*, directed by John Singleton, 1991. Source: https://www.imdb
.com/title/tt0101507/mediaviewer/rm810947584/.

mise-en-scène to stories about blackness and urban culture. These filmmakers did not promote a singular Black aesthetic—presenting only natural hair,
for example—but instead portrayed textural variety as part of authenticating
Black life on screen. However, questions of racial acceptance appeared even in
those works described as "sellout films" by Racquel Gates, with titles that "focus[ed] on adults undergoing identity crises as a result of their professional am-
bitions" and "the emotional, social, and psychological nuances of 'succeeding'
in a white world."[35] These works portrayed a tension between the value of Black
identity and assimilationism or managing blackness in a white and corporate
environment. Thus, even with Black image makers at the helm, films of the
1990s straddled feelings of outwardly expressed cultural pride, anxieties about
social acceptance, and pessimism about capitalism's impact on Black life.

In this visual climate, documentary approaches to Black issues offered a
decidedly serious tone. Black documentarians issued works that were often

recuperative, characterized by intent to "counter" misrepresentations and mis-understandings about blackness in screen portrayals; filmmakers embraced no-tions of the "real," of truth and authenticity, not as master signifiers but as ways to challenge "the authority of mainstream American history and culture."[36] Read against the grain of major studio productions, Black documentary aimed to create a new "primary source for social political accounts of black life."[37] According to cinema studies scholar Michael Martin, these films "endeavor to give voice to protagonists who otherwise are marginalized and silenced," thus they endeavor to "resist and debunk" popular constructions of African Amer-icans.[38] By deploying experts, archival footage, and firsthand testimony, Black documentaries approach realism as a matter of verifiability, looking to forms of evidence that correct the stereotypical "real" most legible to mainstream au-diences. Such commitments were echoed in the "realism" of independent and documentary films targeting white audiences, notable in movies like Michael Moore's *Roger & Me* (1989) but also in MTV's first season of *Real World* (1992). These works similarly incorporated scenes of exposé and confrontation, rep-resenting fringe, self-governing, and anti-institutional approaches to complex issues that typified documentary; however, as this style of imagery became in-creasingly popular toward the end of the century, the independent ethos of films in the 1990s would be transformed. "By 2004 the worldwide business in television documentary alone added up to $4.5 billion revenues annually."[39] As the visual tropes of outsider storytelling became increasingly popular and lucra-tive, documentaries about Black life continued to revolutionize the field with features by experts of African descent and revelations about political and cul-tural phenomena not frequented in other areas of representation.

Natural hair documentaries contributed to this landscape. Physical touch was a common theme of redress in works that attempted to settle contempo-rary cultural practices and histories of racial animus. *Urban Tribe*, a 2000 film, offers an "inside look" at Black hair culture by taking viewers on location to a salon. In this film, the producers attempted to tackle the suffering associated with harsh and hurtful hair care and aimed to debunk characterizations like "tender headedness" or an innate intolerance for painful grooming. The film-makers redefined these euphemisms and reframed them as based in mechanical errors resulting from styling Black hair with improper implements—echoing Willie Morrow's arguments from four decades earlier. In an effort to educate viewers about Afro-textured hair, the director included archival material on Madam C. J. Walker and the famous Clark Doll Study to historicize hair care practices in an anti-Black past. Harsh grooming is depicted as institutional-ized through beauty culture, but also located in the everyday personal practices discussed in the video. Film subjects discuss the physical touch of styling, with many recounting experiences from childhood, when hair care was sometimes painful. Carla Thompson's *The Root of It All* (1994), also shot in black and white, opens with a discussion of "good hair" among women convened in a living room setting (figure 3.10). Together, they offer definitions of terms like *nappy*, which they define as both a texture and an appearance, while sharing memories of painful childhood experiences with straightening. Although the women featured in the discussion wear various hairstyles, including braids, closely cropped hair, permanently straightened hair, and a textured bun, the conversation still drifts toward the ways in which hairstyle choices indicate self-hatred, as they debate and disagree about whether practices of adornment can reveal self-loathing. Another black-and-white video, *Kitchen Blues*, released in 1994, features Black women and girls sharing hair care practices and conversation about hair. Two girls define "good hair" as unlike the locs worn by the director, while their mother recounts the physical and emotional pain she endured as a child during grooming, a memory that now informs her hair care choices as a parent. Intercut with the narrative of feelings associated with Black hairstyling are scenes of touch as a neighbor braids a young girl's hair, while the girl simultaneously styles her doll's hair. In these inclusions, the director features touch as part of the discussion as well as part of the image. Participants in these documentaries discuss the experience of being touched for grooming, while directors illustrate touch with close-up shots of hairstyling. The combination reoccurs across films and contrasts for viewers a distinction between the memories of painful hair care and the gentleness of new approaches to touch that are prevalent alongside this evolving consciousness.

Camera techniques are central to the work of rethinking physical contact in natural hair documentaries. Directors frequently use zoom shots of coiffure material and wide shots of hairstyling. Images that show hair care providers at work draw on the presentation of "experts" in documentary film but also portray the tactile knowledge of hair styling as part of their expertise. Consider the Canadian film *Black, Bold and Beautiful*, a 1999 documentary about the valuation of Black hair within a straight-versus-natural dichotomy. Director Nadine Valcin takes a diasporic focus by addressing the distaste for dreadlocks among Seventh-day Adventists in Canada, the persecution of Rastafarians wearing dreadlocks in Jamaica, and the donning of colorful wigs among women in Jamaican dance-hall culture. In addition to studio interview footage, the film depicts hair experts at work, shown applying permanent straightening chemicals and handling a hot comb. Women give interviews during braid and loc installation, each shot at a wide angle to capture both the stylists and the clients speak-

3.10

Group interview. Still from *The Root of It All*, directed by Carla Thompson, 1994.
Source: https://www.youtube.com/watch?v=a4AhnK8RelQ.

ing directly to the camera. In such choices, "employing experts in relevant fields
and personal reflections in talking-head formats," these elements elicit the seduction of documentary, creating "a kind of hands-off approach to storytelling
that simply allows the filmed subjects to 'speak for themselves.'"[40] At the same
time, such casting of "expert" and expertise is a salient means by which natural
hair documentaries diverge from masculinist arguments about textured hair in
the twentieth century. They portray the professional at work in the deployment
of tactile knowledge in an effort to reframe both the notion of authority and
the styles of physical contact associated with Black women's approach to hair
care. Not only are stylists using tactile knowledge, they are also listening to intimate feelings about appearance. And through a reoccurring focus on women
and girls who speak directly to each other and to the camera, their "autobio-
graphical expertise" becomes central to the film.[41] Knowledge thus includes
proficiency in hair care along with the expertise of lived experience, drawn from
wearing Black hairstyles, revealing tactile epistemologies and embodiment as
types of expert testimony that directors include in documentary film.

3.11

Curling iron close-up. Still from *The Root of It All*, directed by Carla Thompson, 1994. Source: https://www.youtube.com/watch?v=a4AhnK8RelQ.

But the film material also conjures touch in its depiction of textured hair. *Kitchen Blues* offers close-up shots of hair braiding, illustrating distinct sections of hair coming together in a woven pattern, while *The Root of It All* puts viewers in intimate proximity to a curling iron heating disparate strands of textured hair into a single smooth mound (figure 3.11). Such frames that focus exclusively on the visual material of hair use depth to add to the visual pleasure of the image, creating a touching sensation, conjuring the memory of the heat from a smoky hot comb pressing hair straight, or the moisture from permanent relaxing chemicals weighing down textured hair. These depictions demand embodied viewing. These inclusions bring a sense of "aesthetic pleasure" to cinema, which is usually denied in documentary film because of "its closer indexical relation to the real," and thus to appeals to "truth claims, whether at the level of fact or image."[42] But directors who offer close views of actual touching or an intimate focus on hair material not only inform through the sharing of narrative but also interpellate through the body, conjuring memories via a uniquely filmic capacity for tactile viewing. Touch on the surface of the film also presents a point of experimentation for directors, allowing for the animation of hair itself as a feeling material alongside the wearers of textured hair. The film *Middle Passage-N-Roots* (1995), written and directed by Ada M. Babino, is surely a documentary in genre, but it uses interview footage as well as performance to engage with Black hair. The film combines personal and expert testimony with dramatic vignettes about a woman having her hair heat-straightened (only to get rained on upon leaving the salon). Instead of using the camera to shoot close-up shots of hair material, this film employs sequences of dancers representing hair. Using their bodies, the dancers cringe, sway, and rejoice to signal the experience of hair strands variously burned by a hot comb or washed with shampoo. These techniques demonstrate and even dramatize the impact of touch on coiffure material and underscore the psychological associations attributed to textured and straightened hair.

Natural hair documentaries, then, are explicit in their attempts to reform ideas about desirable hairstyles and to discredit notions of textured hair as unmanageable or unworthy of sensitive touch. While these films utilize the documentary form as a means of signaling their evidentiary value, documentarians also employ the camera in their refutation of empiricism, announcing the camera as an apparatus on the scene and revealing the filmmaker as present in the recorded interactions. The twenty-two-minute film *My Nappy Roots,* which debuted in 2006, utilized all these elements to educate viewers about the history of Afro-textured hair. Also relying on the talking-head format, B-roll from hair shows, and archival newspaper clippings, *My Nappy Roots* (figure 3.12) includes a range of experts such as hair care product executives, a university professor, and various authors and celebrities, including actresses Kim Fields and Ella Joyce. The discussion begins with details about precolonial African hair cultures before moving into slavery's impact on Black hair in the United States, showing images such as the abolitionist slave-ship image. Film producers mix the historical and the popular, including cultural figures such as founder/creator of Sisterlocks, writer Trisha Thomas, author of *Nappily Ever After*. Director Regina Kimbell explains, "My thing is 'edutainment,' making history entertaining and exciting, as well as educational," in order to reach audiences and explore topics ignored through traditional scholastic formats.[43] Although the film attends to stock issues associated with the analysis of Black hair, such as the lack of proper combs in slavery, straightening as an assimilationist aesthetic attributed to Madam C. J. Walker, and the use of permanent straightening chemicals or Jheri curl styles, the documentary is decidedly in promotion of "natural hair." *My Nappy Roots* treats film and the camera as technologies that assist in sharing information but that cannot capture (objectify) an observable phenomenon.

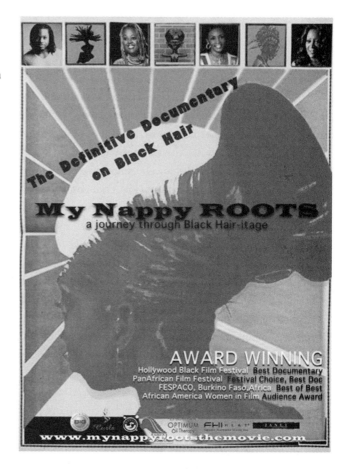

With the exception of the parts from the B-roll insertions, viewers watch as the film margin rolls along the right side of the screen, showing numbers and letters flickering along the screen's edge as an aside to expert testimony framed in film panels. This inclusion is more than a style that adds visual interest to the image. As cinema scholar Tom Gunning explains, "Film's marginal spaces rationalize the moving image and keep it running"; such material exists in service of those handling the film professionally, providing the numbers, letters, and manufacturing information to help with the "ordering of the film image[s] that underlie the spectacle."[44] On screen, however, and in this context, these signs accentuate materiality and functionality to offer the viewer another form of evidence, anticipating and signaling the archival future of the image. These indicators underscore documentary as a record, even if it is subject to editing, and thus gesture toward the development of new evidence about Black hair and its history.

Over time, the documentary format has remained a compelling way to approach the feelings associated with Black hair and to embrace Afro texture. With the emphasis on women's embodied knowledge and expertise, as well as the concentration on sharing information about approaches to care, these films complicate facile notions of hair culture as a simple preoccupation with appearance. Newer works, including Gillian Scott-Ward's *Back to Natural*, build on their predecessors but open onto new representations of authorial voice and the global flows of Black hair culture. Scott-Ward includes visits to a hair salon in France to hear about the twenty-first-century evolution of Black hair from film subjects but also films her own salon experience, depicting the "big chop," cutting her own hair to remove permanently straightened tresses and leaving her with a short natural.[45] Such images speak to the manner in which the experiences resonate with women within the videos, across videos, and across the diaspora, while making the camera a central means of linking these communities around shared relationships to touch.

The seriousness with which women filmmakers engage the question of textured hair underpins the rage with which some viewers have watched Chris Rock's documentary, *Good Hair* (2009). Rock's approach refuted many of the tropes included in the body of films on the subject of textured hair and instead approached the topic with the comedian's signature deployment of classism in Black communities and with little critical thinking about Black women as consumers. Although Rock's film includes interviews from celebrity women, including musicians like Salt-N-Pepa, and women entrepreneurs filmed in their own salons, he also includes music executives like Andre Harrell and politician Al Sharpton, as well as commentary from unnamed men in barbershops. But these interviews fail to situate women as experts and instead emphasize Black women's style choices as financially costly to Black men, reiterating the dated and misogynist claims about mothers making painful grooming choices for their children. Rock also goes on location to the Bronner Bros. International Hair Show in Atlanta, Georgia, and visits religious temples in India, where hair that is cut for sacrifice is then sold to produce hair extensions in the United States. Although Rock employs the documentary tropes of interviews with laypersons and experts, borrowing from (even if without citation of) the larger genre of natural hair documentary from the 1990s and early 2000s, his film is intercut with comedic spoofs rather than archival images.[46] One scene features a bit about Afro-textured hair as valueless, which Rock realizes when he cannot sell it to a Black woman or an Asian man, each employed at a beauty supply store. Rock's suggestion that textured hair is a worthless commodity in a global beauty economy represents an important and biting critique that fails to get unpacked in this comedic approach to the documentary format. Critic Joi Carr argues that Rock's film makes clear that people of African descent prop up a "multi-billion-dollar industry" through the consumption of "black inferiority" and an unattainable "western *notion* of beauty," while paying little attention to issues of history and interiority that proliferate earlier film works.[47] Rock capitalizes on the legacy of critical documentaries that grapple with haptic histories of blackness and commodification, but instead of extending this work, his film anticipates the mainstreaming of images of Black interiority that emerge in the first decade of the twenty-first century.

Aestheticizing Black Hair

Everyday describes the documentary tone shaping much of hair imagery in the twenty-first century, as creatives ranging from aspiring artists to cultural influencers rely on vernacular images to objectify the temporal commonplace into a permanent article. These efforts include photographing textured hair, whether styled or in need of styling, as well as creating videos of an unremarkable hair care routine. A new slate of documentaries also turns to candid interactions but does away with the expert altogether, asking video subjects instead to speak from personal experience, and inviting opinion and conjecture about the signification of textured hair. Rather than studio interviews or visits to salons that suggest some degree of consent among participants, new videos capture the everyday of Black hair on city streets and in public places, depicting the hairstyles of ordinary people or querying their personal grooming habits from the product aisles of retail establishments. The ordinary consumer searching for cosmetics and routines now represents both the audience and the subject in what has been described as the "natural hair movement," a cultural phenomenon organized around efforts to reform attitudes about textures and practices of touch associated with Afro-textured hair. On its face, the natural hair movement encourages the appreciation and promotion of Afro-textured hair through the development of new ways of touching and viewing Black coiffure. Mounted through communication, behavior, political organizing, and, most importantly, visual imagery, purveyors of natural hair tackle the social and psychological imperatives attributed to new methods of hygiene and hair care, while also commodifying textured hair as touchable. Although these new culture makers shift social perspectives, ultimately, this work also serves to entice corporations into the pursuit of textured consumers.

Distinct from the treatment of the Afro in the mid-twentieth century, this new incarnation of texture as popular renders the *display* of Afro-textured hair as the commodity, selling not simply natural hair but also pictures and videos of styling to a diverse audience of laypersons and corporate entities. This version of textured hair is relevant to a "visual economy" where its production is closely tethered to its spectacle and bears no specific indication of "culture" or way of life.[48] Whereas illustrations of natural hair coincided with particular lifestyle choices in twentieth-century representations—anticapitalist activism among the Black Panthers or members of MOVE, for example—more recent depictions portray natural hair with little or no context, showing textured hair in order to simply display the hair. These images circulate within "economies of visibility," as Sarah Banet-Weiser terms them, where visual representation is "the beginning and the end of political action," and "visibility itself has been absorbed into the economy" as inherently political.[49] The flaunt and exhibition of a racial characteristic become political in such a market configuration. Textured hair maintains its signification in a "visible economy of race," part of a calculation of racial "veracity" in addition to the flesh, marking people as "black" or denoting African descent.[50] These displays move in a global flow without clear assertions about whether producers aim to resist slavery's haptic racism or to capitalize on the embrace of texture, instead asserting the embrace of visibility as transformative. Thus, the image of Afro-textured hair, preferably styled by an amateur, is the product, as both the appearance and its corresponding gestures are packaged into images that let viewers glimpse the process of producing the new natural. These economies distinguish recent hair films and photographs from works of the twentieth century, as new material is produced at greater volume and distributed more quickly and directly, with an emphasis on accessibility rather than exaltation.

A prominent new image type, natural hair selfies capture the everyday appreciation of textured hair. As vernacular photographs, selfies correspond to the ordinary, common, and personal; and those selfies that focus on hair are constructed to invite admiration from viewers and suggest the pride of the photographed subject. These images, as Brian Wallis explains, are defined by disinterest in "photography's fine-art status."[51] Selfies, frequently snapped via cell phone camera, illustrate photo subjects wearing hairstyles in kinky and curly textures, sometimes revealing the process by which the woman styled her hair and, more often than not, indicating a pleasing result. These images are self-admiring and are commonly shared on social media. Selfies are celebratory images, most often displaying a "sense of pride and exhibitionism" that is characteristic of Black portraiture, maintaining a racial and aesthetic tension between brazen pride and self-assurance.[52] Whereas Ojeikere photographed "quotidian hairstyles" to reveal their aesthetic value, selfies represent a quotidian photographic practice that renders the embrace of texture as commonplace. The images unify issues of race, beauty, and pleasure by portraying subjects in poses of self-adoration despite the ways in which their hair texture has been used to separate them from the mainstream norms of beauty that extol long, straight hair as preferential. In this way, natural hair selfies are important for viewers interested in a different visual representation of blackness.

Quotidian portrayals of "self-styling" have transformed video as well, even as documentary film has maintained its standing as a critical tool for examining the social significance of textured hair. As self-styling videos moved online to platforms such as YouTube and Vimeo, and as modes of distribution made for quick releases, they also expanded to reveal the diversity of perspectives codified under a "natural hair movement." No longer focused on introspection about childhood grooming practices or the legacy of slavery, online documentaries about textured hair attend less to intimate touch and more to questions of representation. These works are part of the contextual landscape theorized by Aymar Jean Christian, in which "few black female leads in television or in films in the early 2010s had dark skin or natural hair"; in this moment, online platforms transformed into hubs for depictions that appealed to diverse viewers who were previously ignored by legacy platforms.[53] In this way, online videos about Black hair are constitutive of a larger transformation in media representation, with viewers interested in a deepening of intraracial diversity—from documentaries to sketch comedy—created for niche audiences. Creators of such content ruminate on questions of inclusion, such as in the *HairSay: A Natural Hair Documentary*, a student work completed at the University of Missouri, that features interview footage from a conversation with an Asian store-owner about natural hair as well as interviews with stylists about the impact of natural hair on the hair care business. Textured hair is a business in this video, and the producers query the inclusion of people of African descent in the beauty supply chain, from store ownership to product creation. Among such online producers, the documentary format appeals because it is unscripted with impromptu discussion of textured hair captured in ordinary occurrences; these directors shoot in common areas and converse with film subjects who are already engaged in daily activities, with no clear presuppositions about the history or significance of textured hair.

Along these lines, the visual construction of touch disappears from natural hair documentaries distributed online. Although these works provide content that has been absent from television and print, camera techniques that emphasize touch—such as the up-close shots of hair and wide-angled scenes of styling—have vanished. Distinct from their predecessors, online documentaries have evolved aesthetic approaches to suit these new modes of distribution, employing what Craig Hight describes as "a kind of 'YouTube' aesthetic; amateur footage, edited on a desktop, intended almost as throwaway pieces of culture, often produced as a direct response to other online material."[54] The online video *4c: Documentary on A Natural Hair*, another student film project, features twenty-something men and women reflecting on the value of textured and straightened styles. Speaking directly to the camera, it substitutes evidentiary B-roll footage with a news story on Black hair taken from MSNBC's *Melissa Harris-Perry* show. The *4c* of the video title employs the idea of "hair type," based on a scale used for describing differences in coarseness and curl, ranging from 1 through 4, with 4c denoting the kinkiest of textures.[55] In *4c*, the subjects discuss locs and Afros, as well as the "natural hair movement," which is scrutinized for its absent politics and its construction of Black hair. By including this new vocabulary, the contingent of online hair videos assumes a broad cultural awareness about the meaning and value of "natural" and loses the sense of marginality that punctuated earlier films, while still relying on the documentary format to convey a critical tone. Meanwhile, aesthetic practices such as the inclusion of hair material and the visual construction of touch remain prevalent in works with higher production values. Footage from natural hair salons, close-up shots of hair twisting, and images of hair being swept up from the ground appear in *This Is Good Hair, Too*, a short documentary featuring women who share the process by which they "became natural" or stopped using chemical straighteners. This film intercuts archival footage of activist Kathleen Cleaver explaining the movement to embrace Black beauty and the Afro. Here, it is the "Black Panther Iconography" of the 1960s, rather than a postslavery legacy, that offers historical context.[56] The legacy of textured hair is located in its importance to the twentieth century, not the nineteenth, and it is connected to civil rights activism, not colonization.

Representations of touch circulate differently when associated with the natural hair movement. "Touchable" hair gets commodified via the online tutorial video—educational clips where consumers demonstrate on themselves how to wash and style textured hair. These videos portray women testing and reviewing products, creating their own cosmetics, and speaking directly to other women about how to care for Black hair, frequently filming within their own bathrooms or bedrooms. The VHS was once the predominant medium for the circulation of tutorial videos about Black hair care, largely produced by hair care professionals and cosmetic manufacturers, such as Willie Morrow, who used the long format of VHS to help consumers understand how to use their products or how to create styles protected under trademark.[57] Online tutorials instead seek to promote natural hair as accessible, teaching a generation of viewers experienced in caring for straightened hair how to manage texture without chemicals or heat. Their vernacularity is conversant with online documentaries, suggesting a casualness about the filmed interaction, but tutorials also show the consumer-stylist in the image frame, washing her hair in the shower or twisting her hair in the bathroom mirror. In these images, the viewer becomes privy to the creation of textured styles and gains an inside look at private grooming practices. Rather than recounting the painful touch, as discussed in nineties documentaries, twenty-first-century tutorials promote self-touch, as these videos characteristically exclude the presence of a second subject helping to create the style. The construction of the everyday and personal physical contact is essential to these images, a devout commitment maintained by image producers who often obscure from the frame the team of editors and social media experts who help these creatives produce and circulate their online content. This brand of depiction takes corporations as audiences as much as individual consumers.

Tutorial videos, in particular, became prime image space for cosmetic companies to place products in the hands of consumers, employing a vernacular aesthetic of the layperson turned at-home stylist. A report by the global market research firm Mintel explained that "Black hair care expenditures reached $2.7 billion in 2015—up 7% from two years ago," with "more robust growth expected over the next five years" thanks to the natural hair movement.[58] Based on these numbers, Mintel directed advertisers toward "influencer partnerships [that] can help brands better understand what their audience seeks and how to reach them"; "influencer" refers to people who create tutorial videos with test products, thereby "influencing" viewers to purchase.[59] According to Mintel, "leading influencers offer consumers what many brands are lacking—personalized, relevant content that speaks to the specific needs of Black hair care consumers." Mintel named the top natural hair influencers by number of followers—from 150,000 to 386,000—and ranked the most influential social media platforms, listing Instagram first, then Twitter, then blogs, and finally Facebook. Such reporting reveals the close attention that corporations have paid to independent hair communities as well as the influencers' desire to maintain a sense of vernacularity in new portrayals, even as they are sponsored by corporate funds. Turning away from the complex narratives and film sets used to produce Afro Sheen commercials, for instance, marketing textured hair now utilizes images of the consumer engaging the product in real time. In these partnerships, images of natural hair have been transformed by the *shadow* presence of corporate sponsorships, selling audiences to companies and transforming textured hair from a matter of self-acceptance into an issue of know-how.

3.13

Glenford Nuñez, *Yoko, The Coiffure Project*, 2012. Reproduced by permission of the artist.

Some creatives have attempted to transition the vernacular aesthetics of the natural hair movement into photographic works for exhibition. Artist Glenford Nuñez and his *Coiffure Project*, a collection of portraits of Black women and natural hair, represent an effort to take the visual signs born of the moment and create work for museum shows. Nuñez emphasizes motion and light in his black-and-white prints, setting Black women against blank backdrops in studio but also in cityscapes, photographing loose curl patterns and tightly coiffed hair (figure 3.13). Although these images found their circulation through the spectacular representations ignited by the natural hair movement, Nuñez described himself as unfamiliar with some of the terms and concerns taken up by Black women in online natural hair communities. For example, the critique about "hair type" in Nuñez's work—that his images emphasize wavy and loosely curled textured hair—makes his photographs of the moment, when natural hair conversations simultaneously focus on the racial particularities of hair and the nebulous language of "curl" that makes for a multiethnic approach to beauty. The present moment in representations of textured hair provided a catalyst for artists like Nuñez, with his debut work *The Coiffure Project*. He explains, "It's always been a goal of mine to have a show with my work and I'm hoping 'The Coiffure Project' is my ticket."[60] At the same time, because of such saturation, where vernacular photographs appear in exhibition spaces and online, as liminal spaces for thinking about beauty and fully embraced by corporations, gaining recognition as an artist and maintaining authorial control over one's material becomes increasingly complicated. Images of textured hair travel in various economies and garner value that does not always translate to the larger valuation of individual artists. Thus, turning to other modes of presentation has been important for creatives wanting to share photographs of textured hair. Michael July's *Afros: A Celebration of Natural Hair*, a lifestyle and coffee-table book of images and stories about the choice to wear an Afro, locates contemporary wearers of the Afro across races, including Blacks, whites, and Asians, situated in a variety of settings on city streets and in studios. Taking the perfectly rounded Afro of the mid-twentieth century as a subject, July's illustrations are also of the moment, depicting the complicated legacy of Black Power aesthetics emblazoned on T-shirts, perhaps reiterating the very concerns expressed by Angela Davis, and the sexual fantasy attached to natural hair in Blaxploitation representations. While July's vision is less conversant with the manner in which many women represent themselves and their hair in self-portraits, his images also signal the multiple economies in which textured hair now circulates.

In the production and circulation of these works, the camera remains an essential tool as photographs reach wide audiences online and inspire the production of still images off-line. Creatives who turned their cameras on natural hair helped to drive a cultural shift in the perceptions of Black hair. Operating outside of the institutional fetters of product manufacturers and major film studios, independent filmmakers and everyday people imaging Black hair, whether celebratory or investigative, helped to promote conversations on touch and texture. Photographs and videos on Afro-textured hair illustrate the camera as a fluid apparatus for bringing diverse issues related to hair into focus—from the visual, material qualities of hair fiber to new modes of caring for hair that hail individual and corporate viewership. In terms of composition, these representations not only show hair as aesthetically pleasing, they also begin an engagement with Black hair as a visual material in and of itself. Close-up images of Black hair helped to accentuate its racial distinctiveness but obscure the body, while experiments with light, shadow, and form reveal hair as a material that can *make* images.

SURFACE

This chapter explores the work of four Black women artists who create representations of hair in contemporary art. Issues of archive, texture, and touch coalesce in the artmaking that constructs blackness not as biologically determined, not as an interior that manifests on the surface, but as an exterior forged through shared practices of making. Although countless artists contend with the symbolism and significance of Black hair—straight and textured—Black women's centrality to coiffure as a site of invention cannot be overstated. Kellie Jones argues that Black women's culture provides the "material underpinnings" for artist David Hammons's installations made of hair clippings, since "the manipulation of hair is largely identified with a female creative space" and is often produced with a "feminist vision," operating as "a tangible symbol of African American women's creativity and joy."[1] Where hair is a locus of haptic blackness, as I have illustrated in this book, visual representations of coiffure material compound the possibilities for contending with the haptic as historically and culturally constituted. But the haptic has also been central to Black women's artmaking on an array of subjects. Huey Copeland argues that Black women artists have engaged the haptic as a means of "self-fashioning and for the preservation of memories," circumventing fantasies about Black visibility in favor of a focus on "the feel of the subject's psychic and corporeal position."[2] The artists explored here address the sensation of blackness on the surface as construed through coiffure, treating the pictorial surface in ways that approach Black raciality as construed and created, rendered in modes of touch and feeling sensed with the eyes. Jennifer Fisher argues that haptic art "functions by contiguity, contact and resonance" to render "surfaces of the body porous," placing perception inside the body, "on the skin's surface, and in external space."[3] Black women artists depicting Black hair in works that invite touch intertwine the particular histories of touching Black coiffure and the modern museum's prohibition on patrons' contact with artworks.[4] In their representations, these artists emphasize the trace of touch on the pictorial surface and collectively provide a framework for thinking about the human exterior and about Black exteriority, in contradistinction to interiority. These works portray the human surface as textured by history and practices of touch, as realized in the handling of the pictorial plane. The artists discussed here reimagine haptic blackness and the Black exterior by depicting hair in ways that propose the human surface as handmade and as visually marked by the entanglements of racial capitalism.

Sonya Clark's body of work uses human hair, beads, yarn, canvas, and photography to reveal hair as a craft material and to portray hair braiding as an art form. Likewise, with handmade paper, diverse printing techniques, and assemblage, Alison Saar presents the textural distinction of Black coiffure as steeped in the postslavery legacies of Black labor and spiritualism. Finally, Lorna Simpson and Ellen Gallagher reconstruct material taken from the Johnson Publishing Company's (JPC) archive and use collage, paint, and other materials to create new depictions from these familiar illustrations. These artists underscore the haptic construction of blackness through representations of hair, presenting Black hair as a vessel for shared histories and treating the pictorial surface in ways that focus our attention on blackness as a contrived surface. The recurring issues of history, labor, and cultures of adornment flow through the Black female form in this collection of objects. These artists present blackness as a haptic inheritance, where the surface is made by touch, feeling, and the past.

Paper Dolls: Ellen Gallagher and Lorna Simpson

Vintage prints get a rough cut at the hands of Ellen Gallagher, who in 2001 began a series of illustrations that comically revise Black representations from the mid-twentieth century, including images from *Ebony* as well as from *Sepia* and *Our World*. Gallagher offers a makeover of advertising materials for skin bleach and hair pomades in her *Falls & Flips, Double Natural, Pomp Bang, Afrylic,* and *eXelento*. These grids, each composed of 396 portraits cut from archival periodicals, present new profiles of women, as the artist has cut incisions into the paper and improves upon the original images via the application of yellow Plasticine wigs. In the revised images, the ordinary flap of yellow putty reads as an imposition, weighing down the face of the subject when presented as bangs or as a parted comb-over, forming two sets of contrasting surfaces—the putty and the print. Even when Gallagher applies the material in strips to follow the outline of the originals, her revised wigs seem to offer an obscuring adornment, whether she creates long, languishing hairstyles or stately beehives hoisted up with Plasticine patches. The collection of edited materials presents several hundred faces recognizable from the iconic archive of the JPC and ferociously edited by Gallagher with blobs of yellow and ice-blue or with whiteout eyes. On some images, long strips of putty forge a new, rounded Afro in the halo shape of the 1960s, while others get cinnamon-bun swirls and corkscrew squiggles of the contrasting yellow material. Plasticine revises the figures in a series, as in *Afrylic* (plate 13), for example; but these subjects still converse with original advertisements for Murray's Natural Sheen and Johnson's Ultra Wave. After Gallagher's "edits," the new hairstyles, covered faces, and absent eyes trouble the surface, leaving enough print material to indicate where these subjects have come from but not enough information about where they might be headed.

Gallagher refuses the smooth surface, whether human or pictorial, with her transformations that assert the textural quality of the original image. In *DeLuxe* (2004–5; plate 14), a grid of sixty photogravures, she employs various printing techniques from aquatint to tattoo engraving and embellishes her signature Plasticine wigs with coconut oil (used as hair ointment), as well as pomade, velvet, glitter, crystals, foil paper, gold leaf, toy eyeballs, and imitation ice cubes. This array of additions does not allow the eyes to rest on a flat plane and instead draws the viewer into different degrees of depth from the flat page to the frame of each illustrative detail. Here, her choice of putty extends to strands of blue on her *American Beauty*, a detail from *DeLuxe*, as well as white Plasticine to forge exaggerated barristers' and judges' wigs modeled after the English court. Gallagher's edit comments on race and colonization when the first figure in *DeLuxe* wears one such cover while toting a gun; the result is a figure that references British judicial history and a totem of colonial rule. In *Wiglette* (plate 15), Gallagher's combination of yellow and white Plasticine creates sixteen distinct looks. While her use of yellow has been read for blond, making these wigs a "metaphor for white power and manipulation," or operating "as a superimposition on Black identity," Gallagher's color combinations also complicate assumptions about the human surface.[5] The Plasticine hairpieces are shown as varied within themselves, such as the combination of yellow and white triangles that make up the Mini (row 3) or the distinct swirls of the Coquette (row 2). Yellow offers a highlighting material in these instances, allowing Gallagher to forge hairstyles that refute the racialization of hair texture as aligned with skin color or racial identity. In yellow, Gallagher's figures deny resonance with a racial identity, such as what one might be promised with a new "Afrylic" wig, for example. Instead, her yellow Plasticine renders the wig as a raised surface among other kinds of surface and provides a textured image or an incoherent exterior.

The grid itself is central to the representation, allowing the artist to create uniformity around a variety of depictions. Gallagher became adept at making boxes alongside her study of artmaking. Born in Rhode Island, Gallagher studied at Oberlin College and the School of the Museum of Fine Arts at Tufts University, but she points to her work experience in carpentry and bridge building as an important element of her practice. In these works, the grid invites the viewer to toggle between viewing each distinct image and reading them together. Consumed as a collection, as a single grid, the wigged figures demonstrate a dizzying lack of discrepancy, as the collection of gray faces recedes beneath the collective yellow material. Presented in a grid, the structure helps to convey the illusion built into the intimate production of blackness. While the boxes frame each figure, cordoning off one subject from the other, the grid also invites reading all 396 images together as one picture—in unison. Accordingly, distinct figures become a unified mass when taken in from a distance, drawn together through adornment, through the practices Gallagher employs to make the surface. Gallagher's archival paper taken from JPC, where hair illustrations are part of the source material, is distinct from artist Mark Bradford's found papers, for instance, which he uses for his signature grid style. Bradford's abstract works, *Dreadlocks Caint Tell Me Shit* and *Enter and Exit the New Negro*, that use permanent wave endpapers commonly found in Black hair salons, at once assert Black folk culture as high art and proclaim that the meticulousness of textured hair as a visual project might be applicable across the textural spectrum of Black hair treatments. In *Dreadlocks*, in which the artist's signature layering of squares forms a textured whole, Bradford's use of "everyday materials reflects

African American folk art" while providing an "unconventional way to interpret 'high' art."[6] Here, according to Sarah Lewis, "found paper" offers a "conceptual device" resisting "racial and social exclusion."[7] By contrast, Gallagher's use of magazine paper from a recognizable source portrays a certain irreverence for the original, a refusal to maintain the initial illustration's legibility, and thus a refusal of the original's claims about repairing or improving Black aesthetics with cosmetics.

In working the surface with a diverse array of materials, Gallagher asserts the exterior as a production, whether hair or flesh, and she suppresses the ideal of a "natural" beneath her impositions of added materials on the surface. "Gallagher plays with the relationship between wigs and skin as transformation," according to Robin Kelley, as the repeated occurrence of the "skinatural" wig advertisement builds irony about nature and artifice, forging "deliberate evocations of skin—colored skin, all-seeing skin, sensuous skin, warring, aggressive skin, armor."[8] Layering such marketing material with plastic eyeballs and glitter, Gallagher compounds the textural details in ads selling "Afro wigs" with "oddly appropriate names like 'Afrilon' and 'Afrylic,'" or at other times "'Nu Nile,' 'Kongolene,' and 'Freedom Puff.'" Her practice adds to, or "doubles," the natural; with Plasticine Gallagher explains that these surfaces "are built up into a thick relief," so that when "seen from the side, the gray tones of the ads disappear and the yellow plasticine Afros become like lily pads, a strange surface that also, uncannily, looks like skin."[9] Her destruction and enhancement suggest a racial ontology steeped in transformation, forged through her willingness to defy the sacredness of the publishing archive that promoted packaged improvements on Black aesthetics.

This grid series is one of many works emanating from a generation of artists born in or after the 1960s, who find in the pages of the JPC magazines an archive of Black beautification. *Ebony* and *Jet* magazines had an indelible influence on the image of Black hair and skin, as the magazines presented bodily aesthetics through the marketing of material such as Afro Sheen and Raveen hair care products and through editorials. However, *Ebony* in particular constructed a larger ethos around Black middle-class consumption, garnering a diverse and lucrative array of advertising support in the safe space of a periodical that once proposed integration. However, the persistence of the Black freedom struggle transformed the magazine; by the late 1960s, *Ebony* "abandoned" the periodical's commitment to respectability and joined the fight for racial equality.[10] This willingness to pivot from a focus on celebrating class ascension to support of the political concerns of the masses has been central to the archival life of the JPC. In the twenty-first century, *Ebony* and *Jet* have come to function as an archival catalog of iconicity, representing Black life with an identifiable aesthetic. This circulation has made the JPC archive into source material for understanding a bygone era; it also offers a historical inventory of images of Black beauty, thus making this print material inspirational for numerous contemporary artists. *Speaking of People:* Ebony, Jet *and Contemporary Art*, curated by Lauren Haynes, at the Studio Museum in Harlem in 2015, featured numerous works representing Black hair, in part because of the JPC preponderance of advertising material for cosmetics that were featured in the JPC archive. While some of these works did not explicitly portray hair material, such as Glenn Ligon's *Untitled (Dax Pomade)* and *Endless Column/Nu Nile*, works that couple Black hair products and modernist sculptural objects, many of the works within the show reflected on the marketing and the history of Black hair care without representing hair fiber. Ligon's works are among the many works on paper in an exhibition that was also about paper, as demonstrated by artists such as Gallagher, who cut up the pages of the magazines and put them back together in new ways.

Lorna Simpson has also spliced the iconic pages from the JPC archive to insist on the surface as a production. Her collages of hair speak back to Simpson's larger oeuvre, in which hair has reccurred across projects since the late 1980s. Simpson has deployed hair that has been straightened and textured, braided, painted, and pasted together in a representative patchwork of paper collage, even when the subject of the illustration was not about Black hair in particular. Trained in New York City, and working in conversation with other photographers including Carrie Mae Weems and the Kamoinge Workshop, Simpson explored various approaches to photography before moving to California to complete an MFA at the University of California, San Diego, where photography, performance, and texture also became part of the practice she would be exposed to through her teachers.[11] In 2010, Simpson started to remove faces from photographs she found in JPC periodicals, cutting and pasting the torn pages into new pictures. With collage, Simpson insisted on the surface signification in her work, providing audiences with a pictorial surface that asserted its hewn nature. Collage, a technique and a composition, creates a new picture, a new whole, from fragments cut from elsewhere; and in its overt lack of cohesion, collage announces the artist's hand in creating an irregular surface. Elizabeth Alexander argues that "collage constructs wholes from fragments in a continual, referential dialogue between the seemingly disparate shards of various pasts and the current moment of the work itself," indicating a past and a future.[12] In these works, Simpson takes her figures from advertisements, often for hair products promoted in the glossy pages of JPC material, repositioning them in collages with the application of paint and other kinds of paper, sometimes taken from science textbooks and books of minerals. Where Black hair is variously a mountain terrain, a reflective bubble, or brilliant pools of inky blue and bright yellow, Simpson's collages suggest that the exterior can be anything and can be several things at once. Embellishing figures with new hairstyles, from strokes of paint to scenes clipped from other print materials, Simpson creates a mash-up that is obvious at its seams, where her newly formed hairlines sit back, allowing the final representation to include traces of the hairstyle from the original publication along with Simpson's new additions.

In these works, and across different hair motifs, Simpson confronts notions of surfacism. Her images insist that the exterior can yield no insight about the interior, that coiffure yields no useful information about the subject at hand, and that Black exteriority is distinct from issues of interiority. Her fabricated surface is a site for the production of blackness rather than the fact of blackness. Such an approach refutes the abusive constructions of "the black surface" rendered as "only the visible . . . the seen" for the white gaze and construed as a "sealed exteriority epidermalized" that emphasizes the outside.[13] In Simpson's hands, the exterior is not limited to a vapid shell rendered opposite the interior and void of any value with regard to Black subjectivity. Instead, the human exterior exists as a purposeful construction and not simply a racial imposition. Simpson layers a conception of the surface in such a way as to expound on the issue of composition by deepening surfaces, putting disparate elements together in ways that announce the exterior as made.

Borrowed photographs of Black women seem to impose themselves on nature in Simpson's *Earth & Sky* series, where her strategic application of cut paper allows gemstones from science textbooks to mimic the height, expanse, and texture of Black hair. Images such as *Earth & Sky #24* (plate 16) portray Black hair in a cluster of geometric shapes, with samples of gems appearing on a page, describing various "sulphates" of "anglesite" and "celestite." The collection of minerals replaces the subject's hair, coiffed upward in a manner reminiscent of the bouffant style, while the JPC material provides contrasting pictorial textures from different issues. Together, this combination forges a distinction between the human likeness clipped from the periodical and the extraterrestrial images taken from textbooks. These couplings emphasize relations of form and scale, where the organic shapes from the scientific material—in a play on "nature"—get coded as Black hair through Simpson's organization. There is no premade connection between the Black figures of the JPC's pages and the hairdos they are made to wear, and thus anything from gemstones to the stars can offer a stand-in for all the suppositions read into Black coiffure. The nebulae signify Black hair in a detail from *Phenomena* (plate 17), the image of a woman with curled bangs on straightened hair, which covers her forehead to emphasize her downcast gaze and false eyelashes. Simpson's clipped figure, removed from Black print, is encased in the seams of the cut, the gloss of her paper distinct from that of the sheet torn from a textbook, which Simpson inverts to situate her figure with a new hairdo. In Simpson's collages, blackness can live on the surface, in the adornment, not just in the racial constitution of the flesh. In these illustrations, the pictorial surface is an obvious fabrication that loses the mythology of biological cohesion.

Borrowed photographs give history to Simpson's new images. By leaving the original image legible in her collages, Simpson keeps intact those historical images she describes as "amazing portraits" that bear a "subtext of political strife" where the cultural productions (including ads) still convey the angst of the civil rights era.[14] Some works include headlines from front covers or text, such as *Jet #21*, *'55* (plate 18), the collage that positions an editorial on white terror against Black homeowners as the subject's hair, alongside a query about the third man involved in lynching Emmett Till and the headline "Why American Girls Become Singers Abroad." Such compositions maintain Simpson's signature textual inclusions, while overtly announcing the political context of the JPC publications from which Simpson clips her paper. The commingling of different materials to create new pictorial surfaces becomes central to the body of work, even where Simpson employs paint for hairstyles. In these instances, the textual distinction between paint and cut paper underscores surfacism as a central focus. Paint and ink also appear in Simpson's *Reunite & Ice* series, created from advertisements for alcoholic beverages that are frequently depicted in *Ebony* magazine. In the images from this series, the subject of each portrait remains the same, while her outward appearance constantly transforms. Simpson's muse wears jewels and directly engages the viewer, while the representation of her hair moves from mountain scenes to a cloudy sky to Simpson's own paint strokes. Repeating the face of the subject but changing her adornment in reoccurring images, Simpson offers repetition to insist on the exterior as the focus of each image. Her subject remains the same while her figurative hair transforms over and again.

This combination of paint and archival print also relies on the viewer to make meaning from the hair illustrations, as the artist refuses smooth connections by maintaining the sharp edges of the cut paper as distinct from her painted plumes of color. JPC's legacy of selling middle-classness alongside consumer goods in the face of political strife becomes the archival past, but with no illustrative context in Simpson's new images. Meanings about the exterior and its connection to the interior must be fabricated by the viewer of Simpson's collages. Conversely, hair figures into the "extreme marketability of abject black corporeality" that art historian Derek Conrad Murray locates at the forefront of Kehinde Wiley's work, in which, in his embrace of capitalism's demand for excess, the artist emphasizes "the black body as commodity."[15] In Wiley's *Conspicuous Fraud* series, Black coiffure has movement and might reach beyond the frame of the painting. *Conspicuous Fraud Series #1* (2001) depicts a Black man dressed in a suit, in which the triangles of his shirt collar and lapel give way to the rounded softness of deep, black tresses that flow out of and back into the frame, the hair contrasting with the restricting containment of his professional attire. Likewise, a climbing coiffure connects two men in *Conspicuous Fraud Series (Fragonard)*, showing hair as figurative but also supernatural, seeming to have motion or the ability to touch others rather than waiting to be touched. These works, "arresting portraits of young black men with their Afros exploding into halos of serpentine swirls," as Jeffrey Deitch describes them, make hair an active element of the figures' tense relationship to commoditization.[16] Alternatively, Simpson's paint swirls refashion the torn image, highlighting the print material as someone else's photographic work, and literally separating the story about the print subject from the conception of the coiffure.

Hair is ornamentation on a forward-facing portrait in Simpson's collages, but perhaps it has always been so, even in Simpson's larger body of work. The artist's "anti-portraits," as they have been described, put hair in plain view, where instead of presenting the subject's face, Simpson portrays the back of her head.[17] As the debut of her photo-text works in 1985, these images seemed to have made coiffure an essential and yet useless part of the story. In works such as *Screen 2* that provide commentary on hair—"Sandy's head was foreign to a comb"—but that photograph the subject before breaking her into discrete parts, Simpson portrays an experience of judgment rather than of hair in particular. Her subject's straightened hair is gathered haphazardly but makes no clear connection to the phrase printed on the image. Subsequent works such as *Twenty Questions*, *Waterbearer*, and *Completing the Analogy* (plate 19) put the subject's hair at the center of the image, but through Simpson's attention (or seeming inattention) to hair's style, they continue her exploration of text and image forcibly conjoined in search of deeper meaning. When Simpson produced *Stereo Styles* in 1988, her feature showing ten different straightened hairstyles on her model, each with accompanying text, the treatment of coiffure was central, as was its lack of information yielded about the subject. In other words, while the hair along with skin color helped to indicate the figure's blackness, Simpson refused to have these elements yield any other data, thus affirming that the story created by the viewer between the photograph and the text would have to be their own fabrication. Simpson moved on to textured hair, which still appeared as a focus, even if not the subject, in works produced for 1989. Pieces including *Easy for Who to Say*, *Dividing Lines*, and *Guarded Conditions* maintain her refusal to display the figure's face, either through back poses or masking the subject's face with vowel signs. However, in each of these representations, the switch toward textured twists and away from the smooth and straightened styles of the above-mentioned works helps to establish the timelessness of these images. Hair is relevant to these "shift-dress works," as Nika Elder describes them, as they explore visual representations associated with slavery as well as current perceptions of African American women, enabling Simpson to make "literal and visible the cultural work that photography, clothing, and language did within the context of slavery and continues to do within its representation in film and on television."[18] Insisting we view the subjects from behind, Simpson hides the faces and thus highlights the hair of her subjects.

Hair as a signal to the surface makes the exterior a link to the past and to other people. Braiding is another motif for Simpson and represents coiffure in her photo-text works of the early 1990s, even as it becomes severed from the figure. Simpson uses braids to create boxes or to signify the lynched body in works such as *Double Negative*, *ID*, *Square Deal*, *Outline*, *Two Frames*, and *Two Tracks*. Braided hair is used as a textured and a tethering material in her work. Sometimes braids provide viewers with only the textured surface for reading alongside her textual inclusions, such as in *1978–1988*, a print that features eight single braids, some knotted, each with signs attached (1991; plate 20). Huey Copeland argues that "the artificial braid in Simpson's oeuvre figures a contingent form of relation across space and time that must be fabricated," where the connections that it signifies are not only "the unchanging facts of black female oppression, but a willingness to be connected."[19] Thus, the braids conjoin figures in *Same Two* and *Two Sisters, Two Tongues* (1991), just as mythologies of race and gender are used as tethers as well; the braid portrays attachment as a choice rather than an inevitable consequence of the exterior. Through the inclusion of braids, Simpson's works also more forcefully asserted hair as something put on, but not endemic to the individual. That hair is part of reading a surface exclusively is a point made more explicitly in *Coiffure* (1991; plate 21), in which Simpson provides the viewer with three images: the back view of her model, a coiled braid of a wig, and the inside view of an African mask. The accompanying text suggests directions for a braided style—"part into eight sections/from the crown" and "over-hand/under-hand/whichever you prefer"—but none of these actions have been taken up in the picture, or even appear possible on the model's shortly cropped hair. The story then appears to be one of "putting on" where the images reveal what we cannot possibly grasp: the interior of the figure who has donned the mask, the wig, or the braids. Moreover, the hair gets added to the surface for the creation of an image, but as ornamentation, it lends no insight about the interior. It is in these works that the Black female figure becomes "phantasmic," according to Huey Copeland, allowing critics to more easily observe Simpson's deconstruction of "the visual and the sensate," which has always been a part of the artist's body of work.[20] Simpson's point is asserted in *Wigs* (1994), the serigraph prints of various hairpieces applied to felt—a textile material made of matting and pressing together wool fibers—in which the artist plays with the picture's surface to force her argument about the human surface. The matting and condensing required for felt, which make gnarly strands into a smooth surface on which to portray other illustrations, make it a metaphor for hair as a material capable of producing an image.

Simpson's insistence on the exterior's distinction has been carried over into works on paper. While Simpson's photography has also queried ideas about cohesive meaning and subjectivity, her evolution into other materials has also demanded that viewers focus on the exterior. Whereas audiences have consistently looked to photographs for information about the Black subject, there has been an overreliance on the camera's penchant for objectivity as a chance to fix the meaning of the surface and to verify its significations in Simpson's texts. But Simpson also turned to paper and performance to explore the merits of exteriority and adornment, continuing to portray the back of her subjects' heads and hair in other media. Her *Gold Heads* series, works using ink and embossing powder on paper, similarly refuse access to the subject's face, giving full view only of wispy fluffs of shimmering gold hair and an occasional gold eyelash from partial profile view. Here, all coiffures seem to fluff and rise upward, a shift from her *Heads* series (2008)—the graphite and ink on paper illustrations—that play with a variety of hair textures, some blowing in the wind and others curling upward and outward. Movement is a possibility in *Gold Heads*, and the images are inspired by Simpson's film *Momentum*, a two-channel video installation that captures twenty-four dancers, each clad in gold-powdered Afro-textured wigs, golden costumes, and body glitter, preparing and then performing before Simpson's camera. Read together, *Momentum* reveals the motion captured in *Gold Heads*, as the movement and bounce of the Afros is replicated in the motion realized on paper, created with flourishing brush strokes. In Simpson's video, the textured Afros on her gilt ballerinas hold the golden dust in cloud-like formation, which Simpson reproduces on paper, but in the posterior view, the drawings do not lend themselves to assertations about the person in the illustration, especially as Simpson excludes the text material that viewers might rely upon in her other works. In her evolving treatment of the pictorial plane, whether photographs, paper, or collage, Simpson exacerbates the duplicitous nature of surfaces, as built upon and impermanent. In these techniques, she offers a metaphor for the ongoing production of blackness, showing that raciality is not simply a final form of visibility but an ongoing making through cutting, combining, remixing.

A Touch of Craft: Sonya Clark

If Sonya Clark's world of intraracial contact created a founding regard for diaspora, her formal training helped to hone it into expertise. For over twenty years, artist Sonya Clark has been using diverse materials—whether beads, cloth, hair combs, currency, or human hair—to craft objects that contemplate beauty, Black cultures, and belonging. The signature of this American artist of Afro-Caribbean descent might be the head and its adornment, as indicated in her sculpted headdresses, her displays of styled hair on mannequin heads, and, most notably, the reoccurrence of hair as both a subject and a craft material. Clark's exploration of hair engages diasporic approaches to blackness, and over time it becomes more explicit about the human form. Her work combines her personal history as well as her artistic and academic training, as she situates her storytelling within craft art. Born in the United States to immigrant parents, a Trinidadian psychiatrist father and a Jamaican nurse mother, Clark also acknowledges the influence of her maternal grandmother, a professional tailor who taught her to sew while telling her stories. Clark lists these elements as essential to her work, along with her upbringing as part of a transnational community that extended beyond her immediate family. She talks about "growing up in D.C.," next door to the "Ambassador of Benin and his family of fourteen," and describes how she and her sister would return home with "elaborate hairstyles" after visits with the neighbors. It is in her formal training that Clark explored "Yoruba culture and reinforced those early notions of hairdressing not as vanity, but as ritual." These experiences fortified her formal study and helped Clark identify her "authentic obsessions: textiles and hair."[21] She studied African art at Amherst College and went on to examine craft at both the Art Institute of Chicago and Cranbrook Academy of Art. Clark's practice handles touch as a means for conveying diaspora, where hair braiding is a tactile expertise that translates aesthetic values from hand to head.

Early works, including her sculptural pieces, imagine the head as a site for ornamentation and the point from which individual characteristics spring. Created on hat stands, these works "resist categorization" by bleeding distinctions between "hat, hair, and monument"; these objects "pay homage to the gendered head" by featuring hairstyles that include ponytails and braids.[22] In *Dryad* (1998), Clark styles hair as a baobab tree, a genus of trees indigenous to continental Africa. Similarly, works like *Onigi 21 Sticks* (1997) reveal the artist moving "closer still to the body itself" but also communicating "a philosophical principle." She uses the Yoruba word for *sticks* as the title of the work to address the hair both as projectile and as the branches of a living tree.[23] In these works Clark's focus "on the head" as an adorned, "intellectual base" expanded into greater attention paid to the adornment alone, whether or not the head or human form was present.[24] In Clark's Afro-diasporic head coverings, one sees her moving from a representational focus on the body into using hair as material.

A commitment to craft defines Clark's uniqueness among artists interested in Black hair. In much of craft, the artist's hand is "embedded" in the work, forging a "connection" between the creator and the viewer.[25] For Clark, as hair came into greater focus, so too did her own hand become more present as the creator who manipulates the craft object to forge the finished product. Her use of beads and cloth, or combs and human hair, explicitly gestures toward materials that demand the hand to become something other than an everyday object. At the same time, these items indicate the need for physical connections, demanding the gestures of threading and combing that are required in their use. With these materials that help create sculpted objects and wearable materials, Clark imbues her work with an emphasis on the handmade. In her progression as an artist, she moved from works that underscored an everyday materiality to those that make the human hand visible in the piece itself. In *Mother's Wisdom or Cotton Candy* (plate 22), for instance, the photograph shows Clark's two hands cradling a ball of her mother's white hair to represent the wisdom of age and the tender care of a precious object, signified by the open hands. She continued to explore the hand in beaded works as well, such as in *handy ii*, *Palm Masks*, and *Golden Touch*, items that feature representations of hands, remade through beads and accentuating the lines in the palms or the separate-yet-connectedness of fingers.

The exemplification of touch as a means to connect and communicate is central to Clark's *Hair Craft Project* (plates 23 and 24). Organized around twelve canvases and twelve photographs, these works depict not only the art of hair braiding but also the centrality of the hair artist's touch to the production of the image. The photographs capture styles braided into Clark's own hair, while the canvases portray the craft of hair braiding through the braiding of silk thread suspended from a canvas. Clark is the creator of the project, but by photographing the hair braiders beside their creations, she reveals the hands of these stylists as central to the illustrations. Taken as a whole, the many instances of touch create the *Hair Craft Project* to include Clark in conjunction with twelve Black women who style hair in the Richmond, Virginia, area. Working under the "premise that these talented hairdressers are also talented fiber artists," Clark asked each woman to demonstrate her expertise through the medium of hair and to "translate" that to canvas. The craft reveals the skill of the hair artists, as Clark explains: "Their hands embody an ability to map a head with a comb and manipulate the fiber we grow into complex form."[26] Hairstyles range from cornrow braids to loosened twists and include styles that feature additional hair and strands chalked with bright colors and decorative objects. In addition to the photographs and works on canvas, *Hair Craft Project* employed performance art through a live recreation of hair braiding in the space of the art museum. In its various components, this work compounds its latent questions: "Who is an artist?" and "What is art?" Advancing Clark's concerns for history and cultural transmission, the *Hair Craft Project* forces the audience to engage the head *and* the fibrous specificity of Black hair in the process of engaging the art.[27]

Hair Craft Project also invites embodied viewing to understand the representative distinctions of the collected images. The textured canvas depictions of hair via the draped silk thread present a raised surface, inviting museumgoers to stand close to the canvas. Stylist Marsha Johnson turns her canvas sideways to braid a butterfly pattern between two ponytails. The whimsy of her creation suggests a style for a girl, complete with a yellow ribbon wrapped around a single dangling braid. Although the decorum of the modern museum discourages touching, both the pattern of the styles and the textural distinction of the braided thread invite contact, an embodied viewing to conjure a sensation of the thread as representative of, but dissimilar from, the feel of Black hair.[28] Conversely, the flat surface of the photograph documents a style braided through Clark's hair—Johnson's style features cornrow braids patterned on a downward diagonal, with loose ends that emphasize Clark's waves and curls. The photograph also invites close inspection of the textural variations within Clark's head of hair, as well as differences between the hair artists and the exhibition artist. Similar to the canvases, the photographs bring the viewer up close to the meticulous skill required in producing the styles, giving them the opportunity to view the intricacy of individual braids, the craft of well-formed parts that separate the hair into sections, and the diverse textures present on a single head of hair. Where the canvases ask us to think about race, craft, and palpability in absence of a body, the photographs index the human form. Together, these illustrations draw the viewer in to engage the surface of each representation—

the smoothness of the photographic surface and the soft density of the thread on canvas. Not simply visual, they indicate the haptic as the sense by which Black hair might be engaged in the use of thread as a surrogate.

Touch, between the hair artist and the hair fiber, is also the means by which African aesthetic practices are translated. Hair braiding fits within a larger design history through the use of geometry. Ron Eglash identifies "African fractals," or repetition in patterns on an increasing or decreasing scale, as a knowledge practice. Examining the persistence of fractals in architecture, weaving, sculpture, and hair styling, Eglash notes that whether by "stacking, braiding, [or] coiling," the practice of recursion construction ensures that the "output of one stage becomes the input of the next stage."[29] Hair braiding employs "adaptive scaling," which means that the scale of a pattern is altered to fit various forms, such as the human head. Adaptive scaling involves "conformal mapping" where "the pattern simply fits along the contours of a concrete, preexisting structure."[30] In *Hair Craft Project*, recursive structures are revealed in the braids on canvas and in Clark's hairstyles, which illustrate the braided designs in patterns that swirl and expand. Kamala Bhagat's canvas design, winner of two awards at Art Prize, features delineated box braids—titled for the box created by parting the hair at the scalp—connected by wrapping fabric around the silk thread. These separate but adjoined braids come together to resemble the "iterative braiding" from Yaounde, Cameroon.[31] On canvas, Bhagat's image repeats boxes, but in adjusting to the flat surface, she attaches hair loops along the outer edge to create a framing effect. Her precision on the flat surface is reiterated in Clark's hairstyle; Bhagat's thoughtfulness about each individual hair strand and the precision of her parts begins at the nape of Clark's neck. The image shows the collection of individual hairs organizing into smaller individual braids that meet at the center to contribute to a larger braid moving up the middle to the crown of Clark's head. Likewise, the perfect recursion of Chaunda King's circular style on Clark entails only six or seven braids that begin with only a few hairs but that lead into more hair and larger braids until Clark's entire head is covered. King's ability to adapt the scale of her work is further evidenced in her canvas, also an award winner at Art Prize. King creates smaller individual cornrows from the silk thread and then creates a larger flat and angled cornrow of the smaller braids that moves upward on the figurative head. She closes the braided end with Bantu knots at the top and finishes them with cowrie shells. Decorative inclusions such as the shells are significant, adding to the diasporic nature of the hairstyles, as shells were "not only used as currency and decoration" but are hallowed among Africans and Native Americans as symbols of harmony and reverence.[32]

To regard braiding as artistic is to simultaneously reimagine the hairstylists as artists, and Clark insists on as much through her organization of the installation, with the canvases and photographs positioned on opposite walls. *Hair Craft Project* puts the canvases and the photographs in dialogue with one another. Clark asks viewers to engage each representation as both distinct from and also conversant with one another. The eleven photographs feature each hair artist facing the camera, each beside her work, displayed on Clark's styled head and presented in a view of Clark's back. The accompanying explanation adds that the "photographs document the temporary hairstyles created specifically for the project while the canvases provide a permanent example of the craft."[33] Standing next to Clark in each frame, facing the camera, the stylist herself provides a human connection and gives authorship to a craft that tends to remain anonymous once it transitions out of the salon and onto the street. By showing each hair artist as present and beside her work, styled on Clark's head, the photographs assert hairstylists as artists just as the camera's focus on Clark's head insists on hair braiding as art. Through the structure and content of the exhibition, then, Clark presents Black hair as a means by which to engage the idea of art. Clark conflates the skills that produce the fiber art and the skills that produce the ephemeral hairstyle, asking viewers to envision the two practices as equal participants in a creative arena—where the canvas endures in the museum while the hairstyle disappears.

At the same time, Clark's insistence that hair braiders are artists directly confronts questions of labor and licensure that often cause dispute around the organization of Black hair care. Frequently, such debates fall along lines of ethnicity and national origin. Hair braiding, and, at times, "African hair braiding," in the United States intersects with questions of immigration, ethnicity, and work. Classifications for the labor of hair braiding have been controversial and sometimes divisive, as stylists braiding hair exclusively have been categorized as unskilled and unsanctioned laborers in different cities. Natural styles regained their popularity toward the end of the twentieth century, as "low cost hairstyling services [were] provided by unlicensed hair braiders, many of them African immigrants."[34] Licensure and the bureaucratic monitoring of hair braiding were not legislated in many instances until issues of labor competition emerged among stylists of Black women's hair. By 2010, when this lucrative work created rivalries between unlicensed stylists and licensed cosmetologists serving Black customers, licensure became a way to control competition, but also a way to use ethnicity, class, and nationality to determine which and how stylists entered the hair care business. Hair braiding gained a designation as skilled and licensed work via the market and concerns of interest groups, while hair braiders remained marginalized from conceptions of creativity. In her insistence on treating hair braiding as art, Clark's treatment of hair is conversant with other Afro-diasporic artists using coiffure to reveal a complex aesthetic practice. Artist Meshac Gaba likewise takes seriously the market for hair braiding as labor, using brightly colored synthetic hair as architectural material. In choosing brilliant hues of green, yellow, and orange, Gaba boldly announces the synthetic nature of the hair but also illuminates the texture of the braids, which he uses to replicate notable architecture, such as the Chrysler Building in New York and the SS *Rotterdam* from the Netherlands. Gaba's wigs display the intricacy and delicacy of the braids, rendered modern and on par with the architectural works they replicate, but they also construe the "nouveau tresseur or tresseuse, a traditional Beninese hair braider" as artist, inviting viewers to think of the aesthetic significance of braiding in line with the monumental significance of architecture.[35]

Skilled touch is thus a means of defining a visual blackness. Clark's project emphasizes the touch of the stylist as essential for the translation of aesthetics. Braiding forges contact among African-descended peoples and helps to convey as well as make visible the forms of cultural knowledge that are shared among them. The women who create work for the *Hair Craft Project* bring forth the transnational project of Black hair. Although the exhibition artists "are all African American and one [is] African-Caribbean," according to Clark, the styles these women created together with the performance component of the *Hair Craft Project* help to index a diversely constituted blackness.[36] For instance, in the performance "Hairdressers Are My Heroes," Clark and her accompanying hair artist directly engage Afro-diasporic aesthetic practice as well as their ethnically specific cultural knowledge on the subject of Black hair. Describing the performance component, Clark explains: "For the whole day, a free family day at the [Boston MFA] museum, Kathy Montrevil (a Boston hairdresser from Haiti) did my hair in her interpretation of a Mende hairstyle as depicted in a sculpture on display in the African Gallery. As she did my hair, we both entertained questions about hair, hair politics, hair styling, race, art, craft, etc. from the audience. Hundreds of people came through."[37]

While the aesthetic similarities between the hairstyle and the sculpture situate each image within a concept of African aesthetic practices, the *Hair Craft Project* also reveals physical contact as a means of translation. Touch creates connection among diverse Black women and provides a means by which diasporic aesthetic practices are communicated from one individual to another. Hair braiding is not simply labor, then, but also embodied knowledge, a means for conveying shape and pattern through multiple media. Within all of this, the haptic experience of the silk thread on canvas also challenges notions about Black hair texture by using the thread as metonym. Viewers might look upon the thread to recall, internally, the sensation of Afro-textured hair. The canvases reveal the dexterity required to work with the fiber without the indexed body, while the fine silk thread proposes an alternative textural valence to wool, as prescribed in the nineteenth century, for example. In these details, Black hair is represented as a complicated artistic material. It is sacred visual material, as the management or styling of Black hair is the one domain in which touch among Black people, within and across genders, has been deemed acceptable without regard to respectability; and yet, the museum space provides room to contemplate Black hair as a fetish—a peculiar fiber, at once desirable and uncanny—that simultaneously demands and resists touch from viewers. All these relations invite the rethinking of hair and hair braiders within circuits of capital as the *Hair Craft Project* acknowledges the artistic practice of braiding as craft and troubles conceptions of the value of the labor.

Assembling History: Alison Saar

Artist Alison Saar has insisted on texture as a key element in her storytelling since she began working in the early 1980s. Born in Los Angeles, California, to parents Betye Saar, an artist, and Richard Saar, a conservator, Saar portrays her parents' influence in her reliance on found objects. Saar studied at Scripps College before earning an MFA at the Otis Art Institute. Her earliest works "foreshadowed" her later artmaking, according to Judith Wilson, as Saar's use of "handmade paper" and "a found image" intimate her eventual turn toward craft and "resistant materials."[38] This hankering for the textured surface manifested in Saar's early prints, including *Monte* (1983), that employ engraving techniques such as intaglio to produce a crumpled and colorful image; and this tendency can also be found in her sculptural objects. The textured surface is also manifest in Saar's depiction of the Black female nude, according to Jessica Dallow, where Saar visualizes "black women's historical struggle to reclaim their own bodies, turning themselves from exoticized objects into critical subjects" through her deployment of dirt, wood, and tin.[39] This treatment of the textured surface quickly extended from the body to hair, as Saar has employed metalwork and assemblage in her representations of Black coiffure. In fact, assemblage proved the perfect approach for Saar to take up questions of history, heritage, and spiritualism because of the way in which found objects continually gesture toward their past usage or even previous existence as refuse before being reclaimed for art. The "assemblage aesthetic" emphasized in connections forged among disparate objects—often "scavenged, found, and makeshift materials"— provided Saar's hair sculptures with texture as well as a past.[40] Works such as *Sweeping Beauty* (1997), that repurposed an old broom, inverted the object to render the bristles as hair for an upside figure, and the colorful bust of *Nappy Head Blues* (plate 25), which incorporates junk—scissors, combs, keys—in bright blue, portrays Saar's coupling of salvaged materials and representations of coiffure. In an interview with curator Thelma Golden, Saar describes herself as "hair obsessed," with works like *Nappy Head Blues* treating hair as "biographer," as symbolized in the collection of objects that stand in for tufts of curls or in the spirited figures pressed out of the hair at the handles of various *Hot Comb Haint* works.[41] In her choice to portray the mélange of material on top of a head, or to reveal to viewers the collections of items that seem disparate from one another, texture functions as a verb in Saar's work, an action on the surface that she uses to reveal Black hair as roughed by the past.

Out of Saar's preference for discarded material also comes her assertion of spiritualism, as her particular choice of found material also connects to notions of the spirit world in Black culture. Saar's reference to bottle trees is a popular and recurring spiritual motif in her work. Often made of colored glass—blue or green—bottle trees are produced through hanging empty bottles on tree branches. Robert Farris Thompson attributes these "visual statements," which are prevalent throughout the South and are said to "ward off evil," to the graveyard realms for the ways in which they are variously used to protect the dead and capture spirits.[42] In *Delta Doo* (2002), Saar presents her blank female figure with her hair adorned with bottles, and in a woodcut and Chine collé portrait of a woman facing the viewer, Saar portrays her strands shooting straight up, rather than branching out, with clear bottles adorning the tips (plate 26). The hanging bottles propose Black hair as absorbent, much like the bottles, variously able to catch spirits and defend against the spirit world. With such inclusions, Saar presents "the hoodoo repertoire of vernacular healing practices" prevalent among rural African Americans, which, according to Kobena Mercer, connects a larger world of cultural contact with the Global South through "rhizomatic formulations" that establish "hybrid assemblages."[43] Hair is represented in Black southern symbolism via artmaking practices and in images that assert a spiritual connection and not simply an aesthetic similarity.

The textured pictorial surface is essential to Saar's project, as she uses both two- and three-dimensional representations. Moving between sculptural objects and printmaking, Saar repeats figures using the flat surface to provide additional context. She employs her two-dimensional work for the introduction of "other things that couldn't be part of a sculpture." For example, she adds "smoke, or ghostly figures lurking about" to a print that cannot appear in three dimensions because "sculptures are solitary objects often contextualized by the space they inhabit." The print thus yields "a scene, a tableau, a narrative."[44] Accordingly, in *Compton Nocturne* (1999; plate 27), Saar has created a sculpture of a side-lounging woman who faces the viewer. Constructed from wood, reclaimed ceiling tin, paint, and tar, the figure has a defined face and nude body, crowned with a large loom of textured hair fashioned from a bush of glass bottles hanging from branches. Taken individually, the bottles for single servings of liquor, salt, or pepper signal the hodgepodge of assemblage, where an array of found materials are put together to forge a new illustration. As a sculptural object, *Compton Nocturne* puts the hair and the body into three dimensions and renders the hair texture as delicate, almost fragile, through the use of mixed glass, which in its other life might have been trash. Cobbled together, though, the bottles in their textured variety portray not just textured hair but also the collection, or haunting, of a persistent past that lingers with the individual. Saar repeats her story of this figure in a two-dimensional iteration, *Compton Nocturne* (2012), a lithograph printed on light-gray Yamato paper (plate 28). On paper, the figure's hair extends down the length of her body, as do the bottles, from head to toe, while her figure appears in indigo that bleeds into the backdrop to create a blue woman on a blue background. In two dimensions, the blue of her body mimics the blue context, translating the spiritualism signified in the bottles to the larger environment created in the image.

The indigo of Saar's work is another inclusion that dovetails the legacies of spiritualism with the history of labor among African peoples as indigo production traversed the Atlantic. In the United States, it was cultivated and industrialized by unfree West African communities in the Deep South, on plantations in Mississippi and South Carolina. The women of West Africa had "carried indigo production knowledge systems [with them] across the Atlantic." In West Africa, "indigo production and the dyeing process was usually a woman's art."[45] However, while slavery repressed the skills, such as dying and crafting, for a production focus on fieldwork, such as building vats and boiling plants, it could not suppress the spiritual meanings and values attributed to the crop. "The enslaved also saw within indigo spiritual riches, seeing metaphysical and healing properties in the blue dye" attributed to West or Central African cosmologies; Frederick Knight explains that "Afro-Carolinians attributed spiritual significance to the color blue," finding various uses for it in everyday life.[46] The most common use of indigo in the lives of African descendants in the United States was the painting of doors and window frames, particularly "haint blue" to keep evil spirits from crossing the threshold of the home. "'Haint' is a Gullah dialect word for 'haunt' or 'ghost,'" so that when "haint blue paint was used on ceilings, around doors and windows, and even under furnishings," it carried a spiritual value.[47]

Saar's inclusion of southern Blacks' spiritualism extends her commentary on southern Black labor, as in her hands, postslavery commodities score the human surface. Indigo and cotton combine in *High Cotton* (2017; plate 29), a linocut and offset monotype woodcut printed on handmade chiri kozo paper, which features Saar's muse seated at an angle. Here, indigo colors the background and bleeds into the figure to color her hair; but it is distinct from her charcoal-colored skin. While branches of cotton radiate from her braided hair, the subject holds a single plume of cotton, as if to signify a rose. In its many iterations, the cotton branches are a complicated inclusion. Where other women in Western art hold a single flower—the Virgin Mary holding a rose, Pablo Picasso's *Woman with a Flower*, Fernand Léger's *Two Women Holding Flowers*—Saar's cotton plume bears no connotation of love, romance, natural beauty, or fertility. Instead, cotton signals postslavery labor production—a forced connection to people of African descent as a plant marked with Black tactility through the pain of harvesting. As with indigo, the inclusion of cotton enables Saar to signify on a long labor history for people of African descent in the United States, a history that moves from southern agriculture to northern industrialization. Labor historian Joe William Trotter Jr. argues that Black women, in particular, were central to industrial cotton after 1919, forced into the most difficult jobs in northern garment factories and having their work overseen by white women managers.[48] Likewise, historian Glenda Gilmore argues that the preponderance of "segregated cotton mills" in North Carolina were used to buttress the labor of poor whites and to promote white-supremacist racial animus.[49] Saar's figure is physically attached to cotton, and yet holding a plume of cotton offers guidance on reading the subject.

The legacy and symbolism elicited by cotton allows Saar to put context onto the page and also to create settings for and with sculptural objects. Cotton reoccurs in multiple works such as *White Guise* (2019; plate 30), the print of a figure facing forward, clutching an iron in one hand, and gripping her sheer white gown in the other. Eleven bolls of cotton extend upward, tethered to six hair braids tied by ribbons. The woodcut appears on stained paper, imprinted with cotton bolls to make this crop part of the foreground and background of the illustration. Saar describes this effect as a way to render the subject invisible—a light-skinned house "slave"—unseen in her sheer gown, camouflaged with cotton. Again, such situational context becomes available in the two-dimensional work more easily than in the three-dimensional sculptural object. But Saar creates context in the museum space through repetition, creating a three-dimensional object in sculptural form with *White Guise* (2018; plate 31), made of wood, copper, ceiling tin, bronze, and tar. Here, more cotton juts upward from the figure's hair, similarly laid upon the coif to differentiate the cotton branches from her hair material. The patina on copper gives the sculpture a tinge of blue. The title of the work gestures toward a thin perception of the Black figure in the eyes of the white viewer, making this woman recognizable only for her labor. Saar expands upon the commentary by producing multiple figures for her exhibition *Alison Saar: Topsy Turvy* at the L.A. Louver (plate 32), for which she forged five laboring women who similarly clutch work implements and wear their hair adorned with bolls of cotton. Variously holding a sickle, a bale hook, a hoe, a machete, and a tobacco knife to signify work in rice, cotton, indigo, sugar cane, and tobacco fields, Saar's women provide context for one another. In serial, the cotton branches in the hair gesture toward Harriet Jacobs's assertion that "these God-breathing machines are no more, in the sight of their masters, than the cotton they plant, or the horses they tend."[50] Collectively, the cotton bolls situate this group of workers in the outdoors, as they grasp their work implements; the image conjures scenes of labor but also scenes of revenge. Saar's repetitious treatment of materials, such as cotton as bonded to coiffure, serves to reflect on hair texture through the feel of organic materials and ultimately accentuates the constructed nature of such associations as made and perpetuated, rather than as natural occurrences.

Saar's practice might be read alongside that of other Black women artists as surface work. Her textured pictorial surface emphasizes Black hair as a textured human surface. Each plane circulates as an archive of the past, where coiffure carries forward personal and social histories, spirit worlds, and the culture of labor. Through assemblage, handmade paper, and sculpture, Afro-textured hair is given depth, not just a three-dimensional complexity but a spiritual profundity that is produced through hybridity and cultural retentions. This surface work—the apparent referents to making—is intimately constructed in the practices of touch that Clark makes evident in her efforts to show the artists and their craft alongside one another, as well as in the collaging of disparate elements to make new surfaces in the works created by Simpson and Gallagher, distilling the iconic blackness of JPC publications in order to show its pliability. By emphasizing the surface as *made*—as created in adornment practices or steeped in cultural retention—through hybrid assemblages that texture the surface, and through the collectivity composed in working the surface, Black women artists present the haptic production of blackness in intimate encounters. They contend with surface manifestations of feeling, the palpability of the past, and the embodied knowledge required for its translation. These works employ hair clippings, paper cutting, painting, drawing, and sculpting to revisit the dyeing, straightening, braiding, and slicking of Afro-textured hair. In their aesthetic choices, these artists propose Black raciality as a haptic inheritance transmitted through the touch, texture, and surface rendering of coiffure material. These works reveal touch as a way to communicate a precolonial history through African hair braiding, to theorize blackness and texture as forged in postslavery labor practices, and to indicate the human surface as remade in the repetitious ornamentation that is a communal practice. Women artists producing haptic art illustrate a haptic blackness as bequeathed through the haptic engagements of touch, texture, and surface.

CROWNING GESTURES

Afro-textured hair reveals the visual and tactile constitution of blackness as produced in slavery's capitalism and reimagined through ongoing struggles for liberation. Haptic blackness—the sense that the racial surface is textured in feeling and in touch as historically informed experiences—offers a way to think through the commoditization of Black peoples, and a way to think through the means by which aspects of the Black body become disaggregated from one another. Where slavery's capitalization of the Black body into units of labor helped to couple hair and flesh, emancipation presented the dispersal of commodification, so that Black hair found new exchange value as distinct from the flesh and as a salable commodity taken up by diverse entrepreneurs. In the twentieth century, in the face of rampant commoditization of the Afro and of Black hair culture, this construction of blackness served the cultural interests of activists, artists, and businesspersons, marking the complicated and multiple notions of "liberation" in the visual material centered on Afro-textured hair.

The legacy of these multiple freedoms has been stimulating for contemporary artists who depict Black hair and Black hair culture as ways not only to signal a textured concept of race, but also to reference particularly iconic moments in the Black freedom struggle. The comb remains central among these representations, just as it was for Willie Morrow, functioning as what Cheryl Finley calls a "mnemonic aesthetics," where remembering, reclaiming, and reinterpreting the past and its "important emblems and icons of history" enable artists to comment on the present.[1] Kori Newkirk's *Legacy,* a crown made from human-size Afro picks with one missing tooth to gesture toward the strife and labor of caring for blackness, pays homage to this period through the comb. Similarly, in another large-scale portrayal, Hank Willis Thomas's *All Power to All People* (2017), the eight-hundred-pound sculpture presenting the Afro comb clad with a Black Power fist at the top, erected near Philadelphia's city hall, is conversant with Claes Oldenburg's *Clothespin,* meant to address "equal justice and belonging" with public art in order to fill the lack of sculptures related to blackness by offering a work that asserts "community, strength, perseverance, comradeship, and resistance to oppression."[2] Thomas's reclamation of space uses the iconic symbol of Black aesthetics and liberation embodied in the object. These combs gesture toward the commodification and accumulation driving Black capitalists of the mid-twentieth century, who pursued liberation in upward mobility and efforts to capitalize on racial blackness.

Works of art about the comb are conversant with but distinct from the exhibition of the comb as a Black artifact. Renderings of the comb as anthropological object mobilize it as an unifying emblem in which histories of racialization muddle the role of capitalism in the construction of Black racial distinction. Repetition and resonance uncover community, as seen in exhibitions such as the 2014 show *Doing Hair: Art and Hair in Africa* at the Wits Art Museum in Johannesburg, South Africa, and in the 2013 exhibition *Origins of the Afro Comb: 6,000 Years of Culture, Politics, and Identity* at the Fitzwilliam Museum at the University of Cambridge in England. Useful for lengthening the arc of time wherein Black hair matters, these shows offer sometimes "spurious historical links" between objects—an Ibo mask, an Egyptian headrest, combs from across the continent—so that the idea of race is held together by common cultural practices. The comb "made and used by Black people—in ancient Egypt and Sudan, in 'modern' Africa, and in the US"—forges the connection.[3] But moving from the African comb, to Morrow's *400 Years without a Comb* in slavery, to the Afro picks sold in *Ebony* and then revisited by contemporary artists, Black hair and hair culture's evolution over time is about transformations in both commodification and practices of physical contact.

Haptic notions of Black raciality conscript two approaches to feeling. Whereas racial capitalism has organized textured hair as a material proving biological distinction, with blackness as an objectifiable commodity recognized by its particular racial characteristics, people of African descent have also organized textured hair as visual material that can be acted upon in ways that imbue it with other modes of sensuousness and sentimentality. Such affective variety has meant "texturism," as curator Tameka Ellington describes it—the sense that the "straighter (less wool-like) the hair, the more beautiful society claims it to be"—and a resistant spiritualism, as ascribed to the textured aesthetic of Black hair.[4] Cultural producers examining Black hair through film and photography frequently turned to the camera's status as an objectifying tool to assert these values and to filter questions of touch through the pictorial surface. Many of these efforts were birthed by liberation struggles against colonization, by the absorption of Black racial distinction into conceptions of the state, and by new approaches to cultural nationalism. Where the exchange of blackness became an ongoing by-product of slavery's capitalism, the value of coiffure distinguished itself from the flesh. Not only were people commodified into units of labor, with commodification resulting not simply in association with the agricultural goods they produced, but blackness also became a visual product with an exchange value that persisted in the afterlife of slavery. It is for these reasons that the language of liberation and struggle recur on the subject of Black hair as representation—the characterization of Black hair as coarse and requiring management is born of the struggle with racial capitalism.

Along these lines, it becomes difficult to settle matters of "freedom" associated with the visual material of Black coiffure. Recently, public figures have turned to the assertion of the law to address attacks against wearers of Afro-textured hair, first with California lawmakers passing the CROWN Act—the Creating a Respectful and Open World for Natural Hair Act—to protect against discrimination based on hair. Introduced in January 2019 and signed into law on September 21, 2020, the CROWN Act expands the definition of race-based discrimination in the Fair Employment and Housing Act (FEHA) and the state Education Code, offering protection at work and at K-12 schools. Since then, seven additional state legislatures have debated the topic, passing successive CROWN Act bills to legislate against discrimination based on "hair texture or hairstyle if that style or texture is commonly associated with a particular race or national origin," and "against those participating in federally assisted programs, housing programs, public accommodations, and employment."[5] In September 2019, the US House of Representatives passed the bill, stating, "Persons shall not be deprived of equal rights under the law and shall not be subjected to prohibited practices based on their hair texture or style." Supporting these efforts in March 2021, New Jersey senator Cory Booker reintroduced the bill to the US Senate, arguing that people of African descent are "deprived of educational and employment opportunities" when "adorned with natural or protective hairstyles" as well as by wearing "cornrows, twists, braids, Bantu knots, or Afros." The Senate document goes on to cite transformation in the US military's grooming policies—which once described textured hairstyles as "unkempt"—and aims to "institute definitions of race and national origin for Federal civil rights laws that effectuate the comprehensive scope of protection Congress intended to be afforded by such laws," which, until now, have too narrowly defined race and racial discrimination.[6] Along these lines, the CROWN Act proposes the law as a means to acknowledge and protect people of African descent from harassment and social exclusion, and to "enforce procedures" meant to contend with discrimination as associated with civil rights. Such measures are important as countless children are repeatedly punished at school for their hairstyles—including documented reprimands such as school suspension—while adults are barred from work and places of business on the grounds of their textured hair. The CROWN Act presents a means to confront school boards that disallow dreadlocks at high school graduation or during athletic events, as well as colleges and professions that once looked askance at natural hairstyles.[7] The CROWN Act is important, in part, for its visibility as a campaign that incorporates hair in efforts to eradicate discrimination. Where lawmakers in various states take up the charge of the CROWN Act, they help to promote the idea that racial bias predicated on hair is unacceptable.

However, concerns about access also retain issues related to the market. "The construction and application of the law," which Sarah Haley argues is constitutive of gendered racial capitalism, is exacted in such an approach to hair.[8] The CROWN Act uses legal means to deal with Black hair as imbricated in the selling of Black labor or the buying of property. This approach offers a packaged "freedom," levied in "the freedom to own, to enter the market, or to buy and sell one's labor."[9] Such an approach maintains reliance upon corporate partnerships for ascendancy in political institutions. The "Official Campaign of the CROWN Act" has been fueled by the CROWN Coalition, founded by the Dove personal care brand, in cooperation with the National Urban League, Color of Change, and Western Center on Law and Poverty. The presence and financial sponsorship of a cosmetic company has been central to the visibility of the CROWN Act, as Dove funded the survey research to determine the "magnitude of racial discrimination experienced by women in the workplace based on their natural hairstyles." Publicized findings include incidents such as Black women receiving materials on corporate grooming policies earlier in the hiring process and more frequently than non-Black women. Researchers argue that "Black women's hair is more policed in the workplace, thereby contributing to a climate of group control" and increased encounters with "professional barriers."[10] On the basis of hair, Black women are more policed, more targeted, and deemed less ready for the job, according to Dove's research, which is helping to fuel legislative protections against discrimination in the workplace. And yet, it remains difficult to settle issues of extraction and violence through more capitalism. The experience of police harassment and verbal abuse suffered by members of MOVE or by Rastafarians, for example, finds no panacea in questions of access. Likewise, the historical legacy of forcible cutting is not easily resolved by the law when it was once sanctioned by the law. The racism meted out through tactile encounters with Black hair warrants rethinking both the distant visual perspectives on the value of texture and the intimate practices of touch.

New approaches to physical contact include acts of personal care as well as touch in social interaction. Transformations in the haptic encounters with Black hair do not simply mean making it accessible to others, an assumption that undergirds projects like "You Can Touch My Hair," a media event staged in Union Square, New York City, that invited passersby to touch women of African descent.[11] Although organizers meant to confront curiosities about the texture and feel of Black hair, detractors gathered to protest the spectacle, arguing that such public groping only conjured the treatment of Sarah Baartman's body in nineteenth-century Europe. Organizers had to turn to hosting talk-backs with public figures, like image activist Michaela Angela Davis, and creating online content with the support from their corporate partner, Procter & Gamble's Pantene Pro-V hair care, to transform the event into a teachable moment. In their use of personal testimony, street interviews, and the language of "public art," producers of "You Can Touch My Hair" called upon more than twenty years of critical visual material contending with haptic blackness to emphasize the liberatory intentions of the project. Theirs was an attempt to use touch as a correction to practices of looking. And where "the capitalist tendency [is] to render meanings as easily consumable and translatable signs," images are a powerful shorthand that demands a "tactile epistemology" to foster critique "in postindustrial, capitalist society."[12] But Afro-textured coiffure has a unique history, as I have illustrated here. Not everyone can touch Black hair. Touch and the visual together remain central to transforming the cultural significations of Afro-textured hair, and that physical engagement cannot be democratized. Touching Black hair has involved repetitive gestures that have forged legacies in the structurally violent mundane, legacies that cannot be easily remade in disparate everyday encounters. These tangible ways of knowing and feeling cannot be severed from histories of racialization.

The diverse examples of visual culture that I have discussed create an opportunity to reconsider Black hair and latent beliefs about blackness with regard to feeling and touch. The hidden suppleness of Black coiffure offers the chance to contend with the residual legacies of slavery and colonialism. Along with their visual aspect, sentimental and tactile matters of feeling inform the sense of blackness in intimate encounters. As Black hair has been produced and reimagined in the hands and on the heads of artists and wearers of natural hair, its value evolves to become a site of remembrance: a repository for a broadened affective value, a revision on conceptions of texture, a revered spirit world, and a resistant aesthetic for people of African descent.

INTRODUCTION. NEW GROWTH

1 Through the book I use *dreadlocks* and *locs* interchangeably to describe the style of twisting Afro-textured hair to mat and tangle. Locs have a complicated history that also frames the terminology used to describe this hairstyle. In *Hair Story*, Ayana Byrd and Lori Tharps offer the term *dredlocs* to avoid the "dreadful" characterization of Black hair in bondage, a designation from slavery "when Africans emerged from the slave ships after months spent in conditions adverse to any personal hygiene." The authors go on to discuss the commoditization of dredlocs among US Americans, buttressed by popular culture, where fashion separated the style from its radical roots. Along these lines, however, *dread* as a term maintains significance even if its use emerged in the context of slavery, which I have not uncovered in the following research. *Dread* offers an important distinction from *combsome* among Rastafarians, marking loc'd hair as counter to grooming with combs. Barry Chevannes argues that the "institutionalization of the locks" began in 1930s Jamaica, with growing beards and with early debates about combing hair, which was controversial "because society simply did not accept unkempt hair. Not to comb one's hair was to declare oneself not merely antisocial but extra social, like mad derelicts and outcasts." Accordingly, "One who earned that name inspired dread in other brethren by the forthrightness and frankness of his critical remarks and the defense of the principles essential to the Youth Black Faith. 'Dreadful' or 'Dread' was therefore synonymous with 'upright.'" I maintain the use of *dreadlocks* to mark this counterhegemonic significance, even where some wearers of loc'd hair refute these politics. Byrd and Tharps, *Hair Story*, 121; Chevannes, *Rastafari: Roots and Ideology*, 156.

2 See the image by Joseph T. Zealy, *Daguerreotype, Renty, frontal*, 1850. Peabody Museum of Archaeology and Ethnology, Harvard University, Cambridge, MA. For more on the posing of Zealy's subjects, see Lewis, "Insistent Reveal," 299.

3 Hall, "Missing Dolly, Mourning Slavery."

4 Lucy Cottrell was held in bondage by George Blaetterman, a professor at the University of Virginia, and had been sold to him by the estate of Thomas Jefferson after his death in 1826. For more on such images see Fox-Amato, *Exposing Slavery*.

5   S. M. Smith, *Photographic Returns*, 27.

6   Copeland, "Rashid Johnson," 303.

7   Mercer, "Black Hair/Style Politics," 44.

8   Wilson, "Beauty Rites"; Willis, "Black is Beautiful: Then and Now," 139.

9   P. C. Taylor, *Black Is Beautiful*, 12; Gordon, "Black Aesthetics, Black Value," 26.

10 Artists who survived slavery, such as painters Bill Traylor (1854–1949) and Joshua Johnson (1763–1862), or ceramicist David Drake (1801–65), are often treated as exceptional individuals and their artworks are treated archivally.

11 Morgan, *Laboring Women*, 12.

12 Bristol, *Knights of the Razor*; Mills, *Cutting Along the Color Line*.

13 Rooks, *Hair Raising*, 30.

14 Rooks goes on to say that "because female slaves probably looked to the values and materials of the white mistress with regard to clothing, they may have done the same with hair, although their practices would have differed," presuming that "house slaves whom the master held in particularly high esteem were held in high regard" and might have set a tone for the values of hair culture in these communities. Rooks, *Hair Raising*, 25.

15 Gill, *Beauty Shop Politics*, 122.

16 Ford, "SNCC Women," 657.

17 Davis, "Afro Images."

18 Ellis, "New Black Aesthetic," 236.

19 Sheumaker and Wajda, *Material Culture in America*, xii. The study of material culture, especially with regard to people of African descent, is typified by a focus on objects or things, such as the search for personal possessions among enslaved Blacks or for utilitarian artifacts excavated on the continent of Africa. Moving between "'form'-based and 'context'-based analyses" scholars use material culture to piece together life worlds. Arnoldi and Hardin, *African Material Culture*, 1. See also Katz-Hyman and Rice, *World of a Slave*.

20 Crawford, *Dilution Anxiety*. "Light skin, straight noses, and long, straight hair" signify "civility, rationality, and beauty," in contrast to "dark skin, broad noses, and kinky hair, [which] represent savagery, irrationality, and ugliness." Hunter, *Race, Gender*, 3.

21 Powell, *Black Art*, 16.

22 B. H. Edwards, *Practice of Diaspora*.

23 K. Jones, *Eyeminded*, 250.

24 Harney and Moten, *Undercommons*, 98.

25 Bradley, "Introduction," 130.

26 Spillers, "Mama's Baby, Papa's Maybe," 67.

27 Weheliye, *Habeas Viscus*, 2.

28 Snorton, *Black on Both Sides*, 34.

29 Cole, "True Picture of Black Skin."

30 Spillers, "Shades of Intimacy."

31 Metz, *Imaginary Signifier*, 61.

32 Jay, *Downcast Eyes*, 9.

33 Martin Jay points to Luce Irigaray's critique of touch as feminine, rooted in the sex organ that "keeps woman in touch with herself." Jay, *Downcast Eyes*, 292; Irigaray, *This Sex Which Is Not One*, 26.

34 Marks, *Touch*, 7.

35 Campt, *Listening to Images*, 72; Campt, *Image Matters*, 32.

36 Marks, *Touch*, 13.

37 Jacobs-Huey, *From the Kitchen*, 122. With the explosion of new entrepreneurs, Lanita Jacobs-Huey explored language in everyday conversation, including online communities at the turn of the twentieth century, to find "nappy as a controversial and complex signifier," 128.

38 Banks, *Hair Matters*, 172. Banks discusses slavery, as do her interview participants; she explains that "slavery has ended, but the psychological scars remain, as do more subtle forms of devaluing Black physical characteristics" (76). Banks also clarifies that "black women still have to deal with the mental chains of slavery and Jim Crow that are exacerbated by mainstream standards of beauty that black women in general cannot meet" (46).

39 Best and Marcus, "Surface Readings," 9.

40 On insensate blackness, see Bernstein, *Racial Innocence*; Solange, "Don't Touch My Hair."

41 Levenson, Yang, and Gonzales-Day, "Haptic Blackness."

42 Mitchell, *Vénus Noire*, 9.

43 Murrell, *Posing Modernity*, 20.

44 O'Grady, "Olympia's Maid."

45 Curry-Evans et al., *HairStories*, 13.

46 K. Thompson, *Shine*, 229.

CHAPTER 1. ARCHIVE

1 Ruth Cox took the name Harriet Bailey to avoid recapture when she escaped from slavery, likely fleeing to avoid a liquidation sale upon the death of John Leeds Kerr. Born between 1818 and 1822 in Talbot County, Maryland, Adams absconded to Pennsylvania where she met Douglass, and the two believed they were siblings. Bailey would join the Douglass household in Lynn, Massachusetts, to support Anna Douglass, especially with reading and writing, so that she could communicate with Douglass during his tour of Great Britain. In November 1847, Bailey married Perry Frank Adams, and although still a fugitive, she returned to using her given name and became Ruth Cox Adams. Fought, *Women in the World*, 67; Blight, *Frederick Douglass*, 163–66.

2 Adams's collection of hair mementos includes a clipping from her daughter, labeled with extensive identifying details: "Ebby B. Adams 9 months old born in Springfield Mass"; she lists her date of birth as February 22, 1852, and she uses the initials of her "Mother & Father" to refer to Ruth Cox Adams and Perry Francis Adams. Likewise, Adams kept a clipping from her mother, Ebby Cox Bruce, taken at the time of her death on December 20, 1883, and sent from Louisiana by

Adams's brother, Daneal Bruce. For more, see the Alyce McWilliams Hall collection of the Nebraska Historical Society.

3   The Douglass family valued hair as sentimental tokens. The Nebraska Historical Society holds locks of hair identified with notes for Lewis Henry Douglass, Frederick Douglass Jr., and Rosetta Douglass. Each token is marked with the child's age and, like their father's, places the family in Lynn, Massachusetts, at the time of the clipping. The activist may have made regular gifts of his hair clippings, with tokens found among his materials collected by Mississippi State University (1876) as well as by the University of Rochester (1869).

4   Holm, "Sentimental Cuts," 140.

5   Douglass, "Frederick Douglass to Francis Jackson," 90.

6   Douglass, "John Jacobus Flournoy to Frederick Douglass," 327.

7   Cvetkovich, *Archive of Feelings*, 7.

8   D. Taylor, *Archive and the Repertoire*, 19.

9   W. Johnson, *River of Dark Dreams*, 179; Smallwood, *Saltwater Slavery*, 160.

10 Franklin and Schweninger, *Runaway Slaves*, 224.

11 Palmer, "'What Feels More Than Feeling?'" Palmer unpacks "affect theory's lack of interrogation of the particularities of Blackness and its circulation within affective economies" (35).

12 Bernasconi and Lott, *Idea of Race*, 28.

13 Anthropometric studies of the body, and the head in particular, were popular from the late eighteenth through the nineteenth century: physiognomy (1772), which related facial traits to character; phrenology (1796), which used the shape and size of the head to determine character; and craniology (1770), or the study of the shape/size of skulls differentiated by race. Sharrona Pearl argues that physiognomy outlasted phrenology as race science because the former required less physical interaction or consent than the haptic engagement of skull-reading through touch. Pearl, *About Faces*, 191.

14 White and White, "Slave Hair," 46.

15 Latrobe, *Journal of Latrobe*, 64.

16 Latrobe, *Journal of Latrobe*, 177.

17 C. Colbert, *Measure of Perfection*, 13.

18 Dawson et al., *Science Periodicals*, 97.

19 Rusert, *Fugitive Science*, 78.

20 Debret, *Voyage pittoresque et historique*.

21 French artists traveling to France include François-Auguste Biard, Jean Baptiste Debret, and Johann Moritz Rugendas.

22 Aidoo, *Slavery Unseen*, 17.

23 Araujo, *Brazil through French Eyes*, 47.

24 Araujo, *Brazil through French Eyes*, 77.

25 Morton, *Crania Americana*, 85, 4.

26 Fabian, *Skull Collectors*, 88.

27 P. A. Browne, *Trichologia Mammalium*, 67.

28 P. A. Browne, *Trichologia Mammalium*, 53.

29 P. A. Browne, *Trichologia Mammalium*, 30.

30 P. A. Browne, *Trichologia Mammalium*, 90.

31 In southern newspapers, advertisements of enslavers seeking to recover runaways frequently described "wooly hair" among people of African descent. For more see Hodges and Brown, *"Pretends to Be Free,"* 157; Bly, *Escaping Bondage*, 151. Likewise, other academics debated this subject: "Frizzled hair is very prevalent in Africa, arising frequently from the commixture of Nigritian blood, as in Egypt, in Abyssinia, amongst the Gallas, etc. . . . The crisp hair predominates in Africa among the Negroes, the Hottentots, and in Melanesia." Pruner-Bey, "On Human Hair," 5. Or: "The structure of human woolly hair is altogether different from that of sheep's wool. Crisp or woolly hair is fine or coarse, and presents itself in various aspects. It is long, and falls down in twisted curls which resemble thick fringes . . . or long and bristly, thus forming a round mass." Topinard, *Anthropology*, 351.

32 White, *Stylin' African-American Expressive Culture*, 47.

33 Jordan, *White over Black*, 12.

34 P. A. Browne's collection includes ten volumes of separate scrapbooks. Therein he cataloged hair from white men, some of whom served as president of the United States; people identified as Israelite, African, and of African descent; Native Americans of the Cherokee, Creek, Muskogee, Sioux, and Pawnee nations; and people imprisoned in the Ohio Lunatic Asylum. Some entries refer to specimens taken from animals, including "whiskers" attributed to possums, cats, racoons, and horses.

35 *Peter Arrell Browne (1762–1860) Papers*, 1842–43, Archives of the Academy of Natural Sciences of Drexel University.

36 P. A. Browne, *Trichologia Mammalium*, 65.

37 Snorton, *Black on Both Sides*, 24.

38 Hartman, "Seduction and the Ruses."

39 M. Smith, *Sensing the Past*, 109.

40 M. Smith, *How Race Is Made*, 14.

41 Bernstein, *Racial Innocence*.

42 Formerly described as "Gordon" but since identified as "Peter" or "Whipped Peter." Although reproduced many times over, the original image (captured in Baton Rouge, Louisiana, on April 2, 1863, and held at the Library of Congress) includes writing on the reverse side. Dr. J. W. Mercer, assistant surgeon with the Forty-Seventh Massachusetts Volunteers, wrote to Colonel L. B. Marsh, "Colonel, I have found a large number of the four hundred contrabands examined by me to be as badly lacerated as the specimen represented in the enclosed photograph."

43 Baptist, *Half Has Never Been Told*, 142. Baptist explains that drivers whipped enslaved people both to punish them for picking too little cotton and to maintain a fervor to pick the most.

44 Campt, *Image Matters*, 31–32.

45 Campt, *Image Matters*, 33.

46 Clegg, "Credit Market Discipline," 346.

47 Clegg, "Capitalism and Slavery," 283.

48 Spillers, "Mama's Baby, Papa's Maybe," 75.

49 Berry, *Price for Their Pound of Flesh*, 2.

50 Harris, "Whiteness as Property," 1720.

51 Jacobs, *Incidents in the Life*, 118.

52 Gross, *Hannah Mary Tabbs*, 53.

53 Bourdieu, *Language and Symbolic Power*, 238; Guillory, "Bourdieu's Refusal," 28.

54 Patterson, *Slavery and Social Death*, 60.

55 W. Johnson, *Soul by Soul*, 155.

56 "$100 Reward," *American Beacon*, July 4, 1835.

57 Foreman, "Who's Your Mama?," 133.

58 Hardt and Negri, *Empire*, 292.

59 Oksala, "Affective Labor and Feminist Politics," 284.

60 Palmer, "'What Feels More than Feeling?,'" 37.

61 Federal Writers' Project, US Works Progress Administration, *Slave Narrative Project, Vol. 16, Texas, Part 1, Adams–Duhon*, 1941. Library of Congress, Manuscript Division, https://www.loc.gov/item/mesn161/. Victor Duhon is listed as ninety-seven years old in the WPA narrative, dated 1936–38.

62 C. A. Nelson, *Slavery, Geography and Empire*, 306.

63 Glymph, *Out of the House*, 33.

64 T. R. R. Cobb, *Inquiry into the Law*, civ.

65 Din, *Spaniards, Planters, and Slaves*, 125.

66 R. M. Browne, *Surviving Slavery*, 52.

67 Paton, *No Bond but the Law*, 104.

68 "Practice of Cropping Hair of Female Prisoners as Punishment," November 2, 1877, The National Archives, Kew, England 14273/1877. See also Allain, "'They Are Quiet Women Now.'"

69 Morgan, *Laboring Women*, 105.

70 Holland, *Frederick Douglass*, 224.

71 Chesnutt, *Frederick Douglass*, 108.

72 Chesnutt, *Frederick Douglass*, 126.

73 Washington, *Frederick Douglass*, 185.

74 Washington, *Frederick Douglass*, 303.

75 Stauffer, Trodd, and Bernier, *Picturing Frederick Douglass*.

76 Wallace and Smith, *Pictures and Progress*, 48.

77 Douglass, *Narrative of the Life of Frederick Douglass*, 68.

78 Douglass, *Narrative of the Life of Frederick Douglass*, 69.

79 Douglass, *My Bondage and My Freedom*; and in both editions of *Life and Times of Frederick Douglass Written by Himself*, 160.

80 On the contributions of Garrison and antislavery lawyer Wendell Phillips, John Ernest cites their "presumption of authority" as well as "a hint of patronage and benevolent condescension." Ernest, *Douglass in His Own Time*, xiii. Robert Stepto argues Garrison is at "war" with Douglass for authorial control in the text. Stepto, *From behind the Veil*, 18. William Andrews contends that the break from

Garrisonian abolition in 1845 made for greater authorial control for Douglass in his 1855 autobiography. Andrews, *To Tell a Free Story*, 217.

81   Larson, *Bound for the Promised Land*, 42.
82   Larson, *Bound for the Promised Land*, 42.
83   Emily Howland, collector, and Caroline N. Lacy, inscriber, [Emily Howland photograph album], ca. 1861–80, Library of Congress, Prints and Photographs Division, https://lccn.loc.gov/2017656258.
84   Adair, *Kinship across the Black Atlantic*, 21. Wilma King argues that "in the absence of relatives, surrogates or fictive families were valuable assets to the slave community." King, *Stolen Childhood*, 64.
85   Williams, *Help Me to Find My People*, 31.

CHAPTER 2. TEXTURE

1   Higginbotham, *Righteous Discontent*; Ransby, *Ella Baker and the Black Freedom Movement*.
2   Theoharis, "Black Freedom Studies," 358.
3   Thanks to Grace Hong for directing me toward the symbols of student activism in this commercial clip.
4   Ferguson, *Reorder of Things*, 55.
5   George E. Johnson Sr. founded Johnson Products Company in 1954 with Ultra Wave, a hair straightener for men, before creating Ultra Sheen and then Afro Sheen in the late 1960s.
6   Lehman, *Critical History of Soul Train*, 40.
7   Ford, "This Black, Buy Black," 44.
8   Rooks, *Hair Raising*.
9   Kelley, "Nap Time," 342.
10 Ford, *Liberated Threads*, 104.
11 Gill, *Beauty Shop Politics*, 122.
12 Scott, *Refashioning Futures*, 124.
13 This lengthy list of titles ranges from stage works such as Amiri Baraka's *Slave Ship* (1967) to Octavia Butler's *Kindred* (1979). Many of the male-centered works used a "Black Power discourse [that] invokes slavery to name a paralyzing burden of psychological dependency." See Dubey, "Freedom Now," 30. For more on slavery in performance and literature, see Elam, *Taking It to the Streets*; S. D. Colbert, *Black Movements*.
14 Mercer, "Black Hair/Style Politics," 44.
15 Ford, *Liberated Threads*, 28.
16 "Nkrumah led Ghana to independence from Britain in 1957. From Ghana, African and global forces came together in support of African independence to such an extent that the United Nations (UN) declared 1960 the year of Africa." That year, seventeen African countries reclaimed independence. Zuberi, *African Independence*, 49.

17 Brown, Gomez, and Sellers, "Relationship between Internalization and Self-Esteem," 56.

18 Scholarship of this ilk includes works beginning in the 1930s and continues to the present. K. Clark and M. Clark, "Development of Consciousness of Self"; K. Clark and M. Clark, "Emotional Factors in Racial Identification"; Baldwin, "Theory and Research."

19 Quashie, *Sovereignty of Quiet*, 20.

20 Ball and Jackson, *Reconsidering Roots*, 5.

21 Delmont, *Making Roots*, 159.

22 Delmont, *Making Roots*, 112–13.

23 Van Deburg, *Slavery and Race*, 155.

24 J. N. Cobb, "Directed by Himself."

25 Morrow's list of inventions includes the Afro pick and the Jheri curl, among other hairstyling products distributed from his offices at California Curl. Morrow credits California—including the presence of the Black Panthers and urban centers as bastions that helped support his entrepreneurship—as central to what he has been able to establish. Among his entrepreneurial pursuits, Morrow has been the proprietor of his own marketing vehicles, publishing numerous books, including *Workbook for Styling Curly Hair* and *Black Stylist*; a weekly newspaper, the *San Diego Monitor*; and a radio show. DeWyze, "Willie Morrow."

26 Morrow, *400 Years without a Comb*; Morrow and Jefferson, *400 Years without a Comb*.

27 Kragen, "Black Hair Story." Morrow's archive has been exhibited at the Museum at the California Center for the Arts. Items from his personal collection include an array of combs but also tools of enslavement such as shackles.

28 Morrow, *400 Years without a Comb*, 19. Brown, Gomez, and Sellers, "Relationship between Internalization and Self-Esteem," 57.

29 Grier and Cobbs, *Black Rage*, 198.

30 Grier and Cobbs, *Black Rage*, 198.

31 Morrow, *400 Years without a Comb*, 19.

32 Kelley, "Nap Time," 346.

33 Price and Price, *Maroon Arts*, 38.

34 Combs are one instance of carved objects that change over time to reflect the influences and innovations in various artistic materials. The authors describe a collection of combs gathered by Melville Herskovits where "forty-nine of the fifty-three combs collected" in the 1920s "were flat, while the very great majority of combs" gathered "in the field in the 1960s were curved. During the 1970s, flat combs again came into fashion, and today they represent at least half of those being made." Price and Price, *Maroon Arts*, 155.

35 Antiri, "Akan Combs," 32.

36 Tulloch, "Resounding Power," 125.

37 M. Wilson and Russell-Cole, *Divided Sisters*, 131; see also T. Jones, *American Marriage*.

38 Tulloch, "Resounding Power," 133.

39 Morrow, *400 Years without a Comb*, 70.

40 Bristol, *Knights of the Razor*, 11. Bristol describes the cultural appropriation of European aristocracy by enslavers in the United States through the use of unfree Blacks as personal servants. Mills, *Cutting Along the Color Line*, 17. Mills unpacks a complex web wherein Black barbers were hired out by enslavers but were also engaged in the personal care of other people of African descent on plantations, in addition to cutting hair for free African Americans.

41 Morrow and Jefferson, *400 Years without a Comb*.

42 Morrow, *400 Years without a Comb*, 27.

43 Avilez, *Radical Aesthetics*, 7.

44 Farmer, *Remaking Black Power*, 62.

45 Douglas and Durant, *Black Panther*, 94.

46 In addition to fighting police brutality, the Black Panthers actively focused on "the failure of a capitalist system to provide for poor and oppressed communities" by instituting programs to fight food insecurity and disease. For more, see A. Nelson, *Body and Soul*, 151.

47 Powell, "Conversation with Barkley Hendricks," 45.

48 Jarrell, AFRICOBRA, 204.

49 Marable, *How Capitalism Underdeveloped Black America*, 172.

50 Marable, *How Capitalism Underdeveloped Black America*, 172–73.

51 Baradaran, *Color of Money*, 178.

52 The monthly magazine *Jet* began publication in 1945. Johnson Publishing Company (JPC) was founded in 1942 by John Harold Johnson, a Chicago-based insurance agent. Johnson began with subscribers to *Negro Digest*, before releasing *Ebony* in 1945. In time JPC would grow to become the largest African American–owned publishing company in the United States.

53 Weems, *Desegregating the Dollar*, 74.

54 Weems, *Desegregating the Dollar*, 76.

55 Llorens, "Natural Hair."

56 Carby, *Race Men*, 48.

57 E. R. Edwards, *Charisma and Fictions*, 7.

58 Ford, *Liberated Threads*, 108.

59 Llorens, "Natural Hair," 144. David Llorens served as director of Black studies at the University of Washington in Seattle and as an associate editor of *Ebony* magazine. He joined *Ebony* as an assistant editor in 1967 after working at *Negro Digest*. His writerly interest focused on "the position of black people in America." Llorens was a veteran of the Air Force and became an activist working with SNCC in Mississippi. He died at the age of thirty-four after a high-speed chase with the Washington State Patrol. "David Llorens, 34, Writer and Editor," *New York Times*, December 2, 1973.

60 Llorens, "Natural Hair," 141.

61 Llorens, "Natural Hair," 141.

62 Llorens, "Natural Hair," 143.

63 Llorens, "Natural Hair," 144.

64 Llorens, "Natural Hair," 143; Leslie, "Slow Fade to?," 432. Ads for hair straighten-

ers declined going into the sixties, although they never disappeared completely; models with natural hairstyles increased in promotional campaigns beginning in the sixties and remained present into the 1980s, although natural hair models never usurped the number of models with straight hair.

65 *Ebony*, January 1969, 23.

66 *Ebony*, March 1970, 39.

67 *Jet*, October 19, 1972, 34.

68 Acham, *Revolution Televised*, 61.

69 Questlove, *Soul Train*, 29.

70 Lehman, *Critical History of* Soul Train, 59.

71 Danois, *Love, Peace, and Soul*, 27. Cullers is also responsible for advertising Newport Menthol Cigarettes through a soul aesthetic, using the tagline "Bold Cold Newport." Weems, *Desegregating the Dollar*, 77.

72 Danois, *Love, Peace, and Soul*, 27.

73 Danois, *Love, Peace, and Soul*, 26.

74 Crawford, *Black Post-Blackness*.

75 For examples of these ads, see Afro Sheen "Queen of Sheba" commercial, https://www.youtube.com/watch?v=XmNt5zDOUd8; Afro Sheen "Windy City" commercial, https://www.youtube.com/watch?v=IQq-UIkfuqA; Afro Sheen "Tab Dancing" commercial, https://www.youtube.com/watch?v=oArOnOouwYs; Afro Sheen "Afro as Symbol" commercial, https://www.youtube.com/watch?v=IrZ3cox14TE; Afro Sheen "Office Cooler" commercial, https://www.youtube.com/watch?v=apf2KPgBoSM.

76 Kanogo, *Squatters*, 6.

77 Mwanzia Koster, *Power of the Oath*, 21.

78 Branch, *Defeating Mau Mau, Creating Kenya*, 7.

79 Tully, "All's Well in the Colony," 61.

80 Branch, *Defeating Mau Mau, Creating Kenya*, 5.

81 "Mau Mau Massacres 150 Natives in Night Raid near Kenya Capital," *New York Times*, March 28, 1953, 1; "Soviet-Trained Mau Mau Terrorist Is Sentenced to 7 Years' Hard Labor," *New York Times*, April 9, 1953, 1; "Captured Mau Mau Urges Truce on Other Chiefs as British Watch," *New York Times*, March 4, 1954, 1.

82 MacArthur, *Dedan Kimathi on Trial*, 11.

83 Barkham, "Man against Man in the Jungle."

84 "Mau Mau Men to Attend Kenya Celebrations," *New York Times*, December 9, 1963, 8.

85 "Repatriation is a theological, not a political, concept." It has three aspects: (1) "Repatriation is a divine not a human act"; (2) "Repatriation means the return of Africans not to any country of Africa, nor even to West Africa, but specifically to Ethiopia"; (3) "Repatriation also includes the concept of justice, by which Europeans would give up the lands they have seized from the Amerindians and return to Europe." Chevannes, *Rastafari and Other African-Caribbean Worldviews*, 31.

86 Kuumba and Ajanaku, "Dreadlocks," 231.

87 Clarke, *Black Paradise*, 90.

88 Botchway, " . . . The Hairs of Your Head," 33.

89 Goldenberg, *Curse of Ham*.

90 D. A. Thomas, *Exceptional Violence*, 200.

91 D. A. Thomas, *Exceptional Violence*, 200.

92 Fraser, "Two Portraits of Rastafarians." Beginning in 1960, the *New York Times* associated Rastafarianism with crime, printing stories that included the term *Rastafarian* along with words like *cult* and *cult killing*. These stories continued into the mid-seventies, when *Rastafarian* became associated with reggae and musician Bob Marley.

93 Pollard, "Social History of Dread Talk," 23.

94 Wagner-Pacifici, *Discourse and Destruction*, 14.

95 Evans, MOVE, 38.

96 James, *John Africa*, 58.

97 Louise Africa authored the first column, "ON THE MOVE: From the Writings of John Africa," *Philadelphia Tribune*, June 28, 1975, 17. Louise Africa, "ON THE MOVE," *Philadelphia Tribune*, May 15, 1976, 6.

98 Anderson and Hevenor, *Burning Down the House*, 11.

99 Anderson and Hevenor, *Burning Down the House*, 23.

100 Harry, "*Attention, MOVE!*," 100.

101 D. A. Thomas, *Exceptional Violence*, 204.

102 Robinson, *Black Marxism*, 73.

103 Hong, *Death beyond Disavowal*, 19.

104 Iton, *In Search*, 102.

CHAPTER 3. TOUCH

1   Colucci, "Black Is and Black Ain't."

2   A. Edwards, *Blackness in Abstraction*, 174.

3   Gillman, *Inscribing the Other*, 32.

4   Beugnet, *Cinema and Sensation*, 65.

5   Marks, *Skin of the Film*, 118.

6   Hartman, "Seduction and the Ruses."

7   Miles, *Photography, Truth and Reconciliation*.

8   Vokes, *Photography in Africa*, 12; see also Newberry, *Defiant Images*.

9   Herreman and Sieber, *Hair in African Art*.

10 Sieber and Herreman, "Hair in African Art," 57.

11 Poole, "Excess of Description," 167.

12 K. Thompson, "Sidelong Glance," 13.

13 Museu de Arte Moderna do Rio de Janeiro, *African Photography*, 14.

14 Diawara, "1960s in Bamako," 254.

15 Pinney, "Notes from the Surface," 216.

16 Olin, *Touching Photographs*, 3.

17 Ojeikere, *J. D. 'Okhai Ojeikere*. Ojeikere is said to have photographed more than one thousand hairstyles in his forty years of working. See Bromwich, "Nigerian Women's Elaborate Hairstyles—in Pictures."

18 Museu de Arte Moderna do Rio de Janeiro, *African Photography*, 16.

19 Museu de Arte Moderna do Rio de Janeiro, *African Photography*, 55.

20 Museu de Arte Moderna do Rio de Janeiro, *African Photography*, 53.

21 Museu de Arte Moderna do Rio de Janeiro, *African Photography*, 51.

22 Museu de Arte Moderna do Rio de Janeiro, *African Photography*, 49.

23 Fleetwood, *Troubling Vision*, 58.

24 Oguibe, "Photography and the Substance," 579.

25 Giacalone, "Collecting Images for the Future," 198.

26 Okeke-Agulu, *Postcolonial Modernism*, 261.

27 Hair and photography also provide visual evidence of war in Nigeria, as fight-ing impacted dress and hairstyles among Igbo women. These shifts are evident in "several photographs of Biafrans taken during the war show[ing] that many women shaved their hair" and discontinued "elaborate self-fashioning for cere-monial purpose." See Nwigwe, "Igbo Women's Fashion," 173.

28 Haney and Bajorek, "Vital Signs," 220.

29 Gaskins, *Good and Bad Hair*, preface.

30 Kelley and Lewis, *To Make Our World Anew*, 318–19.

31 Coleman, *African American Viewers*, 97.

32 Gray, *Watching Race*, 61.

33 Guerrero, *Framing Blackness*, 160.

34 Gillespie, *Film Blackness*, 76.

35 Gates, *Double Negative*, 83.

36 Klotman and Cutler, *Struggles for Representation*, xvii.

37 Richardson, "Our Stories," 102.

38 Martin, "Madeline Anderson in Conversation," 73.

39 Aufderheide, *Documentary Film*, 6.

40 J. N. Cobb and Jackson, "They Hate Me," 263.

41 Hankin, "And Introducing," 64.

42 Grant, *Documenting the Documentary*, xxiv.

43 Kimbell and Huelsbeck, "Nappy or Straight," 55.

44 Gunning, "Peter Tscherkassky," 102.

45 "Transition" refers to the lengthening of permanently straightened hair before cutting it off, to leave only textured hair remaining.

46 Kimbell sued Rock unsuccessfully for copyright infringement, claiming his film was inspired by *My Nappy Roots*, which she shared with the comedian. Kennedy, "Judge Dumps Lawsuit against Good Hair."

47 Carr, "Paraphernalia of Suffering," 58.

48 Poole, *Vision, Race, and Modernity*, 8.

49 Banet-Weiser, *Empowered*, 23.

50 Wiegman, *American Anatomies*, 21.

51 Wallis, "Dream Life of a People," 9.

52 Powell, *Cutting a Figure*, 10.

53 Christian, *Open TV*, 122.

54 Hight, "Field of Digital Documentary," 5.

55 The system—originally attributed to Andre Walker, stylist to Oprah Winfrey and product entrepreneur—is also critiqued for promoting racial hierarchy that values European hair textures. Walker's system differentiates hair texture by curl pattern but can often distinguish hair along racial lines, categorizing coiffure on a scale from 1 to 4. Afro hair textures fit into categories 3 and 4, which Walker explains are "kinky, or very tightly curled," perhaps "very wiry, very tightly coiled," appearing coarse, "but . . . actually quite fine, with lots and lots of thin strands densely packed together. Healthy Type 4 hair won't shine, but it will have sheen"; it "looks tough and durable, but looks can be deceiving." Walker, *Andre Talks Hair!*, 34.

56 Raiford, *Imprisoned in a Luminous Glare*, 166.

57 *Sisterlocks* is a proprietary textured style protected from copyright infringement. See the trademark/copyright acknowledgment at http://www.sisterlocks.com /uploads/8/3/4/6/8346058/trademark_acknowledgement.pdf.

58 "Executive Summary," 2.

59 Ornelas, *Black Consumers and Haircare*, 1.

60 Julee Wilson, "Natural Hair Book."

CHAPTER 4. SURFACE

1 K. Jones, "In the Thick of It," 22.

2 Copeland, "In the Wake of the Negress," 490.

3 Fisher, "Relational Sense," 4.

4 "Visitors" to collections and museums "touched objects" in order to "experience them intimately" before learning deference toward objects, fear of their ruin, and that "touch had no cognitive or aesthetic uses and thus was of no value in the museum," where these values were essential. Classen, *Deepest Sense*, 141–45.

5 Hanna, *Women Framing Hair*, 181.

6 Curry-Evans et al., *HairStories*, 14.

7 Lewis, "Groundwork," 94.

8 Kelley, "Fugitives from a Chain Store," 13.

9 Hudson, "1000 Words."

10 Carter-David, "'To Mirror the Happier Side,'" 38.

11 Simon, "Easy to Remember," 12.

12 Alexander, "Genius of Romare Bearden," 62.

13 Gordon, *Existence in Black*, 74.

14 Zuckerman, "Daring as a Woman."

15 Murray, "Kehinde Wiley," 97.

16 Deitch, "Representing Kehinde Wiley," 41.

17 Enwezor, "Repetition and Differentiation."

18 Elder, "Lorna Simpson's Fabricated Truths," 53.

19 Copeland, *Bound to Appear*, 92.

20 Copeland, "'Bye, Bye Black Girl,'" 77.

21 Pandolfi, "1858 Prize Profile: Sonya Clark."

22 Francis, "Art about Hair," 37.

23 Clark and Rovine, *African Inspirations*, 18.

24 jegede, *Encyclopedia of African American Artists*, 39.

25 Held and Lineberry, *Crafting a Continuum*, 9.

26 S. Clark, "Hair Craft Project," 91.

27 *Hair Craft Project* was displayed at the 1708 Gallery in Richmond, Virginia; at the
    Kendall College of Art and Design in Grand Rapids, Michigan; and at the Museum of Fine Arts, Boston. I viewed the work in Boston, which was also the setting for Clark's performance work "Hairdressers Are My Heroes," on October 12,
    2015.

28 I asked Clark about this distinction within the exhibition, but she explained that
    a label was unnecessary. "No need to do that in a museum as people tend to know
    that touching the art is off limits." Sonya Clark, message to the author, March
    28, 2016. Along these lines, the *Hair Craft Project* was the only display within the
    Crafted Objects exhibition without a label warning "Do not touch."

29 Eglash, *African Fractals*, 112.

30 Eglash, *African Fractals*, 81.

31 Eglash, *African Fractals*, 113.

32 "Hair is not just a 'personal effect'; it holds a much deeper significance when it
    comes to working gris gris. Hair represents an important part of the soul called *ni*.
    When you take a piece of a person's hair and work gris gris with it, you are working
    with a sympathetic link to that person's soul. Cowry shells are significant because
    they were not only used as currency and decoration, but are sacred today because
    they come from the deep waters from the bed of Faro, the androgynous water spirit
    whose job it was to reinstate harmony between the sexes. This reverence to the
    earth as Mother and sacredness is one of many beliefs that were held in common by
    the Africans and the Native Americans." Alvarado, *Voodoo Hoodoo Spellbook*, 204.

33 S. Clark, *Hair Craft Project*, ix.

34 K. S. Johnson, "Political Hair," 418.

35 *Meschac Gaba: Tresses*, installation at the Studio Museum in Harlem, January 26
    to March 27, 2005. https://studiomuseum.org/exhibition/meschac-gaba-tresses.

36 Sonya Clark, message to the author, March 28, 2016.

37 Sonya Clark, message to the author, March 28, 2016.

38 Judith Wilson, "Down to the Crossroads," 107.

39 Dallow, "Reclaiming Histories," 93.

40 K. Jones, *South of Pico*, 68.

41 "Alison Saar and Thelma Golden."

42 R. F. Thompson, *Flash of the Spirit*, 145.

43 Mercer, "New Practices, New Identities," 254.

44 Saar, "Fighting Flatness," 96.

45 Libby, *Slavery in Frontier Mississippi*, 32. Libby explains how the labor-intensive
    process of creating the blue dye, once industrialized and subsidized by the British Crown, transformed the artisanal work of dye making in West Africa into the

grueling work of harvesting, boiling, churning, and draining, all done by unfree Blacks on plantations.

46 Knight, "In an Ocean of Blue," 74.

47 Telfair Museum of Art, *Collection Highlights*, 45. A haint/hant is considered an "evil witchlike supernatural being that is believed to chase its victims to their death"; and haint blue—"a deep, rich sky blue color believed to repel haints"—is a paint used by "believers" and said "to protect their windows and doors from entry by a haint." See Hazzard-Donald, *Mojo Workin'*, 207.

48 Trotter, *Workers on Arrival*.

49 Gilmore, *Gender and Jim Crow*, 23.

50 Jacobs, *Incidents*, 16.

CONCLUSION. CROWNING GESTURES

1 Finley, *Committed to Memory*, 11.

2 H. W. Thomas, "All Power to All People."

3 Coote, "Exhibition Review," 81.

4 Ellington, "Conception of *Textures*," 16.

5 Between July 2019 and May 2020, some states passed the CROWN Act or amended human rights laws. These include California, Colorado, Maryland, New Jersey, New York, Virginia, and Washington.

6 CROWN Act of 2020, H.R. 5309, 116th Cong. (2020).

7 DeAndre Arnold was excluded from graduation proceedings at Barbers Hill High School in Mont Belvieu, Texas; student-athlete Andrew Johnson of Buena Regional High School in New Jersey had his locks forcibly cut on the sidelines of a wrestling match as a condition of competition; twin sisters Deanna and Mya Cook were sentenced to school detentions for box braids at Mystic Valley Regional Charter School; students protested at Pretoria High School for Girls in South Africa after harassment to "fix" their hair from the administrators. Lattimore, "When Black Hair Violates"; Mahr, "Protests over Black Girls' Hair."

Natural hairstyles were cited as the cause for termination of one meteorologist at a Louisiana news station in 2013 and were discouraged by the MBA program at Hampton University, a historically Black college. Julee Wilson, "Black Women Worry."

8 Haley, *No Mercy Here*, 5.

9 Chambers-Letson, *After the Party*, 6.

10 In a 2019 survey commissioned by the CROWN Coalition, 1,017 Black women and 1,050 non-Black women, ages twenty-five to sixty-four, who had worked full time in an office or in sales within the past six months, answered questions about their experiences around hair in the workplace. Dove, *CROWN Research Study*. The CROWN Coalition, founded in 2019, is a national alliance founded by Dove, the National Urban League, Color of Change, and Western Center on Law and Poverty to end race-based hair discrimination in the United States.

11 Staged in Union Square, New York City, on June 6, 2013, "You Can Touch My Hair" was organized by Un-ruly, an online platform dedicated to the discussion of race and beauty and founded by entrepreneur and former advertising executive Antonia Opiah.

12 Marks, *Skin of the Film*, 139.

Acham, Christine. *Revolution Televised: Prime Time and the Struggle for Black Power*. Minneapolis: University of Minnesota Press, 2004.

Adair, Gigi. *Kinship across the Black Atlantic: Writing Diasporic Relations*. Liverpool: Liverpool University Press, 2019.

Aidoo, Lamonte. *Slavery Unseen: Sex, Power, and Violence in Brazilian History*. Durham, NC: Duke University Press, 2018.

Alexander, Elizabeth. "The Genius of Romare Bearden." In *Something All Our Own: The Grant Hill Collection of African American Art*, edited by Alvia Wardlaw, 57–70. Durham, NC: Duke University Press, 2004.

"Alison Saar and Thelma Golden at L.A. Louver." Interview by Thelma Golden. February 14, 2020. YouTube, March 13, 2020. https://www.youtube.com/watch?v=1qdo6ek_ZBc.

Allain, Jacqueline Mercier. "'They Are Quiet Women Now': Hair Cropping, British Imperial Governance, and the Gendered Body in the Archive." *Slavery and Abolition* 41, no. 4 (April 7, 2020): 772–94.

Alvarado, Denise. *The Voodoo Hoodoo Spellbook*. Newburyport, MA: Red Wheel Weiser, 2011.

Anderson, John, and Hilary Hevenor. *Burning Down the House: MOVE and the Tragedy of Philadelphia*. New York: W. W. Norton, 1987.

Andrews, William L. *To Tell a Free Story: The First Century of Afro-American Autobiography, 1760–1865*. Urbana: University of Illinois Press, 1986.

Antiri, Janet Adwoa. "Akan Combs." *African Arts* 8, no. 1 (Autumn 1974): 32–35.

Araujo, Ana Lucia. *Brazil through French Eyes: A Nineteenth-Century Artist in the Tropics*. Albuquerque: University of New Mexico Press, 2015.

Arnoldi, Mary Jo, and Kris L. Hardin. *African Material Culture*. Bloomington: Indiana University Press, 1996.

Aufderheide, Patricia. *Documentary Film: A Very Short Introduction*. New York: Oxford University Press, 2007.

Avilez, GerShun. *Radical Aesthetics and Modern Black Nationalism*. Urbana: University of Illinois Press, 2016.

Baldwin, Joseph A. "Theory and Research Concerning the Notion of Black Self-Hatred: A Review and Reinterpretation." *Journal of Black Psychology* 5, no. 2 (1979): 51–77.

Ball, Erica, and Kellie Carter Jackson. *Reconsidering Roots: Race, Politics, and Memory.* Athens: University of Georgia Press, 2017.

Banet-Weiser, Sarah. *Empowered: Popular Feminism and Popular Misogyny.* Durham, NC: Duke University Press, 2018.

Banks, Ingrid. *Hair Matters: Beauty, Power, and Black Women's Consciousness.* New York: New York University Press, 2000.

Baptist, Edward E. *The Half Has Never Been Told: Slavery and the Making of American Capitalism.* New York: Basic Books, 2016.

Baradaran, Mehrsa. *The Color of Money: Black Banks and the Racial Wealth Gap.* Cambridge, MA: Belknap Press of Harvard University Press, 2019.

Barkham, John. "Man against Man in the Jungle: *Man Hunt in Kenya*, by Ian Henderson." *New York Times*, August 31, 1958.

Bernasconi, Robert, and Tommy L. Lott, eds. *The Idea of Race.* Indianapolis: Hackett, 2000.

Bernstein, Robin. *Racial Innocence: Performing American Childhood and Race from Slavery to Civil Rights.* New York: New York University Press, 2011.

Berry, Daina Ramey. *The Price for Their Pound of Flesh: The Value of the Enslaved, from Womb to Grave, in the Building of a Nation.* Boston: Beacon Press, 2017.

Best, Stephen, and Sharon Marcus. "Surface Reading: An Introduction." *Representations* 108, no. 1 (Fall 2009): 1–21.

Beugnet, Martine. *Cinema and Sensation: French Film and the Art of Transgression.* Carbondale: Southern Illinois University Press, 2007.

Black Consumers and Haircare, US, August 2015. "Executive Summary." Mintel Reports Database. Accessed March 13, 2022. https://reports.mintel.com/display/716774/.

Blight, David W. *Frederick Douglass: Prophet of Freedom.* New York: Simon and Schuster, 2018.

Bly, Antonio T. *Escaping Bondage: A Documentary History of Runaway Slaves in Eighteenth-Century New England, 1700–1789.* Lanham, MD: Lexington Books, 2012.

Botchway, De-Valera N. Y. M. " . . . The Hairs of Your Head Are All Numbered: Symbolisms of Hair and Dreadlocks in the Boboshanti Order of Rastafari." *Africology: The Journal of Pan African Studies* 12, no. 8 (December 2018): 20–38.

Bourdieu, Pierre. *Language and Symbolic Power.* Translated by Gino Raymond and Matthew Adamson. Cambridge, MA: Harvard University Press, 1991.

Bradley, Rizvana. "Introduction: Other Sensualities." *Women and Performance: A Journal of Feminist Theory* 24, nos. 2–3 (2014): 129–33.

Branch, Daniel. *Defeating Mau Mau, Creating Kenya: Counterinsurgency, Civil War, and Decolonization.* Cambridge: Cambridge University Press, 2009.

Brathwaite, Kwame. *Kwame Brathwaite: Black Is Beautiful.* New York: Aperture, 2019. Exhibition catalog.

Bristol, Douglas W., Jr. *Knights of the Razor: Black Barbers in Slavery and Freedom.* Baltimore, MD: Johns Hopkins University Press, 2009.

Bromwich, Kathryn. "Nigerian Women's Elaborate Hairstyles—in Pictures." *Guardian*, June 23, 2018. https://www.theguardian.com/artanddesign/gallery/2018/jun/23/nigerian-womens-elaborate-hairstyles-in-pictures.

Brown, Tony N., John P. Gomez, and Sherrill L. Sellers. "The Relationship between Internalization and Self-Esteem among Black Adults." *Sociological Focus* 35, no. 1 (February 2002): 55–71.

Browne, Peter A. *Trichologia Mammalium; or, A Treatise on the Organization, Properties, and Uses of Hair and Wool; Together with an Essay upon the Raising and Breeding of Sheep.* Philadelphia: J. H. Jones, 1853.

Browne, Randy M. *Surviving Slavery in the British Caribbean.* Philadelphia: University of Pennsylvania Press, 2017.

Byrd, Ayana D., and Lori L. Tharps. *Hair Story: Untangling the Roots of Black Hair in America.* Rev. ed. New York: St. Martin's Griffin Books, 2014.

Campt, Tina. *Image Matters: Archive, Photography, and the African Diaspora in Europe.* Durham, NC: Duke University Press, 2012.

Campt, Tina. *Listening to Images.* Durham, NC: Duke University Press, 2017.

Carby, Hazel V. *Race Men.* Cambridge, MA: Harvard University Press, 1998.

Carr, Joi. "The Paraphernalia of Suffering: Chris Rock's Good Hair, Still Playing in the Dark." *Black Camera* 5, no. 1 (Fall 2013): 56–71.

Carter-David, Siobhan. "'To Mirror the Happier Side of Negro Life': *Ebony* and *Jet* in Black Cultural and Print History." In *Speaking of People:* Ebony, Jet *and Contemporary Art,* edited by Lauren Haynes, 36–41. New York: Studio Museum in Harlem, 2014. Exhibition catalog.

Chambers-Letson, Joshua Takano. *After the Party: A Manifesto for Queer of Color Life.* New York: New York University Press, 2018.

Chesnutt, Charles Waddell. *Frederick Douglass.* Boston: Small, Maynard, 1899.

Chevannes, Barry, ed. *Rastafari and Other African-Caribbean Worldviews.* New Brunswick, NJ: Rutgers University Press, 1998.

Chevannes, Barry. *Rastafari: Roots and Ideology.* Syracuse, NY: Syracuse University Press, 1994.

Christian, Aymar Jean. *Open TV: Innovation beyond Hollywood and the Rise of Web Television.* New York: New York University Press, 2018.

Clark, Kenneth B., and Mamie P. Clark. "The Development of Consciousness of Self and the Emergence of Racial Identification in Negro Pre-School Children." *Journal of Social Psychology* 10, no. 4 (1939): 591–99.

Clark, Kenneth B., and Mamie P. Clark. "Emotional Factors in Racial Identification and Preference in Negro Children." *Journal of Negro Education* 19, no. 3 (1950): 341–50.

Clark, Sonya, and Victoria L. Rovine. *African Inspirations: Sculpted Headwear by Sonya Clark.* Iowa City: University of Iowa Museum of Art, 2001. Exhibition catalog.

Clark, Sonya. *The Hair Craft Project.* Richmond, VA: 1708 Gallery, 2014. Exhibition catalog.

Clark, Sonya. "Hair Craft Project." *Nka: Journal of Contemporary African Art,* 37, no. 1 (November 2015): 90–92.

Clarke, Peter B. *Black Paradise: The Rastafarian Movement.* San Bernadino, CA: Borgo Press, 1986.

Classen, Constance. *The Deepest Sense: A Cultural History of Touch.* Urbana: University of Illinois Press, 2012.

Clegg, John J. "Capitalism and Slavery." *Critical Historical Studies* 2, no. 2 (Fall 2015): 281–304.

Clegg, John J. "Credit Market Discipline and Capitalist Slavery in Antebellum South Carolina." *Social Science History* 42, no. 2 (Summer 2018): 343–76.

Cobb, Jasmine Nichole. "Directed by Himself: Steve McQueen's *12 Years a Slave*." *American Literary History* 26, no. 2 (Summer 2014): 339–46.

Cobb, Jasmine Nichole, and Jackson, John L. Jr. "They Hate Me: Spike Lee, Documentary Filmmaking, and Hollywood's 'Savage Slot.'" In *Fight the Power! The Spike Lee Reader*, edited by Janice Hamlet and Robin Means Coleman, 251–72. New York: Peter Lang, 2009.

Cobb, Thomas R. R. *An Inquiry into the Law of Negro Slavery in the United States of America*. Philadelphia: T. and J. W. Johnson, 1858.

Colbert, Charles. *A Measure of Perfection: Phrenology and the Fine Arts in America*. Chapel Hill: University of North Carolina Press, 1997.

Colbert, Soyica Diggs. *Black Movements: Performance and Cultural Politics*. New Brunswick, NJ: Rutgers University Press, 2017.

Cole, Teju. "A True Picture of Black Skin." *New York Times Magazine*, February 18, 2015.

Coleman, Robin R. Means. *African American Viewers and the Black Situation Comedy: Situating Racial Humor*. New York: Garland, 1998.

Colucci, Emily. "Black Is and Black Ain't in Pace Gallery's 'Blackness in Abstraction.'" *Art City*, August 18, 2016. http://artfcity.com/2016/08/18/black-is-and-black-aint -in-pace-gallerys-Blackness-in-abstraction/.

Coote, Jeremy. "Exhibition Review: Origins of the Afro Comb: 6,000 Years of Culture, Politics, and Identity." *African Arts* 50, no. 4 (Winter 2017): 80–82.

Copeland, Huey. *Bound to Appear: Art, Slavery, and the Site of Blackness in Multicultural America*. Chicago: University of Chicago Press, 2013.

Copeland, Huey. "'Bye, Bye Black Girl': Lorna Simpson's Figurative Retreat." *Art Journal* 64, no. 2 (Summer 2005): 62–77.

Copeland, Huey. "In the Wake of the Negress." In *Modern Women: Women Artists at the Museum of Modern Art*, edited by Cornelia Butler and Alexandra Schwartz, 480–97. New York: Museum of Modern Art, 2010.

Copeland, Huey. "Rashid Johnson." *Artforum International* 50, no. 10 (Summer 2012): 302–3.

Crawford, Margo Natalie. *Black Post-Blackness: The Black Arts Movement and Twenty-First-Century Aesthetics*. Urbana: University of Illinois Press, 2017.

Crawford, Margo Natalie. *Dilution Anxiety and the Black Phallus*. Columbus: Ohio State University Press, 2008.

Curry-Evans, Kim, Susan Krane, Neal A. Lester, Pamela Sneed, Charles H. Nelson, and Kevin Powell. *HairStories*. Scottsdale, AZ: Scottsdale Museum of Contemporary Art, 2003. Exhibition catalog.

Cvetkovich, Ann. *An Archive of Feelings: Trauma, Sexuality, and Lesbian Public Cultures*. Durham, NC: Duke University Press, 2003.

Dallow, Jessica. "Reclaiming Histories: Betye and Alison Saar, Feminism, and the Representation of Black Womanhood." *Feminist Studies* 30, no. 1 (Spring 2004): 74–113.

Danois, Ericka Blount. *Love, Peace, and Soul: Behind the Scenes of America's Favorite Dance Show: Classic Moments*. Montclair, NJ: Backbeat Books, 2013.

Davis, Angela Y. "Afro Images: Politics, Fashion, and Nostalgia." *Critical Inquiry* 21, no. 1 (Autumn 1994): 37–45.

Dawson, Gowan, Bernard Lightman, Sally Shuttleworth, and Jonathan R. Topham. *Science Periodicals in Nineteenth-Century Britain: Constructing Scientific Communities*. Chicago: University of Chicago Press, 2020.

Debret, Jean Baptiste. V*oyage pittoresque et historique au Brésil, ou Séjour d'un artiste français au Brésil, depuis 1816 jusqu'en 1831 inclusivement, epoques de l'avènement et de l'abdication de S. M. D. Pedro 1er, fondateur de l'Empire brésilien*. Paris: Firmin Didot Frères, 1834–39.

Deitch, Jeffrey. "Representing Kehinde Wiley." In *Kehinde Wiley: A New Republic*, edited by Eugenie Tsai, 41. Brooklyn: Brooklyn Museum in association with Del Monico Books/Prestel, 2015. Exhibition catalog.

Delmont, Matthew F. *Making Roots: A Nation Captivated*. Oakland: University of California Press, 2016.

DeWyze, Jeannette. "Willie Morrow and How California Curl Made It without San Diego Banks." *San Diego Reader*, October 29, 1981. https://AfroSheen.sandiegoreader .com/news/1981/oct/29/cover-its-curly-at-the-top/#.

Diawara, Manthia. "The 1960s in Bamako: Malick Sidibé and James Brown." In *Black Cultural Traffic Crossroads in Global Performance and Popular Culture*, edited by Harry J. Elam Jr. and Kennell Jackson, 242–65. Ann Arbor: University of Michigan Press, 2005.

Din, Gilbert C. *Spaniards, Planters, and Slaves: The Spanish Regulation of Slavery in Louisiana, 1763–1803*. College Station: Texas A&M University Press, 1999.

Douglas, Emory, and Sam Durant, eds. *Black Panther: The Revolutionary Art of Emory Douglas*. New York: Rizzoli, 2007.

Douglass, Frederick. "Frederick Douglass to Francis Jackson." In *The Frederick Douglass Papers: Series Three, Correspondence*. Vol. 1, *1842–1852*, edited by John R. McKivigan, 89–91. New Haven, CT: Yale University Press, 2009.

Douglass, Frederick. "John Jacobus Flournoy to Frederick Douglass," *The Frederick Douglass Papers: Series Three, Correspondence*. Vol. 1, *1842–1852*, edited by John R. McKivigan, 326–29. New Haven, CT: Yale University Press, 2009.

Douglass, Frederick. *Life and Times of Frederick Douglass Written by Himself . . . With an Introduction by Mr. George L. Ruffin, of Boston*. Boston: De Wolfe and Fiske, 1892.

Douglass, Frederick. *My Bondage and My Freedom. Part I.—Life as a Slave. Part II.—Life as a Freeman*. New York: Miller, Orton and Mulligan, 1855.

Douglass, Frederick. *Narrative of the Life of Frederick Douglass, an American Slave: Written by Himself*. Boston: Anti-Slavery Office, 1845.

Dove. *The CROWN Research Study: Creating a Respectful and Open Workplace for Natural Hair*. Brochure. Accessed April 20, 2022. https://static1.squarespace.com/static /5edc69fd622c36173f56651f/t/5edeaa2fe5ddef345e087361/1591650865168/Dove _research_brochure2020_FINAL3.pdf.

Dubey, Madhu. "Freedom Now: Black Power and the Literature of Slavery." In *Black Cultural Production after Civil Rights*, edited by Robert J. Patterson, 30–47. Urbana: University of Illinois Press, 2019.

Edwards, Adrienne. *Blackness in Abstraction*. New York: Pace Gallery, 2016. Exhibition catalog.

Edwards, Brent Hayes. *The Practice of Diaspora: Literature, Translation, and the Rise of Black Internationalism*. Cambridge, MA: Harvard University Press, 2003.

Edwards, Erica R. *Charisma and Fictions of Black Leadership*. Minneapolis: University of Minnesota Press, 2012.

Eglash, Ron. *African Fractals: Modern Computing and Indigenous Design*. New Brunswick, NJ: Rutgers University Press, 1999.

Elam, Harry Justin. *Taking It to the Streets: The Social Protest Theater of Luis Valdez and Amiri Baraka*. Ann Arbor: University of Michigan Press, 1997.

Elder, Nika. "Lorna Simpson's Fabricated Truths." *Art Journal* 77, no. 1 (2018): 30–53.

Ellington, Tameka N. "The Conception of *Textures: The History and Art of Black Hair*." In *Textures: The History and Art of Black Hair*, edited by Joseph L. Underwood and Tameka Ellington, 13–18. Munich: Hirmer, 2022. Exhibition catalog.

Ellis, Trey. "The New Black Aesthetic." *Callaloo* 38 (Winter 1989): 233–43.

Enwezor, Okwui. "Repetition and Differentiation—Lorna Simpson's Iconography of the Racial Sublime." In *Lorna Simpson*, edited by Okwui Enwezor, 102–31. New York: Abrams and American Federation of Arts, 2006. Exhibition catalog.

Ernest, John. *Douglass in His Own Time: A Biographic Chronicle of His Life, Drawn from Recollections, Interviews, and Memoirs by Family, Friends, and Associates*. Iowa City: University of Iowa Press, 2014.

Evans, Richard Kent. *MOVE: An American Religion*. New York: Oxford University Press, 2020.

"Executive Summary." *Black Consumers and Haircare: US, August 2015*. Mintel Reports Database, 2015. Accessed March 13, 2022. https://reports.mintel.com/display/716774/.

Fabian, Ann. *The Skull Collectors: Race, Science, and America's Unburied Dead*. Chicago: University of Chicago Press, 2010.

Farmer, Ashley D. *Remaking Black Power: How Black Women Transformed an Era*. Chapel Hill: University of North Carolina Press, 2017.

Ferguson, Roderick. *The Reorder of Things: The University and Its Pedagogies of Minority Difference*. Minneapolis: University of Minnesota Press, 2012.

Finley, Cheryl. *Committed to Memory: The Art of the Slave Ship Icon*. Princeton, NJ: Princeton University Press, 2018.

Fisher, Jennifer. "Relational Sense: Towards a Haptic Aesthetics." *Parachute: Contemporary Art Magazine* 87 (July–September 1997): 4–11.

Fleetwood, Nicole R. *Troubling Vision: Performance, Visuality, and Blackness*. Chicago: University of Chicago Press, 2011.

Ford, Tanisha C. *Liberated Threads: Black Women, Style, and the Global Politics of Soul*. Chapel Hill: University of North Carolina Press, 2015.

Ford, Tanisha C. "SNCC Women, Denim, and the Politics of Dress." *Journal of Southern History* 79, no. 3 (August 2013): 625–58.

Ford, Tanisha C. "This Black, Buy Black." In Brathwaite, *Kwame Brathwaite: Black Is Beautiful*, 39–63. New York: Aperture, 2019.

Foreman, P. Gabrielle. "Who's Your Mama? 'White' Mulatta Genealogies, Early

Photography, and Anti-passing Narratives of Slavery and Freedom." In Wallace and Smith, *Pictures and Progress*, 132–66.

Fought, Leigh. *Women in the World of Frederick Douglass*. New York: Oxford University Press, 2017.

Fox-Amato, Matthew. *Exposing Slavery: Photography, Human Bondage, and the Birth of Modern Visual Politics in America*. New York: Oxford University Press, 2019.

Francis, Jacqueline. "Art about Hair." *International Review of African American Art* 15, no. 2 (January 1998): 37–38.

Franklin, John Hope, and Loren Schweninger. *Runaway Slaves: Rebels on the Plantation*. New York: Oxford University Press, 1999.

Fraser, C. Gerald. "Two Portraits of Rastafarians: A Cult of Violence or Righteousness." *New York Times*, June 21, 1977.

Gaskins, Bill. *Good and Bad Hair: Photographs*. New Brunswick, NJ: Rutgers University Press, 1997.

Gates, Racquel J. *Double Negative: The Black Image and Popular Imagination*. Durham, NC: Duke University Press, 2018.

Giacalone, Clara. "Collecting Images for the Future: Rethinking J. D. 'Okhai Ojeikere's Photography as Archival Practice." In *New Spaces for Negotiating Art and Histories in Africa*, edited by Kerstin Pinther, Berit Fischer, and Ugochukwu-Smooth C. Nzewi, 196–213. Berlin: LIT, 2015.

Gill, Tiffany. *Beauty Shop Politics: African American Women's Activism in the Beauty Industry*. Urbana: University of Illinois Press, 2010.

Gillespie, Michael Boyce. *Film Blackness: American Cinema and the Idea of Black Film*. Durham, NC: Duke University Press, 2016.

Gillman, Sander L. *Inscribing the Other*. Lincoln: University of Nebraska Press, 1991.

Gilmore, Glenda Elizabeth. *Gender and Jim Crow: Women and the Politics of White Supremacy in North Carolina, 1896–1920*. Chapel Hill: University of North Carolina Press, 1996.

Glymph, Thavolia. *Out of the House of Bondage: The Transformation of the Plantation Household*. Cambridge: Cambridge University Press, 2008.

Goldenberg, David M. *The Curse of Ham: Race and Slavery in Early Judaism, Christianity, and Islam*. Princeton, NJ: Princeton University Press, 2003.

Gordon, Lewis R. "Black Aesthetics, Black Value." *Public Culture* 30, no. 1 (2018): 19–34.

Gordon, Lewis R., ed. *Existence in Black: An Anthology of Black Existential Philosophy*. New York: Routledge, 1997.

Grant, Barry Keith. *Documenting the Documentary: Close Readings of Documentary Film and Video*, 2nd ed. Detroit, MI: Wayne State University Press, 2014.

Gray, Herman. *Watching Race: Television and the Struggle for "Blackness."* Minneapolis: University of Minnesota Press, 1995.

Grier, William H., and Price M. Cobbs. *Black Rage*. London: Jonathan Cape, 1968.

Gross, Kali Nicole. *Hannah Mary Tabbs and the Disembodied Torso: A Tale of Race, Sex, and Violence in America*. New York: Oxford University Press, 2016.

Guerrero, Ed. *Framing Blackness: The African American Image in Film*. Philadelphia: Temple University Press, 1993.

Guillory, John. "Bourdieu's Refusal." In *Pierre Bourdieu: Fieldwork in Culture*, edited by Nicholas Brown and Imre Szeman, 19–43. Lanham, MD: Rowman and Littlefield, 2000.

Gunning, Tom. "Peter Tscherkassky Manufractures Two Minutes of (Im)Pure Cinema." In *Process Cinema: Handmade Film in the Digital Age*, edited by Scott MacKenzie and Janine Marchessault, 96–107. Montreal: McGill–Queen's University Press, 2019.

Haley, Sarah. *No Mercy Here: Gender, Punishment, and the Making of Jim Crow Modernity*. Chapel Hill: University of North Carolina Press, 2016.

Hall, Rachel. "Missing Dolly, Mourning Slavery: The Slave Notice as Keepsake." *Camera Obscura* 21, no. 1 (61) (2006): 71–103.

Haney, Erin, and Jennifer Bajorek. "Vital Signs: 21st-Century Institutions for Photography in Africa." In *The African Photographic Archive: Research and Curatorial Strategies,* edited by Christopher Morton and Darren Newbury, 215–30. New York: Bloomsbury Academic, 2015.

Hankin, Kelly. "And Introducing . . . the Female Director: Documentaries about Women Filmmakers as Feminist Activism." *NWSA Journal* 19, no. 1 (Spring 2007): 59–88.

Hanna, Heather. *Women Framing Hair: Serial Strategies in Contemporary Art*. New Castle upon Tyne, UK: Cambridge Scholars Publishing, 2015.

Hardt, Michael, and Antonio Negri. *Empire*. Cambridge, MA: Harvard University Press, 2000.

Harney, Stefano, and Fred Moten. *The Undercommons: Fugitive Planning and Black Study*. Wivenhoe, UK: Minor Compositions, 2013.

Harris, Cheryl I. "Whiteness as Property." *Harvard Law Review* 106, no. 8 (June 1993): 1707–91.

Harry, Margot. *"Attention, MOVE! This Is America!"* Chicago: Banner Press, 1987.

Hartman, Saidiya. "Seduction and the Ruses of Power." *Callaloo* 19, no. 2 (1996): 537–60.

Hazzard-Donald, Katrina. *Mojo Workin': The Old African American Hoodoo System*. Urbana: University of Illinois Press, 2013.

Held, Peter, and Heather Sealy Lineberry, eds. *Crafting a Continuum: Rethinking Contemporary Craft*. Santa Barbara: Perpetua Press, 2013. Exhibition catalog.

Herreman, Frank, and Roy Sieber, eds. *Hair in African Art and Culture*. New York: Museum for African Art, 2000.

Higginbotham, Evelyn. *Righteous Discontent: The Women's Movement in the Black Baptist Church, 1880–1920*. Cambridge, MA: Harvard University Press, 1993.

Hight, Craig. "The Field of Digital Documentary: A Challenge to Documentary Theorists." *Studies in Documentary Film* 2, no. 1 (2008): 3–7.

Hodges, Graham Russell Gao, and Alan Edward Brown, eds. *"Pretends to Be Free": Runaway Slave Advertisements from Colonial and Revolutionary New York and New Jersey*. New York: Fordham University Press, 2019.

Holland, Frederic May. *Frederick Douglass: The Colored Orator*. New York: Funk and Wagnalls, 1895.

Holm, Christiane. "Sentimental Cuts: Eighteenth-Century Mourning Jewelry with Hair." *Eighteenth-Century Studies* 38, no. 1 (Fall 2004): 139–43.

Hong, Grace Kyungwon. *Death beyond Disavowal: The Impossible Politics of Difference*. Minneapolis: University of Minnesota Press, 2015.

Hudson, Suzanne P. "1000 Words: Ellen Gallagher." *Artforum International* 42, no. 8 (April 2004). https://www.artforum.com/print/200404/1000-words-ellen -gallagher-6573.

Hunter, Margaret L. *Race, Gender, and the Politics of Skin Tone*. New York: Routledge, 2005.

Irigaray, Luce. *This Sex Which Is Not One*. Translated by Catherine Porter with Carolyn Burke. Ithaca, NY: Cornell University Press, 1985.

Iton, Richard. *In Search of the Black Fantastic: Politics and Popular Culture in the Post-Civil Rights Era*. New York: Oxford University Press, 2008.

Jacobs, Harriet A. *Incidents in the Life of a Slave Girl: Written by Herself*. Edited by L. Maria Child. Boston: Published for the Author, 1861.

Jacobs-Huey, Lanita. *From the Kitchen to the Parlor: Language and Becoming in African American Women's Hair Care*. New York: Oxford University Press, 2006.

James, Louise Leaphart. *John Africa . . . Childhood Untold until Today*. Bloomington, IN: Xlibris, 2013.

Jarrell, Wadsworth. *AFRICOBRA: Experimental Art toward a School of Thought*. Durham, NC: Duke University Press, 2020.

Jay, Martin. *Downcast Eyes: The Denigration of Vision in Twentieth-Century French Thought*. Berkeley: University of California Press, 1993.

jegede, dele. *Encyclopedia of African American Artists*. Westport, CT: Greenwood Press, 2009.

Johnson, Kimberley S. "Political Hair: Occupational Licensing and the Regulation of Race and Gender Identity." *Du Bois Review* 8, no. 2 (2011): 417–40.

Johnson, Walter. *River of Dark Dreams: Slavery and Empire in the Cotton Kingdom*. Cambridge, MA: Belknap Press of Harvard University Press, 2013.

Johnson, Walter. *Soul by Soul: Life inside the Antebellum Slave Market*. Cambridge, MA: Harvard University Press, 1999.

Jones, Kellie. *Eyeminded: Living and Writing Contemporary Art*. Durham, NC: Duke University Press, 2011.

Jones, Kellie. "In the Thick of It: David Hammons and Hair Culture in the 1970s." *Third Text* 12, no. 44 (1998): 17–24.

Jones, Kellie. *South of Pico: African American Artists in Los Angeles in the 1960s and 1970s*. Durham, NC: Duke University Press, 2017.

Jones, Tayari. *An American Marriage*. Chapel Hill, NC: Algonquin Books of Chapel Hill, 2018.

Jordan, Winthrop D. *White over Black: American Attitudes toward the Negro, 1550–1812*. 2nd ed. Chapel Hill: University of North Carolina Press, 2012.

July, Michael. *Afros: A Celebration of Natural Hair*. Brooklyn, NY: Natural Light Press, 2013.

Kanogo, Tabitha. *Squatters and the Roots of Mau Mau, 1905–63*. London: J. Curry, 1987.

Katz-Hyman, Martha B., and Kym S. Rice. *World of a Slave: Encyclopedia of the Material Life of Slaves in the United States*. Santa Barbara, CA: Greenwood, 2011.

Kelley, Robin D. G. "Fugitives from a Chain Store." In *Ellen Gallagher: Preserve* 11–20. Des Moines: Des Moines Art Center, 2001. Exhibition catalog.

Kelley, Robin D. G. "Nap Time: Historicizing the Afro." *Fashion Theory* 1, no. 4 (1997): 339–51.

Kelley, Robin D. G., and Earl Lewis, eds. *To Make Our World Anew: A History of African Americans*. Vol. 1, *To 1880*. New York: Oxford University Press, 2005.

Kennedy, John. "Judge Dumps Lawsuit against Good Hair." Vibe.com, October 9, 2009. https://www.vibe.com/news/national/judge-dumps-lawsuit-against-good-hair-47048/.

Kimbell, Regina, and Mary Huelsbeck. "A Black Camera Interview: Nappy or Straight—Must We Choose? Regina Kimbell on Black Hair-Itage." *Black Camera* 22/23 (Spring 2008): 49–59.

King, Wilma. *Stolen Childhood: Slave Youth in Nineteenth-Century America*. Bloomington: Indiana University Press, 1998.

Klotman, Phyllis R., and Janet K. Cutler, eds. *Struggles for Representation: African American Documentary Film and Video*. Bloomington: Indiana University Press, 1999.

Knight, Frederick. "In an Ocean of Blue: West African Indigo Workers in the Atlantic World to 1800." In *Diasporic Africa: A Reader*, edited by Michael A. Gomez, 59–86. New York: New York University Press, 2006.

Kragen, Pam. "The Black Hair Story: '400 Years without a Comb.'" *San Diego Union-Tribune*, January 15, 2016. https://AfroSheen.sandiegouniontribune.com/lifestyle/people/sdut-400-years-without-a-comb-exhibit-2016jan15-htmlstory.html.

Kuumba, M. Bahati, and Femi Ajanaku. "Dreadlocks: The Hair Aesthetics of Cultural Resistance and Collective Identity Formation." *Mobilization: An International Quarterly* 3, no. 2 (1998): 227–43.

Larson, Kate Clifford. *Bound for the Promised Land: Harriet Tubman, Portrait of An American Hero*. New York: Ballantine, 2004.

Latrobe, Benjamin Henry. *The Journal of Latrobe*. New York: D. Appleton, 1905.

Lattimore, Kayla. "When Black Hair Violates the Dress Code." NPR, July 17, 2017. https://www.npr.org/sections/ed/2017/07/17/534448313/when-black-hair-violates-the-dress-code.

Lehman, Christopher P. *A Critical History of Soul Train on Television*. Jefferson, NC: McFarland, 2008.

Leslie, Michael. "Slow Fade to? Advertising in Ebony Magazine, 1957–1989." *Journalism and Mass Communication Quarterly* 72, no. 2 (Summer 1995): 426–35.

Levenson, Cyra, Chi-ming Yang, and Ken Gonzales-Day. "Haptic Blackness: The Double Life of an 18th-Century Bust." *British Art Studies* 1 (November 2015): 1–38. https://doi.org/10.17658/issn.2058-5462/issue-01/harwood.

Lewis, Sarah Elizabeth. "Groundwork: Race and Aesthetics in the Era of Stand Your Ground Law." *Art Journal* 79, no. 4 (2020): 92–113.

Lewis, Sarah Elizabeth. "Insistent Reveal: Louis Agassiz, Joseph T. Zealy, Carrie Mae Weems, and the Politics of Undress in the Photography of Racial Science." In *To Make Their Own Way in the World: The Enduring Legacy of the Zealy Daguerreotypes*, edited by Ilisa Barbash, Molly Rogers, and Deborah Willis, 297–325. Cambridge, MA: Peabody Museum Press/Aperture, 2020.

Libby, David J. *Slavery in Frontier Mississippi, 1720–1835*. Jackson: University Press of Mississippi, 2004.

Llorens, David. "Natural Hair—New Symbol of Race Pride." *Ebony*, December 1967.

MacArthur, Julie, ed. *Dedan Kimathi on Trial: Colonial Justice and Popular Memory in Kenya's Mau Mau Rebellion*. Athens: Ohio University Press, 2017.

Mahr, Krista. "Protests over Black Girls' Hair Rekindle Debate about Racism in South Africa." *Washington Post,* September 3, 2016. https://www.washingtonpost.com /world/africa/protests-over-black-girls-hair-rekindle-debate-about-racism-in-south -africa/2016/09/02/27f445da-6ef4-11e6-993f-73c693a89820_story.html.

Marable, Manning. *How Capitalism Underdeveloped Black America: Problems in Race, Political Economy, and Society*. Chicago: Haymarket Books, 2015.

Marks, Laura U. *The Skin of the Film: Intercultural Cinema, Embodiment, and the Senses*. Durham, NC: Duke University Press, 2000.

Marks, Laura U. *Touch: Sensuous Theory and Multisensory Media*. Minneapolis: University of Minnesota Press, 2002.

Martin, Michael. "Madeline Anderson in Conversation: Pioneering an African American Documentary Tradition." *Black Camera* 5, no. 1 (Fall 2013): 72–93.

Mercer, Kobena. "Black Hair/Style Politics." *New Formations*, no. 3 (Winter 1987): 33–54.

Mercer, Kobena. "New Practices, New Identities: Hybridity and Globalization." In *The Image of the Black in Western Art*. Vol. 5: *The Twentieth Century, Part 2: The Rise of Black Artists*, edited by David Bindman and Henry Louis Gates Jr., 225–300. Cambridge, MA: Belknap Press of Harvard University Press, 2014.

Metz, Christian. *The Imaginary Signifier: Psychoanalysis and the Cinema*. Translated by Celia Britton, Annwyl Williams, Ben Brewster, and Alfred Guzzetti. Bloomington: Indiana University Press, 1981.

Miles, Melissa. *Photography, Truth and Reconciliation*. London: Bloomsbury, 2019.

Mills, Quincy T. *Cutting Along the Color Line: Black Barbers and Barber Shops in America*. Philadelphia: University of Pennsylvania Press, 2013.

Mitchell, Robin. *Vénus Noire: Black Women and Colonial Fantasies in Nineteenth-Century France*. Athens: University of Georgia Press, 2020.

Morgan, Jennifer L. *Laboring Women: Reproduction and Gender in New World Slavery*. Philadelphia: University of Pennsylvania Press, 2004.

Morrow, William (Willie) Lee. *400 Years without a Comb*. San Diego, CA: Black Publishers of San Diego, 1973.

Morrow, William (Willie) Lee, and Albert Jefferson. *400 Years without a Comb: The Inferior Seed*. Video Recording. San Diego, CA: California Curl, 1989.

Morton, Samuel George. *Crania Americana, or, A Comparative View of the Skulls of Various Aboriginal Nations of North and South America*. Philadelphia: J. Dobson, 1839.

Murray, Derek Conrad. "Kehinde Wiley: Splendid Bodies." *Nka: Journal of Contemporary African Art* 21 (Fall 2007): 90–101.

Murrell, Denise. *Posing Modernity: The Black Model from Manet and Matisse to Today*. New Haven, CT: Yale University Press, 2018.

Museu de Arte Moderna do Rio de Janeiro. *African Photography: Gilberto Chateaubriand Collection*. Rio de Janeiro: Museu de Arte Moderna, 2011.

Mwanzia Koster, Mickie. *The Power of the Oath: Mau Mau Nationalism in Kenya, 1952–1960*. Rochester, NY: University of Rochester Press, 2016.

Nelson, Alondra. *Body and Soul: The Black Panther Party and the Fight against Medical Discrimination*. Minneapolis: University of Minnesota Press, 2011.

Nelson, Charmaine A. *Slavery, Geography and Empire in Nineteenth-Century Marine Landscapes of Montreal and Jamaica*. New York: Routledge, 2016.

Newberry, Darren. *Defiant Images: Photography and Apartheid South Africa*. Pretoria, South Africa: Unisa Press, 2009.

Nwigwe, Chukwuemeka. "Igbo Women's Fashion and the Nigeria-Biafra War." In *Women and the Nigeria-Biafra War: Reframing Gender and Conflict in Africa*, edited by Gloria Chuku and Sussie U. Aham-Okoro, 159–80. Lanham, MD: Lexington Books, 2020.

O'Grady, Lorraine. "Olympia's Maid: Reclaiming Black Female Subjectivity." In *The Feminism and Visual Culture Reader*, 2nd ed., edited by Amelia Jones, 174–86. London: Routledge, 2010.

Oguibe, Olu. "Photography and the Substance of the Image." In *The Visual Culture Reader*, 2nd ed., edited by Nicholas Mirzoeff, 565–83. New York: Routledge, 2002.

Ojeikere, J. D. 'Okhai, and Andre Magnin. *J. D. 'Okhai Ojeikere: Photographs*. Zurich: Scalo, 2000.

Okeke-Agulu, Chika. *Postcolonial Modernism: Art and Decolonization in Twentieth-Century Nigeria*. Durham, NC: Duke University Press, 2015.

Oksala, Johanna. "Affective Labor and Feminist Politics." *Signs: Journal of Women in Culture and Society* 41, no. 2 (2016): 281–303.

Olin, Margaret. *Touching Photographs*. Chicago: University of Chicago Press, 2012.

Ornelas, Jeanette. *Black Consumers and Haircare: US, August 2015*. Mintel Reports Database, 2015. https://reports.mintel.com/display/716774/ (accessed March 13, 2022).

Palmer, Tyrone S. "'What Feels More Than Feeling?': Theorizing the Unthinkability of Black Affect." *Critical Ethnic Studies* 3, no. 2 (Fall 2017): 31–56.

Pandolfi, Elizabeth. "1858 Prize Profile: Sonya Clark." *Charleston City Paper*, September 4, 2014. https://charlestoncitypaper.com/1858-prize-profile-sonya-clark/.

Paton, Diana. *No Bond but the Law: Punishment, Race, and Gender in Jamaican State Formation, 1780–1870*. Durham, NC: Duke University Press, 2004.

Patterson, Orlando. *Slavery and Social Death: A Comparative Study*. Cambridge, MA: Harvard University Press, 1982.

Pearl, Sharrona. *About Faces: Physiognomy in Nineteenth-Century Britain*. Cambridge, MA: Harvard University Press, 2010.

Pinney, Christopher. "Notes from the Surface of the Image: Photography, Postcolonialism, and Vernacular Modernism." In *Photography's Other Histories*, edited by Christopher Pinney and Nicolas Peterson, 202–20. Durham, NC: Duke University Press, 2003.

Pollard, Velma. "The Social History of Dread Talk." *Caribbean Quarterly* 28, no. 4 (December 1982): 17–40.

Poole, Deborah. "An Excess of Description: Ethnography, Race, and Visual Technologies." *Annual Review of Anthropology* 34, no. 1 (2005): 159–79.

Poole, Deborah. *Vision, Race, and Modernity: A Visual Economy of the Andean Image World*. Princeton, NJ: Princeton University Press, 1997.

Powell, Richard J. *Black Art: A Cultural History*. Rev. ed. London: Thames and Hudson, 2002.

Powell, Richard J. "Conversation with Barkley Hendricks." In *Barkley L. Hendricks: Birth of the Cool*, edited by Trevor Schoonmaker, 39–57. Durham, NC: Duke University Press, 2008.

Powell, Richard J. *Cutting a Figure: Fashioning Black Portraiture*. Chicago: University of Chicago Press, 2008.

Price, Sally, and Richard Price. *Maroon Arts: Cultural Vitality in the African Diaspora*. Boston: Beacon Press, 1999.

Pruner-Bey, Dr. "On Human Hair as a Race-Character, Examined by the Aid of the Microscope." *Anthropological Review* 2, no. 4 (February 1864): 1–23.

Quashie, Kevin. *The Sovereignty of Quiet: Beyond Resistance in Black Culture*. New Brunswick, NJ: Rutgers University Press, 2012.

Questlove. *Soul Train: The Music, Dance, and Style of a Generation*. New York: Harper Design, 2013.

Raiford, Leigh. *Imprisoned in a Luminous Glare: Photography and the African American Freedom Struggle*. Chapel Hill: University of North Carolina Press, 2011.

Ransby, Barbara. *Ella Baker and the Black Freedom Movement: A Radical Democratic Vision*. Chapel Hill: University of North Carolina Press, 2003.

Richardson, Matt. "Our Stories Have Never Been Told: Preliminary Thoughts on Black Lesbian Cultural Production as Historiography in *The Watermelon Woman*." *Black Camera* 2, no. 2 (Spring 2011): 100–113.

Robinson, Cedric J. *Black Marxism: The Making of the Black Radical Tradition*. Chapel Hill: University of North Carolina Press, 2000.

Rooks, Noliwe. *Hair Raising: Beauty, Culture, and African American Women*. New Brunswick, NJ: Rutgers University Press, 1996.

Rusert, Britt. *Fugitive Science: Empiricism and Freedom in Early African American Culture*. New York: New York University Press, 2017.

Saar, Alison. "Fighting Flatness." In *Mirror, Mirror: The Prints of Alison Saar*, edited by Carolyn Vaughn, 95–101. Portland, OR: Jordan Schnitzer Family Foundation, 2019. Exhibition catalog.

Scott, David. *Refashioning Futures: Criticism after Postcoloniality*. Princeton, NJ: Princeton University Press, 1999.

Sheumaker, Helen, and Shirley Teresa Wajda, eds. *Material Culture in America: Understanding Everyday Life*. Santa Barbara, CA: ABC-CLIO, 2008.

Sieber, Roy, and Frank Herreman. "Hair in African Art and Culture: Exhibition Preview." *African Arts* 33, no. 3 (Autumn 2000): 54–69.

Simon, Joan. "Easy to Remember, Hard to Forget: Lorna Simpson's Gestures and Reenactments." In *Lorna Simpson*, edited by Joan Simon, 9–30. New York: Prestel, 2013. Exhibition catalog.

Smallwood, Stephanie E. *Saltwater Slavery: A Middle Passage from Africa to American Diaspora*. Cambridge, MA: Harvard University Press, 2007.

Smith, Mark. *How Race Is Made: Slavery, Segregation, and the Senses*. Chapel Hill: University of North Carolina Press, 2006.

Smith, Mark. *Sensing the Past: Seeing, Hearing, Smelling, Tasting, and Touching in History*. Berkeley: University of California Press, 2007.

Smith, Shawn Michelle. *Photographic Returns: Racial Justice and the Time of Photography*. Durham, NC: Duke University Press, 2020.

Snorton, C. Riley. *Black on Both Sides: A Racial History of Trans Identity*. Minneapolis: University of Minnesota Press, 2017.

Solange. "Don't Touch My Hair." *A Seat at the Table*. New York: Saint Records and Columbia Records, 2016.

Spillers, Hortense. "Mama's Baby, Papa's Maybe: An American Grammar Book." *Diacritics* 17, no. 2 (Summer 1987): 65–81.

Spillers, Hortense. "Shades of Intimacy: What the Eighteenth Century Teaches Us." Paper presented at The Flesh of the Matter: A Hortense Spillers Symposium, Cornell University, Ithaca, NY, March 18–19, 2016.

Stauffer, John, Zoe Trodd and Celeste-Marie Bernier. *Picturing Frederick Douglass: An Illustrated Biography of the Nineteenth Century's Most Photographed American*. New York: W. W. Norton, 2015.

Stepto, Robert B. *From Behind the Veil: A Study of Afro-American Narrative*. Urbana: University of Illinois Press, 1979.

Taylor, Diana. *The Archive and the Repertoire: Performing Cultural Memory in the Americas*. Durham, NC: Duke University Press, 2003.

Taylor, Paul C. *Black Is Beautiful: A Philosophy of Black Aesthetics*. Chichester, England: John Wiley and Sons, 2016.

Telfair Museum of Art. *Collection Highlights: Telfair Museum of Art*. Edited by Hollis Koons McCullough. Savannah, GA: Telfair Museum of Art, 2005.

Theoharis, Jeanne. "Black Freedom Studies: Re-imagining and Redefining the Fundamentals." *History Compass* 4, no. 2 (2006): 348–67.

Thomas, Deborah A. *Exceptional Violence: Embodied Citizenship in Transnational Jamaica*. Durham, NC: Duke University Press, 2011.

Thomas, Hank Willis. "All Power to All People." *Mural Arts Philadelphia*, January 28, 2022. https://www.muralarts.org/artworks/monumentlab/all-power-to-all-people/.

Thompson, Krista. *Shine: The Visual Economy of Light in African Diasporic Aesthetic Practice*. Durham, NC: Duke University Press, 2015.

Thompson, Krista. "A Sidelong Glance: The Practice of African Diaspora Art History in the United States." *Art Journal* 70, no. 3 (Fall 2011): 6–31.

Thompson, Robert Farris. *Flash of the Spirit: African and Afro-American Art and Philosophy*. New York: Vintage, 1984.

Topinard, Paul. *Anthropology*. London: Chapman and Hall, 1894.

Trotter, Joe William, Jr. *Workers on Arrival: Black Labor in the Making of America*. Oakland: University of California Press, 2019.

Tulloch, Carol. "Resounding Power of the Afro Comb." In *Hair: Styling, Culture and Fashion*, edited by Geraldine Biddle-Perry and Sarah Cheang, 123–40. Oxford: Berg, 2008.

Tully, Melissa. "All's Well in the Colony: Newspaper Coverage of the Mau Mau

Movement, 1952–56." In *Narrating War and Peace in Africa*, edited by Toyin Falola and Hetty ter Haar, 56–76. Rochester, NY: University of Rochester Press, 2010.

Van Deburg, William L. *Slavery and Race in American Popular Culture*. Madison: University of Wisconsin Press, 1984.

Vokes, Richard, ed. *Photography in Africa: Ethnographic Perspectives*. Woodbridge, UK: James Currey, 2012.

Wagner-Pacifici, Robin. *Discourse and Destruction: The City of Philadelphia versus MOVE*. Chicago: University of Chicago Press, 1994.

Walker, Andre. *Andre Talks Hair!* New York: Simon and Schuster, 1997.

Wallace, Maurice O., and Shawn Michelle Smith, eds. *Pictures and Progress: Early Photography and the Making of African American Identity*. Durham, NC: Duke University Press, 2012.

Wallis, Brian. "The Dream Life of a People: African American Vernacular Photography by Brian Wallis." In *African American Vernacular Photography: Selections from the Daniel Cowin Collection*, essays by Brian Wallis and Deborah Willis, 9–16. New York: International Center of Photography, 2005. Exhibition catalog.

Washington, Booker T. *Frederick Douglass*. London: Hodder and Stoughton, 1906.

Weems, Robert E., Jr. *Desegregating the Dollar: African American Consumerism in the Twentieth Century*. New York: New York University Press, 1998.

Weheliye, Alexander G. *Habeas Viscus: Racializing Assemblages, Biopolitics, and Black Feminist Theories of the Human*. Durham, NC: Duke University Press, 2014.

White, Shane. *Stylin' African-American Expressive Culture from Its Beginnings to the Zoot Suit*. Ithaca, NY: Cornell University Press, 1999.

White, Shane, and Graham White. "Slave Hair and African American Culture in the Eighteenth and Nineteenth Centuries." *Journal of Southern History* 61, no. 1 (February 1995): 45–76.

Wiegman, Robyn. *American Anatomies: Theorizing Race and Gender*. Durham, NC: Duke University Press, 1995.

Williams, Heather Andrea. *Help Me to Find My People: The African American Search for Family Lost in Slavery*. Chapel Hill: University of North Carolina Press, 2012.

Willis, Deborah. "Black is Beautiful: Then and Now." In Brathwaite, Kwame Brathwaite: Black Is Beautiful, 131–42.

Wilson, Judith. "Beauty Rites: Toward an Anatomy of Culture in African American Women's Art." *International Review of African American Art* 11, number 3 (January 1994): 11–17, 47–53.

Wilson, Judith. "Down to the Crossroads: The Art of Alison Saar." *Callaloo* 14, no. 1 (1991): 107–23.

Wilson, Julee. "Black Women Worry That Their Natural Hair Could Affect Job Employment or Retention." *HuffPost*, March 5, 2013. https://www.huffpost.com/entry/black-women-natural-hair-at-the-workplace_n_2811056.

Wilson, Julee. "Natural Hair Book 'The Coiffure Project' by Photographer Glenford Nunez Hits the Web." *HuffPost*, July 2, 2013. https://www.huffpost.com/entry/natural-hair-book-the-coiffure-project-by-glenford-nunez_n_3535323.

Wilson, Midge, and Kathy Russell-Cole. *Divided Sisters: Bridging the Gap between Black Women and White Women*. New York: Anchor Books, 1996.

Zuberi, Tukufu. *African Independence: How Africa Shapes the World*. Lanham, MD: Rowman and Littlefield, 2015.

Zuckerman, Heidi. "Daring As a Woman: An Interview with Lorna Simpson." *Paris Review*, November 10, 2017. https://www.theparisreview.org/blog/2017/11/10/daring -woman-interview-lorna-simpson/.

Ford, Tanisha, 7, 61
4C: A Documentary on Natural Hair (2017), 127
Franklin, John Hope, 28

Gaba, Meshac, 147
Gallagher, Ellen, 132, 135–36, 152; *Afrylic*, 133,
plate 13; *American Beauty*, 133; *DeLuxe*, 133–34,
plate 14; *Double Natural*, 133; *eXelento*, 133; *Falls
& Flips*, 133; *Pomp Bang*, 133; *Pomp Gang*, 133;
Wiglette (details from *DeLuxe*), 134, plate 15
Garrison, William Lloyd, 51, 166–67n80
Garvey, Marcus, 87
Gaskins, Bill, 23; *Carolyn, World African Hair Care,
Braid, and Trade Show, Atlanta, Georgia*, 113;
Good and Bad Hair, 111; *Red, World African Hair
Care, Braid, and Trade Show, Atlanta, Georgia*,
111–12; *Scarlet, Columbus, Ohio*, 111–12
Gates, Racquel, 116
Ghana, 65, 104, 167n16
Gill, Tiffany, 7
Gillespie, Michael, 115
Gilmore, Glenda, 151
Glymph, Thavolia, 45
Gobineau, Arthur de, 39
Gone with the Wind (1939), 63
Gonzales-Day, Ken: *Digital Composition of "Bust
of a Man*,*"* 17–18
Goodbye Uncle Tom (1971), 64
Goode, Wilson, 88
Good Hair (2009), 123–24
Good Times (television program), 83
Gordon, Peter, 40–42, 51, 165n42
grabbing hair, 48, 94–95
Gray, Herman, 115
Grier, William: *Black Rage*, 66
Griffith, D. W.: *Birth of a Nation* (1915), 63
Gross, Kali, 44
Guerrero, Ed, 115
Gunning, Tom, 122

haint/haunt, 150–51, 174–75n47
hair cutting, forcible, 22, 43–48, 69, 159
HairSay: A Natural Hair Documentary (2011), 126
HairStories (exhibition catalog), 19
hairstylists, 107, 118–19, 126, 128, 144–47, 173n55.
See also barbering
hair typing system (A. Walker), 14, 127, 129,
172–73n55

Haiti, 147; Haitian Revolution, 18
Haley, Alex: *Roots* (book and television series), 64
Haley, Sarah, 158
Hammons, David, 131; *Hair Pyramids*, 10; *Nap
Tapestry*, 10–11
hapticality, definition of, 10–16
haptic art, 132, 153
haptic blackness: and art, 132, 153; and cultural
production, 60–62, 90, 96; definition of,
16–17, 23, 155; and political movements, 84,
90, 95; and slavery, 22, 29, 49, 97; and visual
representation, 97–98, 101–2, 113, 124, 131, 159
haptic images, 14, 16, 42, 102
haptic inheritance, 23, 132, 153
haptic racism, 36, 39, 55, 125
Harney, Stefano, 10
Harper, Frances Ellen Watkins, 68–69
Harper's Weekly (magazine), 40
Harrell, Andre, 123
Harris, Charles "Teenie," 111
Harris-Perry, Melissa, 127
Hartman, Saidiya, 102
Harwood, Francis: *Bust of a Man*, 17–19
Haynes, Lauren, 136
head coverings, 34; scarves, 1, 18, 28, 30–31, 46, 52;
wraps, 31, 69
Hendricks, Barkley L.: *Lawdy Mama*, 73–74,
plate 10
Herreman, Frank, 104
Herskovits, Melville, 168n34
Hight, Craig, 127
Hill, Ginger, 50
Holbein, Hans: *The Ambassadors*, 21
Holland, Frederic May: *Frederick Douglass:
The Colored Orator*, 48
Hong, Grace, 96
Howland, Emily, 52

Ice-T, 115
illustrations, of Black hair: *Black Panther*
(newspaper), 72–73; Black Panther Party, 125;
of Black protest, 7, 9; and race science, 28, 30,
32–37, 42; of slavery, 12; travel, 28, 30, 32–34,
54. *See also individual artists*
Indigenous peoples: in Brazil, 33; in the United
States, 35–36, 170n84
indigo, 150–51, 174–75n45, 175n47
Instagram, 128

Powell, Adam Clayton, 77
Powell, Richard, 73–74
Powelson, Benjamin F., 53
prisoners: cutting hair of, 45–47
Procter & Gamble, 159
Pulliam, Keshia Knight, 115

Quashie, Colin: *SlaveShip Brand Sardines*, 12
Quashie, Kevin, 63

race men, 76, 83
race science, 29–30, 32–40, 48–49, 51, 164n13
racial capitalism, 5–6, 13, 16, 23, 29, 42, 47–48,
    60–62, 96, 132, 157–58. *See also* slavery
racism, 75, 159; and academic writing, 28, 30–31;
    haptic, 39, 55, 125; internalized, 62–63, 66–67,
    114, 118; white supremacy, 9, 76, 151. *See also*
    racial capitalism; slavery
Rastafarians, 87–88, 95, 118, 159, 161n1, 170–71n91
Raveen hair care, 78, 135
Real World (1992), 117
repatriation, 170n84
respectability, 7, 52, 96, 135, 148
Richmond, VA, 144, 174n27
Robinson, Cedric, 95
Rock, Chris: *Good Hair* (2009), 123–24, 172n46
Rooks, Noliwe, 7, 60, 162n14
Root of It All, The (1994), 118–20
Roots (television miniseries), 64–65
Roundtree, Richard, 78
Ruffin, George L., 51
Rusert, Britt, 33

Saar, Alison, 132; *Compton Nocturne*, 150, plates
    27–28; *Delta Doo*, 149, plate 26; *High Cotton*,
    151, plate 29; *Hot Comb Haint*, 149; *Monte*,
    148; *Nappy Head Blues*, 149, plate 25; *Sweeping
    Beauty*, 149; *Topsy Turvy*, 152, plate 32; *White
    Guise*, 152, plates 30–31
Saar, Betye, 148
Saar, Richard, 148
Salt-N-Pepa, 123
San Diego, CA, 65
Sanford and Son (television program), 83
Sawyer, Samuel, 44
Scalphunters (1968), 63
school: hair in, 87, 157–58, 175n7
Schweninger, Loren, 28

science, and race, 29–30, 32–40, 48–49, 51, 164n13
Scott, David, 61
Scott-Ward, Gillian: *Back to Natural* (2019), 123
sculpture, 17, 19–20, 22, 104, 147–50, 152, 156,
    plate 25, plate 27, plates 31–32. *See also
    individual artists*
Selassie, Haile, 87
selfies, 125–26
Sellers, Cleveland, 76
Sepia (magazine), 133
Seventh-day Adventists, 118
sexual violence, 22, 43, 45, 47–48, 64
Shaft (1971), 78
Sharpton, Al, 123
shaved heads, 44–45, 47, 172n27
Sidibé, Malick: *Soirée familiale*, 105–6
Sieber, Roy, 104
Simpson, Lorna, 132, 136–37, 152; *1978–1988*, 140,
    plate 20; *Coiffure*, 140, plate 21; *Completing the
    Analogy*, 139, plate 19; *Dividing Lines*, 140; *Double
    Negative*, 140; *Earth & Sky #24*, 137, plate 16; *Easy
    for Who to Say*, 140; *Gold Heads*, 141; *Guarded
    Conditions*, 140; *ID*, 140; *Jet #21, '55*, 138, plate 18;
    Momentum, 141–42; *Outline*, 140; *Phenomena*,
    137–38, plate 17; *Reunite & Ice*, 138; *Same Two*,
    140; *Screen 2*, 139; *Square Deal*, 140; *Stereo Styles*,
    139; *Twenty Questions*, 139; *Two Frames*, 140;
    Two Sisters, Two Tongues, 140; *Two Tracks*, 140;
    Waterbearer, 139; *Wigs*, 141
Singleton, John: *Boyz n the Hood*, 115–16
Sisterlocks, 121, 173n57
slave narratives, 22, 28, 43–45, 51–52. *See also
    individual narratives*
slavery, 15, 31–33, 57, 150–51, 153, 157, 162n10,
    165n43; and archive of feeling, 25–29; cultural
    legacy of, 9, 16, 102–3, 126–27, 132, 160, 167n13;
    fugitives from, 5, 13, 27–28, 40, 48, 50–52, 55,
    71, 97, 163n1; and gender, 14, 17, 162n14, 163n38;
    and hair, 4–7, 22, 25–30, 34–55, 69–72, 100,
    156, 121, 161n1, 169n40; and haptic blackness,
    14, 16, 22, 29, 84, 87, 155; and haptic racism,
    36, 39–40, 55, 87, 125; and kinship, 167n84;
    material culture of, 162n19, 168n27; and touch,
    53–55, 103; visual legacy of, 12–13, 28–29, 40,
    60–68, 71, 140. *See also* racial capitalism
Slaves (1969), 63
Smith, James McCune, 51
Smith, Lionel, 46
Smith, Mark Michael, 39